ON THE MARGINS OF DISCOURSE

The Relation of Literature to Language

BARBARA HERRNSTEIN SMITH

The
University of Chicago Press | Chicago & London

809
Sm 50
112 473
January 1980

THE UNIVERSITY OF CHICAGO PRESS, CHICAGO 60637
THE UNIVERSITY OF CHICAGO PRESS, LTD., LONDON

BARBARA HERRNSTEIN SMITH, professor of
English and Communications at the University of
Pennsylvania, is the author of *Poetic Closure*, also
published by the University of Chicago Press,
which won the Phi Beta Kappa Christian Gauss
Award and the Explicator Award for 1968.

Library of Congress Cataloging in Publication Data

Smith, Barbara Herrnstein.
  On the margins of discourse.

  Includes bibliographical references and index.
  1. Literature—Philosophy.   2. Style, Literary.
3. Language and languages—Style.   I. Title.
PN54.S6   809   78-18274
ISBN 0-226-76452-4

ON
THE MARGINS
OF DISCOURSE

For Julia and Deirdre,
exemplary daughters

CONTENTS

PREFACE

"And," quipped a friend, "will you tell us next about poetic *aperture*?" Although I replied at the time (it was some years ago) that I had no such plans, "aperture" could indeed be seen as the subject of the present volume: not in the sense of openings but rather of unendings, interminables, indeterminacies. The turn from closure* to openness did not, however, require a turnabout, for, as this study will suggest, it is by virtue of its enclosure that the poem achieves its amplitude and infinitude. From within the circle that marks its margins, the poem extends a parabolic curve; disengaged from historical enactment, it persists in history and acquires historicity through the continued possibility of its reenactment. Like Yeats's golden "form," it may, "once out of nature ..., sing of what is passed, or passing, or to come."

This study was initiated in 1969; a version of it, then entitled *Fictive Discourse*, was completed in 1972. The greater part of the present volume consists of portions of that original manuscript, successively extracted, expanded, and revised for presentation as public lectures or publication as individual articles. The germ of the study and an anticipation of its major topics and arguments appear in the first essay, "Literature as Performance, Fiction, and Art," which,

---

Poetic Closure: A Study of How Poems End (Chicago, 1968).

though composed for a different occasion, can now be read as an introduction to the entire volume. Originally the text of a paper delivered to the American Philosophical Association, it considers a number of questions raised by Nelson Goodman's *Languages of Art*—and, more generally, by traditional philosophic aesthetics—concerning the relation of literature both to language and to other artforms. In the course of the paper, I propose an alternative conception of that relation which involves, among other things, the drawing of a set of distinctions between the texts of verbal artworks and other texts. That particular problem—the possibility and propriety of drawing such distinctions, the clarification and refinement of their formulation, and the pursuit of their implications for literary, linguistic, and aesthetic theory—continued to absorb my attention and eventually became central to the study that here completes itself.

Because I was extracting portions of the manuscript for publication at the same time as I was expanding and revising it (and, over the course of six years, my views on a number of points themselves underwent revision), the individual pieces now reassembled are not in altogether genial alignment with each other. I have not, in preparing this volume, undertaken the sort of wholesale revision that would have been required to so align them, but I have filed some of the rougher edges and, in bracketed footnotes, indicated where points are developed further or significantly modified in later portions.

Some difficulties posed by the two key terms of the study, *natural discourse* and *fictive discourse*, may be eased if I briefly discuss their origin. As noted above, the distinction was initially proposed in a discussion of the relation of literature to other artforms. Accordingly, the term *natural* was chosen as an allusion to the traditional opposition of "art" and "nature," in which each member (as in many traditional oppositions) evokes, and to some extent defines, the identity of the other. The term *fictive* had already been used in *Poetic Closure* in the corresponding sense of "feigned" or "represented," that is, "artificial," but without the suggestion of an inferior substitute or deceptive imitation. Although the study focuses on the relation between fictive and natural *discourse*, that relation is to be seen not as unique to language but rather as one instance of the more general relation between "fictive" and "natural" objects and events. The former include not only most of what we think of as art and artifice—for example, mask, costume, effigy, and illustration, as well as painting, sculpture, music, and dance—but also much else that we think of as play, sport, or simply manufacture. Like the fashioning of tools, the cultivation of plants, or the domestication of animals, the creation of fictive objects and events reflects our impatience with nature, with that which merely *happens* to exist, happens to happen, or happens to "appear." They are the products of our impulse and ability to fabricate, by acts of hand, eye, or mind, *representations* (simulacra, images, quasi-instances) of natural "phenomena": that is, to construct or to *make appear* either counter-forms of phenomena or counter-feit instantiations of *types* of phenomena which, "in nature," exist or occur independent of our designs or desires.

Among the phenomena that we may, in this sense, "represent" (to ourselves and to others) are objects and events that are themselves "artificial," both in being the products of human agency and also in having been fashioned in accord with human designs and desires. Thus, artworks, toys, and illustrations may represent not only sunsets and oranges, but also hats, houses, and, indeed, artworks, toys, and illustrations; and we may represent, in play or drama, not only people sleeping and stumbling, but also people dancing, *speaking*, and, indeed, playing games and performing in dramas. In so representing them, however (even if the representation is created by an act of artistry no more strenuous than placing or imagining a "frame" around them or placing or imagining them on a "stage"), we make each of those objects and events, including those already "fashioned," serve novel or distinctive functions, and thus we make them the instruments and products of our own emergent designs and desires. While discourse itself is certainly the supreme instrument and product of human designs and desires and may therefore seem to be naturally artificial, nevertheless utterances, like other objects and events, can be regarded as "natural" *relative to* such representations of them (that is, "fictive utterances")

xi

as we may produce for special ends, aesthetic and other, and which thus serve novel or distinctive functions.

"Natural discourse," then, is not equivalent to "spoken language," nor is it a substitute for such expressions as "normal," "everyday," or "ordinary" discourse. Similarly, the term *fictive*, as used here, is not equivalent to "false," "imaginary," or, for that matter, to "fictional." Both are terms that I have chosen to designate what I later refer to as "covert categories," that is, categories which, though not consistently marked or labeled by the members of a community, are nevertheless manifested in their behavior as functional discriminations and defined and sustained by relatively distinctive sets of conventions. (The term *covert category* is borrowed from Benjamin Lee Whorf's *Language, Thought and Reality* [Cambridge, Mass., 1956], pp. 87–101 passim, where it is used in a similar sense.)

The second chapter in part 1, "Poetry as Fiction," develops the suggestion that verbal artworks—poems, plays, stories, novels—may be seen as representations of discourse and, in that sense, as "mimetic" utterances. Although the term *mimetic* was later abandoned in favor of its alternative, *fictive*, part of my concern in the original essay was to suggest how the concept of *mimesis*, which figures so largely in Western aesthetic theory and has so often been invoked crudely or inappropriately with respect to literature, *could* be used with some pertinence both to characterize verbal artworks and to illuminate their relation to other artforms.

Although the concept of fictive discourse was initially developed to that end, it was clear that the class of verbal structures that could be described as "representations of utterances" was by no means confined to "works of literature," and that the general nature of fictive discourse was itself a matter worth exploring further. Accordingly, in the title chapter, "On the Margins of Discourse," extensive consideration is given to various verbal structures (for example, logician's examples, advertisements, and quotations) which, as fictive utterances, commonly serve functions other than "aesthetic" ones, and to various "borderline cases" (for example, greeting-card messages and proverbs) that illustrate the functional and conventional nature of the distinction between fictive and natural discourse and thus the potentially multiple functions and contextually variable identity of all verbal structures.

A number of topics and issues touched on only briefly or incidentally in the selections that comprise part 1 had been considered more systematically in other portions of the original (now almost completely cannibalized) manuscript. Those portions were revised and expanded for presentation at the University of California, Berkeley, as The Witter Bynner Lectures in Poetry ("Exchanging Words: On the Economics and Ethics of Verbal Transactions"), the text of which forms part 2 of this volume. Among those topics and issues are (1) the transactional nature of natural discourse and the distinctive functions of language for speakers and listeners, (2) the joint origins, in the dynamics or "economics" of verbal transactions, of the conventions governing natural and fictive discourse, and (3) the muddle of *meaning* (and thereby *intention*), both generally and with respect to literary interpretation.

While the observations on language offered in this study do not constitute an original or comprehensive linguistic theory, they do reflect conceptions of verbal and symbolic behavior that are at considerable variance with the theory of language represented by transformational-generative grammar, and at relative distances from theories or analyses of communication, speech acts, and meaning offered by, among others, ordinary-language philosophers. Some key points of those conceptions are made explicit and elaborated in the first lecture, "In the Linguistic Marketplace."

The second lecture, "Licensing the Unspeakable," returns to fictive discourse, specifically to the possibility (and, indeed, necessity) of verbal "licentiousness," as created by the economics of verbal transactions and as learned and revealed in our earliest experiences with the multiple functions of language. (The discussion here of the relation between art and what I refer to as "cognitive play" will be developed further in a study of aesthetic value which I am now pursuing.)

The term *interpretation* is used throughout part 1 in a quite broad sense, to refer to the process or activity of drawing inferences from, or ascribing meanings to, verbal structures: a process or activity that directs—and may, in the case of literary works, largely constitute—

our response to those structures. As I point out there, the explications, scholia, "readings," and so on offered by professional and/or academic exegetes must be seen as very special cases of "interpretation," for we all (including children, illiterates, and members of cultures where no such professional class exists) must interpret verbal structures if we are to respond to them at all, and even when we do articulate our interpretations publicly, it need not be in the service of instruction. A number of questions concerning meanings ("determinate" and "indeterminate") and literary interpretation (in both the broad and narrow senses), particularly as raised by the work of certain contemporary American critics and theorists (represented, synecdochically, by E. D. Hirsch), are the subject of the third lecture, "The Ethics of Interpretation"—the title of which, as will be seen, is somewhat ironic.

As a diversion from revising part 2 of this study, I undertook to write a brief review of a collection of papers edited by Roger Fowler under the title *Style and Structure in Literature: Essays in the New Stylistics*. The diversion became its own form of obsession and, by the time it was completed, the "brief review"—"Surfacing from the Deep"—was eighty pages long and something other than a review. It appears as part 3 of this volume, the original text somewhat abbreviated, and subsected and subtitled to suggest the various topics considered.

A number of points made in parts 1 and 2 are here extended in directions not accommodated by the scope and momentum of the earlier pieces, and are sharpened with respect to their implications for the study of literature. The most direct extensions appear in the discussion of various attempts by linguists and others to encircle and net the parabolas of poetic meaning, and in a brief outline of how a theory of literary narrative might be pursued in connection with a more general study of the social and potentially aesthetic functions of all verbal narrative. The whole of part 3, however, may be taken as an extension of the conception of literary theory reflected in *Poetic Closure* as well as in the earlier sections of this volume, that is, not as metacriticism, philosophic meditations on literary texts, or a corner of some other intellectual domain or discipline, and not as justified by the practices or confined by the purposes of pedagogy;

but rather as a continuously evolving inquiry into all the phenomena and activities of which literature consists and to which it is related, an inquiry that is responsive and connectible to the general study of social and symbolic behavior, and that dissolves its own margins in the very process of discovering them.

This volume is sparing in citational footnotes. I do, however, wish to acknowledge here some of the more significant sources and conspicuous analogues of the study.

As the numerous domestic examples will suggest, many of the observations made here, especially those on language acquisition and verbal play, are drawn from homegrown sources, among them the two young women to whom this volume is dedicated. (I have, however, been mindful of the tendency of children to acquire language in obedient accord with whatever theory of language acquisition their parents subscribe to.) Other sources, remote in (personal) time and all but obliterated by contributory streams and ultimate depositions, include my happy encounter, at an impressionable age, with selected writings by Charles S. Pierce; Kenneth Burke's *Counter-Statement* (Chicago, 1931); and B. F. Skinner's *Verbal Behavior* (New York, 1957: a little-known work, not to be confused with the well-known review of it by Noam Chomsky [*Language* 35 (1959): 26–58]).

Analogues of the study, that is, recently published—or, in many cases, recently translated—works that, to various extents, parallel or intersect with it, include the following:

Studies originally published in the 1920s by Russian literary theorists, especially the essays by Boris Tomaševskij ("Literature and Biography"), Jurij Tynjanov ("On Literary Evolution"), and V. N. Vološinov ("Reported Speech"), translated and reprinted in *Readings in Russian Poetics*, ed. L. Matejka and K. Pomorska (Cambridge, Mass., 1971); Vološinov's "Discourse in Life and Discourse in Art," reprinted as Appendix 1 in *Freudianism: A Marxist Critique*, tr. I. R. Titunik and ed. with N. H. Bruss (New York, 1976); and Mikhail Bakhtin's *Problems of Dostoevsky's Poetics*, tr. R. W. Rostel (Ann Arbor, Mich., 1973);

Works by other literary theorists, particularly Roman Ingarden,

The Literary Work of Art (orig. pub. 1931), tr. George G. Grabo-
wicz (Evanston, Ill., 1973); Robert Champigny, *Ontology of the
Narrative* (The Hague and Paris, 1972); Wolfgang Iser, *The Implied
Reader* (Baltimore and London, 1974) and "The Reality of Fiction:
A Functionalist Approach to Literature," *New Literary History* 7
(1975): 7–38; Roland Barthes, *S/Z: An Essay* (orig. pub. 1970), tr.
Richard Miller (New York, 1974); John Ellis, *The Theory of Literary
Criticism* (Berkeley, Calif., 1974); and, encountered as this volume
was going to press, Mary Louise Pratt, *Toward a Speech Act Theory
of Literary Discourse* (Bloomington, Ind., 1977);

Various studies of art and symbolic behavior, particularly David K.
Lewis, *Convention: A Philosophic Analysis* (Cambridge, Mass.,
1969); Gregory Bateson, *Steps to an Ecology of Mind* (New York,
1972); Erving Goffman, *Relations in Public* (New York, 1971) and
Frame Analysis (New York, 1974); Arthur Danto, "The Trans-
figuration of the Commonplace," *Journal of Aesthetics and Art
Criticism* 33 (1974): 138–48; Umberto Eco, *A Theory of Semiotics*
(Bloomington, Ind., 1976); and, read in manuscript after this
volume was completed, Morse Peckham, *Explanation and Power:
An Inquiry into the Control of Human Behavior* (New York,
Continuum Books, in press).

A number of friends have given to portions of this study their own
often contentious but always valued attention: at Bennington College, Alvin Feinman, Joanna Kirkpatrick, and Richard Tristman; at
the University of Pennsylvania, Larry Gross, Leonard B. Meyer,
Saul Morson, and the much-missed late Sol Worth. I am grateful,
also, to Tom Wick and Eric Reeves for their heterogeneous helpful-
ness as my research assistants, to Thomas D. Cohen for his
relentless provocations, and to Morse Peckham, who put at my
service his uncanny knack for almost always, ultimately, being
right.

Various phases of the study were aided by leaves and grants from
Bennington College, the University of Pennsylvania, the National
Endowment for the Humanities, and the John Simon Guggenheim
Memorial Foundation. I should also like to thank the Witter Bynner
Foundation and the Department of English at the University of

California, Berkeley, for their invitation to deliver the Poetry
Lectures for 1977 and for their hospitality during my visit.

Permission to publish edited versions of the articles and lectures
assembled here is gratefully acknowledged. The original texts
appeared as follows:

"Literature as Performance, Fiction, and Art," *The Journal of
Philosophy* 47 (1970): 553-63. © 1970 by The Journal of Philosophy, Inc.

"Poetry as Fiction," *New Literary History* 2 (1971): 259-82.
Reprinted in *New Directions in Literary History*, ed. Ralph Cohen
(Baltimore and London, 1974). © 1971, 1974 by New Literary
History.

"On the Margins of Discourse," *Critical Inquiry* 1 (1975):
769-98. © 1975 by The University of Chicago.

"Exchanging Words: On the Economics and Ethics of Verbal
Transactions," The Witter Bynner Lectures in Poetry for 1977,
delivered at the University of California, Berkeley, October–November 1977.

"Surfacing from the Deep," *PTL: A Journal for Descriptive
Poetics and Theory of Literature* 2 (1977): 151-82. © North-Holland
Publishing Co., 1977.

1
TOWARD A THEORY
OF FICTIVE DISCOURSE

1

LITERATURE AS PERFORMANCE, FICTION, AND ART

What Nelson Goodman on occasion calls his "heresies" struck me as not only sound and welcome gospel but of considerable potential value for literary theory. The otherwise inviting prospect of extending *Languages of Art*[1] to the arts of language was initially dimmed, however, by those extensions which Goodman himself provides; for they are in certain respects quite problematic. My hope in bringing one particularly disturbing set of problems to attention here is to persuade him to relinquish some lingering orthodoxies and consider some of the more radical and unexpected implications of *Languages of Art* for the theory of literature.

1. TEXTS AND SCORES

There are two senses in which we commonly speak of *literature*: either as the class of linguistic texts or as the class of linguistic artworks. Thus literature may include, on the one hand, everything written down in orthographic inscription or, on the other, what is sometimes awkwardly referred to as "poetry in the broad sense," meaning that the distinctive feature is not meter. Although the two classes overlap, one is not a subclass of the other. Poems are not certain kinds of linguistic texts; they are certain kinds of linguistic structures, and inscriptions of them may or may not exist. Since the distinction I am speaking of is very gross, and since Goodman is a

3

very subtle man, his failure to heed it in *Languages of Art* must be taken to reflect not a lack of discernment but rather a deliberate decision. I shall attempt to suggest here why, given his objectives and concerns, this decision was mistaken.

In the fifth chapter of the book, "Score, Sketch, and Script" (pp. 177–221), Goodman examines the relation between a number of standard artforms and their respective notational systems, actual or conceivable. He considers in turn music, painting, dance, architecture, and, along the way, something which he refers to variously as "literary arts," "literary works," and "works of literature," and which he exemplifies variously as poems, novels, biographies, and histories of the Civil War. In view of the examples, it would seem that he wants us to understand "literary" here in the relatively undiscriminating sense of *written down*—which is surprising, of course, in the context of an examination of the various arts.

It follows from Goodman's use of the term *literary* that his analysis of "the literary arts" applies to all printed texts from the First Folio Shakespeare to *How to Travel in Europe on $5 a Day*, and also to the note I left this morning for the milkman, but does not apply to a preliterate epic saga or the love poem of an Adaman Islander or the animal fable spun by an unlettered Appalachian farmer. Goodman declares that he is "not concerned with what distinguishes some scripts as 'truly literary' works," but the disclaimer does not answer the objection that he *should* have been concerned with a distinction very much like that. For my point here is not that he failed to assume or ensure an honorific definition for literary art, but rather that he failed to recognize the integrity and significance of what he would call its relevant "antecedent classification," and that he consequently failed to account for literature properly in the terms of his own theory.

Goodman might offer to allow for the illiterate's work of literature by noting that, for it to qualify, a text of the work need not actually exist so long as someone *could* produce an inscription for it which, when read aloud, would be accepted as an instance of that work—presumably in that culture or community. This would not help much, however; for, given any orthographic system, anything speakable is also inscribable. Consequently, lacking some other principle of distinction, every utterance in any linguistic community that had at least one literate member would be a work of literature. Goodman has either excluded from his class of "literary works" all the poems and tales that have never been inscribed, or he has included as literature virtually everything that has ever been uttered.

Goodman's initial identification of literary art with written texts is either responsible for or a reflection of his equally disturbing identification of a poem with the class of its inscriptions and/or utterances. I say "and/or" because it is not clear whether he means, as he says in one place, that "a . . . literary work is not the compliance-class of a text but the text or script itself" or, as he says in another place, that "all and only inscriptions and utterances of the text are instances of the work." In either case, the identification seems improper, because, aside from concrete poetry (that is, "picture poems" or verbal constructions dependent on graphic presentation for their formal properties) and one other important class of exceptions to be mentioned later, the poem or literary artwork cannot be identified with its own inscription. Moreover, it may be identified with the utterance of its inscription only if one understands "utterance" in the sense of "performance" to be described hereafter. Given Goodman's own definitions and analyses, the relation between a poem and its text is readily and, I think, happily conceived as analogous to the relation between a musical work and its score or between a dramatic work and its script. Where a text exists, a "genuine instance" of the poem is a performance defined by and complying with it. When there is no performance occurring, the text has the same ontological status as a score. Thus I regard as baffling Goodman's assertion that "an unrecited poem is not so forlorn as an unsung song."

Imagine, if you will, that a court musician has performed an air, both the lyrics and melody of which he has composed himself. "Lovely," says the Queen, "we must have a copy." What does the musician do? He prepares a score and a text; or, rather, he prepares a score of the entire song, in which certain features are inscribed in one symbolic scheme, musical notation, and other features are inscribed in another symbolic scheme, linguistic orthography. It is

5

not clear why, at this point, or in this state, one inscription should be thought more forlorn than the other. To produce a genuine instance of the air, someone must produce a physical realization of both words and melody; merely playing the lute and displaying the text will not do. Moreover, the relation of the text to the work would not be different if the composer had composed only the lyrics—that is, a poem—and had never intended to set them to music. Or, more to the point, we should then say that all the music he had designed for that poem was to be found in its phonetic and prosodic features insofar as they were specified by the conventions of interpreting poetic texts. That music could not be found in the text itself because texts are altogether mute objects. To translate the inscription of that lyric into an instance of the work, something has to serve as the instrument of its performance.

It is evident from Goodman's discussion that he had considered the possibility of regarding poetry as a mediated or "two-stage" art, with texts functioning as true scores. He rejected the possibility, however, because although he could grant that vocal readings might be construed as performances, the phenomenon of *silent* reading apparently remained an insoluble problem. That the problem was partially created by his own misconception of the matter is suggested by his argument that, if silent readings of a poem could be considered instances of a work, then so could "the lookings at a picture and the listenings to a [musical] performance." A silent reading of a poem, however, is or may be a much more specific and precisely determined activity than looking at a picture or listening to music. The reader is required to produce, from his correct "spelling" of a spatial array of marks on a page, a temporally organized and otherwise defined structure of sounds—or, if you like, pseudo-sounds. The physical or neurophysiological source of the structure generated by the silent reader is of little significance here: it may originate somewhere in his musculature or peripheral or central nervous system, or the source may vary from reader to reader. What is significant is that the structure itself will not vary.

Although, in a silent reading, the performer and audience are necessarily the same person, this should not obscure the fact that the reading consists of two theoretically distinct activities, only one of which is comparable to listening to music or looking at a picture. To be sure, the configuration of physical events that constitutes a genuine instance of an artwork is usually external to the audience's own body or sensory system: the music originates outside our ears, the painting is located outside our eyes. The surface of the skin, however, is an arbitrary boundary line here, and if we can conceive the solitary singer enjoying his own performance, we should not really have any trouble extending the conception to the solitary silent reader.

Goodman's observations on the limits of scores are of considerable interest when extended to poetic texts. "The function of a score," he writes, "is to specify the essential properties a performance must have to belong to the work; the stipulations are only of certain aspects and only within certain degrees." This is a point that could be heeded with profit by contemporary linguists and others who lament what they see as the phonetic inadequacy of texts, especially in indicating the "correct" degree or position of metrical stresses. But phonetic equivalence is no more required of correct performances of poems than of musical compositions. What is required, rather, is compliance with the text according to the conventions of interpretation established by the tradition within which the poem and text are composed and interpreted.

It should nevertheless be noted that the conventions for the interpretation of poetic inscriptions are not the same as those for the ordinary reading of discursive texts. Not every text is a score, because not every linguistic inscription is of a literary artwork. One cannot skim a poem or read it distractedly while listening to a conversation: not, that is, if one is to produce and experience it as an artwork. For the structure of sounds and temporal pacing in a poem are part of what constitutes the work, and the poem has not occurred unless that pacing and structure have been made manifest to its audience.

It is curious, in this connection, that Goodman never mentions one rather striking feature of certain texts, namely their lineation. I trust he is not under the impression that the lines in which poems are printed are merely a typographic ritual, or that they identify poems as a genre but do not otherwise control or define their compliance-classes. For lineation is an integral part of the notational system of poetry; and although it does not control the rhythmic features of a performance as specifically as do the indications of timing in musical notation, it nevertheless does direct and limit them. Consequently, given certain traditionally authorized rules of interpretation, any performance that does not comply with a poem's lineation is not an instance of that poem.

ii. Representations of Discourse

I would like to return now to the class of exceptions mentioned earlier. An interesting case *can* be made for regarding certain literary works as constituted by their own inscriptions, and, although it is not the case that Goodman makes, I think he might find it congenial. Briefly, the argument would go as follows. As a general class, literary artworks may be conceived of as depictions or representations, rather than instances, of natural discourse. (An analogy may be drawn to the familiar Aristotelian conception of drama as the representation of human action. *Hamlet* is a representation, not an instance, of a man avenging his father's murder.) The various genres of literary art—for example, dramatic poems, tales, odes, lyrics—can to some extent be distinguished according to what types of discourse—for example, dialogues, anecdotes of past events, public speeches, and private declarations—they characteristically represent. Thus, lyric poems typically represent personal utterances, or, to use Goodman's picturesquely unidiomatic terms, such poems are *pictures* of utterances. What is significant for the present point is that certain types of discourse are themselves characteristically *textual inscriptions*—for example, chronicles, journals, letters, biographies, and memoirs—and certain genres of literature, roughly what we refer to as "prose fiction," characteristically represent such varieties of *inscribed* discourse. A literary work in such a genre would, then, indeed be constituted by the instances of its own text. (We might say that, if poems are pictures of utterances, novels are pictures of inscriptions or books; and we note that novels, a distinctly post-Gutenberg genre, have typically been representations of chronicles, journals, letters, biographies, and memoirs.)

8

One can readily understand, then, what would lead Goodman to identify at least some literary works with their own inscriptions. His error, however, was to generalize the identification indiscriminately, neglecting to distinguish properly among the following three classes: (1) those instances of "literature," including all ordinary texts or inscriptions, which are not literary artworks at all,[2] (2) those literary artworks which, as representations of *inscribed* discourse, are indeed constituted by their own texts, and finally (3) those literary artworks which, as representations of various kinds of *spoken* discourse, bear the special relation to their own texts[3] that I have just described here, that is, the relation between a performable work and its score.

Goodman observes that literary texts may be conceived of in two ways: first, as phonetic characters in a notational system having utterances as compliants; second, as characters in a discursive language having objects or events as compliants. As to the first part of this formulation, I have been suggesting that the texts of literary artworks have certain features that distinguish them—and their "utterances"—from the inscriptions of ordinary discourse. It is the second part that concerns me now, for it slights the more fundamental distinction between the two senses of *literature* that I alluded to at the beginning. The second part of the formulation is inaccurate because, to the extent that a literary artwork can be conceived as a character in a discursive language, it has *no* objects or events as compliants.

I shall elaborate this in a moment, but first I should say parenthetically that I think the concept of *compliance* is severely strained when Goodman uses it to describe the relation between natural verbal discourse and the world of objects and events. The relation between a given phonetic character and the sound that complies with it is not comparable to the relation between a given utterance and anything at all. The world of objects and events does not comply with our utterances; it contains them and it causes them.[4]

Granting Goodman his terms, however, and also granting that the text of a literary artwork becomes, *through* a performance, a character in a natural language, it remains true that that character has no compliance-class because the literary artwork is *fictive*. Fictiveness, moreover, is precisely what distinguishes the literary artwork from the more general class of verbal utterances and inscriptions. Poems and novels, as opposed to biographies and histories of the Civil War, are linguistic structures whose relation to the world of objects and events is short-circuited. The short circuit operates through a convention according to which certain identifiable utterances are understood to be performances of a verbal action, the occurrence of which *as* an "action" is entirely confined to such performances. The child who asks, "Did it really happen or is it a story?" has already learned the convention, and soon will not have to ask because he will also have learned the cues that identify fictiveness in a narration.

By this convention, Keats's ode "To Autumn," in which the speaker is left unspecified, is precisely as fictive as Tennyson's poem, "Ulysses," in which the speaker is represented as the wily Greek himself. Both poems are understood not as the inscribed records of utterances actually uttered by men who spoke poetically, but rather as linguistic structures composed by men whom we call poets because they compose such structures. No matter how closely the statements in such a composition resemble statements the poet himself as a historical creature might have truly and truthfully uttered, they remain fictive statements in the poem. *As an utterance*, the poem is unmoored from any specific context or occasion in the world of objects and events, and thus, in Goodman's terms, it refers to and denotes nothing. To object that the poem *seems* to imply and evoke such a world is, of course, to speak of the characteristic marvel and object of poetic composition, but it is not an argument. To evoke or suggest is not to denote; it is to *seem* to denote, and that is what is meant by fictiveness and what has traditionally been meant by poetry. In Ben Jonson's words: "Hence hee is call'd a Poet, not hee which writeth in measure only; but that fayneth and formeth a fable, and writes things *like* the Truth. For, the Fable and Fiction is (as it were) the forme and Soule of any Poeticall worke, or Poeme" (*Timber: or, Discoveries,* 1641).

Novels and tales are obviously also fictive, but more radically so than is sometimes supposed. For not only are the characters and the

10

events narrated in a novel fictional, but so also is the narrator whose voice relates the events, and, most significantly, so also are the statements through which the narration is presented. A history of the Civil War may be conceived, in some very peculiar sense, as having the Civil War as its compliance-class, but in that sense no war at all is the compliance-class of the *Iliad* or, indeed, of *War and Peace*. A reader who fails to comprehend the nature of fictions may be as likely to look for Prince Andrey's grave as for Napoleon's Tomb, but the fact that we can locate the latter and not the former does not make one part of Tolstoy's novel any less fictional than another. For the essential fictiveness of literary artworks is not to be discovered in the unreality of the characters, objects, and events alluded to, but in the unreality of the *alludings* themselves.

III. ART AND COGNITIVE ACTIVITY

In the final sections of *Languages of Art* (pp. 241–65), Goodman enlists his theory of symbols in the service of a noble cause, namely the destruction of what he refers to as "the deeply entrenched dichotomy of the cognitive and the emotive." I am in sympathy with the cause, and it seems to me that Goodman's contributions to it here are of great value. Nevertheless, in demolishing the falsely conceived dichotomy, he has unwittingly—and, for his purposes, unnecessarily—obscured a quite validly conceived distinction, namely that between nature and art.

Those who seek to demonstrate the affinity of science and art typically focus on the similarities between the scientist and the artist, observing, for example, that both are engaged in creating or revealing order in nature or experience. Goodman takes a more unusual and interesting line, comparing the activity of the scientist to that of the audience or spectator of a work of art, and emphasizing the degree to which the characteristic *experience* of each is similar. Thus he speaks of the searching, testing, making of delicate discriminations, and discerning of subtle relationships that are involved in one's experience of art; and certainly the activity of the scientist is readily described in such terms. What concerns me, however, is that, whereas the scientist's activities are directed toward the exploration of the natural universe, the "reader" of the painting

11

or poem or musical composition is engaged in the exploration of a structure created by a fellow creature and designed by that artist precisely to encourage and reward such exploration. There is, I believe, no reason to suppose that the structure of nature was designed to engage our interest, to entice us into investigations, and to reward our activities with discovery—although we, of course, have probably been designed by natural selection to find that sort of activity gratifying in any case.

My point here is that we—that is, human beings, but perhaps not uniquely among organisms—do indeed take pleasure in what Goodman calls cognitive activity, and that this pleasure or satisfaction may be diminished or enhanced by various circumstances, and that the artist is one who is skilled at fashioning such enhancing circumstances, and that we call circumstances so fashioned *works of art*. The artist (a gentleman who has perhaps received an inordinate amount of attention in Romantic aesthetics but whom Goodman nevertheless snubs almost, one would think, pointedly)[5]—the artist creates structures that are relatively free of those irrelevancies, irregularities, and monotonies that often frustrate and attenuate our satisfaction in cognitive activity, but structures that are, at the same time, sufficiently complex, rich, or subtle to engage and exercise our cognitive faculties.

The work of art, then, provides the stimulus to and occasion for a highly distilled and rewarding cognitive experience, but also a highly artificial one; for in experiencing a work of art, we may have all the satisfaction that attends the pursuit and acquisition of knowledge without *necessarily* having acquired any knowledge at all. Or, rather, what we acquire knowledge *of* in a work of art is primarily the work itself, a fabricated microcosm designed to be knowable in just that way. What is most important here is that although this knowledge obviously has its sources in nature and reflects it in various ways, it cannot be *generalized* to nature as we generalize knowledge in science—or indeed in our ordinary experiences—from one part of nature to another.

We surely must grant, as Goodman insists, that aesthetic experience is not altogether distinctive. It shares motives and qualities with the experience of scientists doing science and, of course, of philosophers doing philosophy. We should acknowledge that it also shares motives and qualities—perhaps some of the same ones—with scientists, philosophers, and other people making love and playing games. We remain, in all these activities, what we always are: creatures moving about in a world we must seek to know in order to survive and for whom, as Aristotle noted, learning is the liveliest pleasure. It is also true, however, that the sources or objects of our aesthetic experiences may be artificial worlds, fictive "natures," and that the consequences of knowing *them* are confused at one's peril with the consequences of knowing nature proper.[6] Of course, we are usually saved from such peril by the conventions (such as stages, frames, pedestals, and versification) that operate to inform us that we are confronted by art, not nature, so that we are never really deluded by the fictive construction and thus receive no *false* knowledge from it.

The connection between these last remarks and the earlier parts of my paper are, I trust, clear: the distinction that Goodman blurs in identifying literary art with written inscriptions is, in effect, the distinction between fiction and history, and between art and nature. The verbal actions—speech or writing—of other men are a part of nature, as much a part of the natural environment as the behavior of sun, stars, rocks, and trees; and those verbal actions are as much a part of history as all the other actions of our fellow creatures. Furthermore, our lives do depend on our searching, testing, making delicate discriminations, and discerning subtle relationships in the utterances of these fellow creatures. The cognitive explorations thus directed, however, are not always rewarded with discoveries and revelations; for these utterances are often obscure and fragmentary, or predictable and monotonous. If we wish to assure ourselves of a more satisfying cognitive experience with language, we will turn to poems and novels—knowing, of course, that the speech of men in nature and history is distinct from the language of art.

13

2

POETRY AS FICTION

Paradoxes make intriguing titles, but I am not otherwise fond of them and intend, by the end of this article, to dissolve the one that entitles it. I mean to do this by elaborating the proposition that fictiveness is the characteristic quality of what we call "poetry" when we use the term in the broad sense bequeathed by Aristotle, that is, to refer to the general class of verbal artworks. My primary concern will be to develop a conception of poetry that allows us to distinguish it from and relate it to both nonpoetic discourse and other artforms. The view presented here was initially, but rather incidentally, proposed elsewhere.[1] I have found the elaboration of it of continuing interest, however, especially since the grounds for those distinctions and the nature of those relationships remain, to my mind, extremely problematic in contemporary linguistic and aesthetic theory.

Before saying anything at all about poetry, I shall, in what follows, have a few things to say about language generally. Any theory of poetry inevitably, though not always explicitly, presupposes a theory of language. Thus, those who have at various times regarded poetry as inspired speech, or embellished prose, or the language of passion, or "emotive" statements, have obviously had somewhat different notions of what language is when it is *not* poetry—for example, uninspired speech, plain prose, the language

14

of reason, or "verifiable statements." Since, moreover, linguistic theory is now in a very volatile state, no general propositions concerning language can be offered casually or taken for granted. In any case, although I am by no means offering here anything that could be called a theory of language, the first section of this article will develop some general observations on nonpoetic or what I call "natural" discourse, particularly in those respects that are most significant in distinguishing it from poetry. The second section of the article will develop some implications of the conception of poetry as mimetic, or what I shall be calling *fictive*, discourse.

Although the making of distinctions, definitions, and classifications will occupy a good deal of the discussion throughout, it should become clear that my ultimate interest is not in taxonomy but in poetry as an artform. I am concerned with how, on what basis, we actually do identify a verbal structure as poetry, and how that identification directs and modifies our experience and interpretation of that structure both as distinct from a natural utterance and as related to other artforms.[2]

i. Natural Discourse

By "natural discourse" I mean here all utterances—trivial or sublime, ill-wrought or eloquent, true or false, scientific or passionate—that can be taken as someone's saying something, somewhere, sometime, that is, as the verbal acts of real persons on particular occasions in response to particular sets of circumstances. In stressing all these particularities, I wish to emphasize that a natural utterance is a historical *event*: like any other event, it occupies a specific and unique point in time and space. A natural utterance is thus an event in the same sense as the coronation of Elizabeth I on 15 January 1559, or the departure this morning from Albany of Allegheny Airlines flight 617, or the falling of a certain leaf from a certain elm tree. Other events more or less resembling these in various respects may occur at other times or in other places, but the event itself—that coronation, that flight, that utterance—cannot recur, for it is historically unique.

The point requires emphasis because it reflects a fundamental distinction that may be drawn between natural utterances and certain other linguistic structures which are *not* historical events and which can be both defined and described independently of any particular instance of *occurrence*. Dictionary entries, for example, or what we refer to abstractly as "the word *fire*" or "the phrase *law and order*" are not themselves particular events; they are, rather, linguistic *forms*, or the names of certain *types* or *classes* of events. And, as such, certain observations may be made about them: for example, the morphemic or phonetic features that define all members of the class, or the syntactic rules governing their accepted use in English sentences, or, of course, the characteristic features of the circumstances in which they *do* occur as part of utterances—in other words, their "dictionary meanings." But these linguistic forms—words, phrases, and so on—are not themselves historical events unless or until they occur as the verbal responses of particular persons on particular occasions. Obviously "the word *fire*" as a general class is a very different sort of thing from a specific utterance, "Fire!", which may warn a man that his life is in danger or send a bullet speeding toward him, very much depending on the particular circumstances in which the utterance occurs and to which it is a response.

A natural utterance not only occurs *in* a particular set of circumstances—what is often referred to as its *context*—but is also understood as being a response *to* those circumstances. In other words, the historical "context" of an utterance does not merely surround it but *occasions* it, brings it into existence. The context of an utterance, then, is best thought of not simply as its gross external or physical setting, but rather as the total set of conditions that has in fact determined its occurrence and form.[3] That total set of conditions, what makes us say something at a particular time and also shapes the linguistic structure of our utterance—the specific words we choose, our syntax, our intonation, and so on—is likely to be manifold and complex no matter how simple the utterance. Moreover, the total set of conditions that determines what we say and how we speak is by no means confined to the objects and events "spoken about," or what linguistic theorists of various persuasions refer to as "referents," "designations," "denotations," or "significations."

It is worth noting that the existence of an object or event or even, as we say, an "idea," is never a sufficient reason for responding to it verbally. In other words, the fact that something is true is never a sufficient reason for saying it. If I should be heard to say, "It's five o'clock," the reasons for my saying so would clearly include more than what time of day it was just then, for at any moment it is a certain time, but I do not announce the time continuously through the day. Perhaps, on this occasion, I wished to remind someone of an appointment, or perhaps someone had just asked me for the correct time. Certainly these circumstances were as significant in occasioning my utterance as that specific one to which my words, "It's five o'clock," might seem exclusively to "refer," namely the time of day.

Given any utterable fact or state of affairs, gross or subtle, physical or psychological—the state of the weather, the color of swans, or my opinion of the government—whether or not I will actually utter it, and how I will utter it, will always depend on other variables, that is, attendant circumstances other than that fact or state of affairs. These variables will include, among other things, the presence of a potential listener, my relationship to him, the nature of the social occasion, the immediate verbal context (what either he or I have been saying), and, perhaps most significantly, the conventions of the linguistic community to which we both belong.

There is no reason to maintain a sharp distinction between the sort of physical and social variables just mentioned and what might otherwise be thought of as the internal, personal, mental, or psychological springs of speech. It is obvious that among the circumstances that provoke, occasion, and shape an utterance are conditions peculiar to the speaker's current state: his emotions, his feelings, his memories, expectations, beliefs, and desires. I may say "It's five o'clock" partly because I am hungry or anxious or bored, and such conditions must also be recognized as part of the context of the utterance. We should note, moreover, that the speaker's "current state" is inevitably the product of his past as well as his current experiences, including, most significantly, his past *verbal* experiences, and that part of his psychological or mental condition—and therefore part of the context of his utterance—is how he has learned to use language.

Although we may, for certain purposes, describe an utterance exclusively in terms of its linguistic form (for example, as a certain concatenation of lexemes and/or phonemes), a natural utterance can never be adequately specified or described as an *event* except in relation to the context in which it occurred. In other words, a verbal event, like any other event, is individuated as much by its context as by its form. Thus, although we could say that two men each pulling the trigger of a gun are engaged in acts of the same *form*, it is clear that Mr. X shooting Mr. Y is not the same event as Mr. A shooting Mr. B, or as Mr. X shooting Mr. Y again fifteen minutes later. Similarly, when I say, making introductions at a party, "This is my daughter," it may not be a unique event with respect to its linguistic form, but it is certainly not the same event as some other woman saying it of her daughter or, indeed, as my own saying it on some other occasion, either fifteen minutes later to some other guest or even absentmindedly to the same one as before.

Moreover, it is unlikely that any two natural utterances would be even *formally* identical if one extends attention to the more subtle aspects of their linguistic form. For although each utterance could be transcribed with the same symbols, such a transcription preserves only a fraction of the total physical reality constituting each utterance, a reality that would include not only a certain sequence of phonemes, but also intonational features such as pitch contours, stress, pacing, and usually facial expressions and other gestures as well. While some linguists may regard the latter aspects of the utterance with suspicion and dispute their status as linguistic features, it is nevertheless becoming increasingly evident that there is no absolute discontinuity between the part of an act or event that is called "verbal" and the totality of that act or event. In other words, a natural utterance is always continuous with the speaker's total ongoing behavior and also continuous with the total world of natural events. The professional linguist's or our own ordinary description of the utterance reflects an arbitrary demarcation and abstraction from the fullness, the density, and the spatial, temporal, and causal continuity of all human action and all events in nature.

Most of us would agree that it is impossible to provide a complete and exhaustive description of a nonverbal historical event such as

18

the coronation of Elizabeth or the departure of flight 617. What the historian offers will usually be a selection or abstraction of certain features of these events at a level thought adequate for the purpose at hand. It is clear, moreover, that neither an eyewitness report nor, if we had it, even a videotape, would constitute a total record of the event; and neither one, of course, would constitute the event itself. The same limits and distinctions apply to the descriptions and records of verbal events: Elizabeth's first speech to Parliament on 4 February 1559, or my farewells this morning to my family. No description or record would be complete, neither a vocal quotation nor a tape recording, in either of which many features of the original event would be lost. The fact, however, that verbal events can be transcribed in a standard notational system often seems to obscure for us their similarity to other events. It is true that orthography and phonetic notation allows us to record or describe natural utterances with considerable subtlety and specificity of detail through conventionalized symbols. Moreover, a transcription of this kind—that is, a "text" of the utterance—may be an adequate description or record of it for most purposes. Nevertheless, we should not confuse a copy of that text with the verbal event itself, the historical act of a particular speaker on a particular occasion.

The relation of utterances to texts is of special interest to us here since, at least in our own culture, we typically encounter poetry as texts. The relation is extremely complex, however, with respect to both natural and poetic discourse, and, indeed, it is not always the same relation. I have just been speaking of texts that serve as records or descriptions of natural utterances, that is, inscriptions of verbal events that occurred at some specific time, such as Elizabeth's first address to Parliament. Not all texts bear this relation to some natural utterance. Many texts—personal letters, for example—are not records or descriptions of utterances, but constitute utterances themselves, only in written rather than vocal form. It is true, of course, that there are other very significant aspects to the relation between writing and vocal speech, and they are not mutually independent or simply parallel possibilities. Nevertheless, to the extent that the writer's act of composing and inscribing is a historically specific and unique verbal event, it is analogous to the

19

speaker's act of emitting the sounds that comprise spoken discourse. And thus we may regard the product of either act as a natural utterance.

In view of the Gutenberg revolution, the question may arise as to whether printed (or otherwise duplicated) texts can also be regarded as natural utterances, and the answer here is sometimes yes and sometimes no. A printed text may be simply one of many copies of an inscribed record of a vocal utterance that, like Elizabeth's Address, did occur at some specific time and place. In this case, the text is *not* a natural utterance, but the transcription of one. But a printed work may also be a natural utterance itself in written form, exactly like a personal letter—though the letter, of course, usually exists as only a single text. It may be initially difficult to conceive of a printed work as a natural utterance and thus, by our definition here, a historically *unique* event. We should recognize, however, that no matter how many duplications of a text are subsequently produced, the writer's actual composition of the linguistic structure that constitutes that text was and remains a historically unique event. ("Unique" here does not mean *unitary*, and it is understood that the composition of the text will often consist of numerous "acts" dispersed in time, from the initial jottings to the ultimate revisions.)

To summarize these points, then: whether or not a composition was written to be printed, and no matter how long it is, or how long it took to write, and no matter how remote in time or space the writer from his ultimate audience, or how eloquent its style, or how culturally significant and otherwise estimable it is, the composition must still be regarded as a *natural utterance* so long as it may be taken as the verbal responses of a historically real person, occasioned and determined by a historically real universe. And this means that *most* of what we call "literature" in the general sense of inscribed compositions does in fact consist of natural utterances. This would include works ranging from Aristotle's *Metaphysics* and Macaulay's *History of England* to an article in a scientific journal or an editorial in this morning's *New York Times*. These are all as much natural utterances as the remarks exchanged between me and a colleague a few moments ago.

There remains, however, one other class of texts that are neither natural utterances in written form nor the transcription of natural utterances that originally occurred in vocal form, and this class consists of the texts of *fictive utterances*, including most prominently those compositions that we otherwise refer to as works of imaginative literature—poems, tales, dramas, and novels. I shall reserve comment on these texts until later, in connection with the general discussion of fictive discourse; for, as we shall see, fictive utterances bear an altogether distinctive relation to their own texts when indeed (as is not always the case) such texts exist.

But we may return now from the texts to the *contexts* of natural utterances, and thereby to the crucial question of meaning and interpretation. A natural utterance cannot be exclusively identified or described independent of its context, nor can its meaning be understood independent of that context. Indeed, what we often mean by the "meaning" of an utterance *is* its context, that is, the set of conditions that occasioned its occurrence and determined its form. The view of meaning proposed here is not offered as an analysis of all the numerous senses in which the term has been or could be used, and certainly not as a solution to the ever-proliferating number of problems associated with it in contemporary linguistics and philosophy. Nevertheless, a causal conception of meaning—which this is—has much to recommend it, particularly here, since it permits us to appreciate better the distinctive nature of poetic discourse and of its "interpretation." Moreover, it is not so idiosyncratic as may first appear, for "meaning" in the sense of *causes* or *determinants* will often be found to accommodate or correspond to familiar usage of the term.

I must emphasize that I am speaking here of the meaning not of *words* but of *utterances*, a distinction not always grasped even by those most concerned with these problems. One may ascertain the meanings of those abstract classes called *words* by determining the conventions governing their usage in the relevant linguistic community, usually by consulting one's experience of the language or, when difficulties arise, either a dictionary—or an analytic philosopher. Dictionaries and philosophers are of only limited help, however, in ascertaining the meaning of particular verbal events. When we speak ordinarily of the meaning of a particular utterance—

that is, what someone has said—we are usually concerned not with the definitions of the words that compose it or even, in a restricted sense, with what it "refers" to, but rather with *why it occurred*: the situation and motives that produced it, the set of conditions, "external" and "internal," physical and psychological, that caused the speaker to utter that statement at that time in that form—in other words, what we are calling here its *context*.

For example, definitions and referents are not what interest John when he asks, "What do you mean?", in response to his friend's remark, "You know, I think Bill is a fool." Pointing to Bill and offering an analysis of the "concept" of folly will probably not answer his question. Knowing this, his friend is more likely to describe certain circumstances, observations he has made, impressions he has had (and perhaps also his motives for articulating them at that moment), and so forth, until John says, "Oh, well, now I understand what you mean," meaning that he has located to his own satisfaction the reasons for or *causes of* his friend's remark. The qualification here, "to his own satisfaction," is an important one, for it is most unlikely that John would in fact have identified *all* the determinants involved.

We rarely "understand completely" one another's utterances, nor do we need or seek to do so. Criteria for the adequate understanding of an utterance vary widely, depending on the nature of the utterance and the primary purposes and interests of the speaker and listener. And although sometimes—for example, in a psychoanalyst's office—one may probe for increasingly subtle and obscure determinants, both speaker and listener are usually satisfied with considerably less than a total identification of *all* of them. It is usually not necessary, and of course it is usually not possible, for the listener to ascertain all the conditions that make up the context of an utterance. It is not necessary because many of them will be trivial and irrelevant to his concerns. And it is not possible either because the speaker's original context is remote in time or space, or because many of the springs of speech are not apparent from the immediate context or, as we say, are private or internal to the speaker. The listener or audience, therefore, is always obliged to "interpret" what is said or written. That is, to the extent that the listener *has* an interest in those unavailable determinants, he must hypothesize, imagine, or *infer* them.

When we read the inscribed utterance of a friend, such as a letter from him, we may be more aware of interpreting as such than when we listen to him speak, but we do so in both instances and by the same process: partly through inferences based on what we know of him personally, but mostly through inferences based on all our own prior experiences, especially our prior experiences with language. And, when he alludes either in speech or writing to matters of which we have no specific knowledge—for example, a third person whom we have never met, a place we have never visited—we supply our ignorance by an imaginative projection of what we do know generally. It is important to emphasize, however, that these projections are attempts to infer or approximate *actual* circumstances, and thus are subject to correction should our knowledge become more specific. ("Oh, *you're* Charlie's brother. From what he said, I pictured you as much older.")

What makes a letter particularly interesting as an utterance is the fact that, since it lacks the supplementary information usually conveyed to the listener by intonation and gestures as well as by shared physical contexts (we cannot point to things in letters), this sort of information will commonly be supplied by the writer in other ways: by explicit allusions ("As I write this, I am sitting by my study window—you know, the one that looks out over the back garden," and so on), by graphic substitutes for intonation (for example, underlining, punctuation, spacing), and by more subtle modifications of the language itself (for example, in diction, syntax, turns of phrasing, and metaphor). Our syntax in letters, because it carries a greater burden of information than in conversational speech, not only *can* be but *must* be more controlled. To be sure, since we are often more or less conscious of the generic relation of our letters to "literature," we will employ forms such as archaisms and metaphoric imagery that would seem pretentious or otherwise inappropriate in conversational speech. This, however, does not altogether account for the fact that some of us become, in our letters, rather uncharacteristically eloquent and "literary"; for, as we shall see, there are other reasons why the linguistic features of letters often bear an interesting resemblance to those commonly associated with poetic discourse.

II. FICTIVE DISCOURSE

Poems are not natural utterances, not historically unique verbal acts or events; indeed a poem is not an event at all, and cannot be said ever to have "occurred" in the usual sense. When we read the text of a poem or hear it read aloud, our response to it as a linguistic structure is governed by quite special conventions, and it is the understanding that these conventions are operating that distinguishes the poem as a verbal artwork from natural discourse. The operation of these conventions is most readily apparent in dramatic poetry, that is, plays, where it is understood that the acts and events performed on the stage are not *happening* but are being *represented* as happening. When we see a production of *Hamlet*, we do not watch a queen drinking poison, but the enactment of such an event, which may be said to "occur" only in being thus enacted. But among the acts and events represented on the stage are also verbal ones. As the actor who portrays Claudius leans forward and extends his arm in a gesture of horror and abortive warning, thus representing a man leaning forward and extending his arm, and so on, that actor also utters the words, "Gertrude, do not drink," thus representing a man uttering those words. We are not aware here of any radical discontinuity between the enactment of a physical action and the enactment of an utterance—and of course an utterance *is* a physical action, though it has other characteristics that sometimes obscure that fact.

Most of us would be quite willing to grant the existence of what could be called *mimetic* or *fictive discourse*—that is, the representation of speech—at least in dramatic poetry. What I would like to suggest, however, is that *all* poetry may be so regarded, that we could conceive of as fictive discourse not only the representation of speech in drama, but also lyrics, epics, tales, and novels. The conception of poetry as mimetic is, of course, quite ancient, and modern theorists do continue to assert that literature is a representational art. It is by no means clear, however, what or what kind of thing it is that the poem "imitates" or represents. One common

24

notion seems to be that poetry, apparently on the analogy of painting, somehow represents "images in words." Or, in view of the existence of numerous imageless poems and passages in novels, that it represents ideas or feelings, either the author's or those of his characters. Or, in view of how restrictive even this formulation is, it is sometimes suggested that literary works, especially narrative fictions, represent imagined events or even worlds—*in*, it will solemnly be added, *the medium of language*. I will not attempt here to indicate all the problems entailed by such suggestions,[4] for I wish only to point out that they all ignore what might be thought most apparent, namely that what poems do represent "in the medium of language" is *language*, or more accurately, speech, human utterance, discourse. The conception of poetry as fictive discourse proposed here attempts to close in on poetry from two directions: one, as it may be distinguished from other mimetic artforms, and two, as it may be distinguished from other verbal compositions. As a mimetic artform, what a poem distinctively and characteristically represents is not images, ideas, feelings, characters, scenes, or worlds, but *discourse*. Poetry does, like drama, represent actions and events, but exclusively verbal ones. And, as a verbal composition, a poem is characteristically taken to be not a natural utterance, but the *representation* of one.

A poem represents discourse in the same sense as a play, in its totality, represents human actions and events, or a painting represents visual objects. When we speak of the objects represented in or by a painting, it is understood that they need not correspond to any particular objects, but rather to an identifiable class of them. A painting can depict a landscape that exists as a visual object only in the depiction itself. Thus, when we speak of *mimesis* or representation in an artwork, we recognize that it does not constitute the imitation or reproduction of existing objects or events, but rather the fabrication of fictive objects and events of which there are existing or possible instances or types—whether they be rural landscapes, star-crossed lovers, or laments for dead friends. In other words, to say that an artist has represented a certain object or event is to say that he has constructed a fictive member of an identifiable class of natural ("real") objects or events.

Part of what has obscured the relation of poetic *mimesis* to pictorial and other kinds of artistic representation are traditional notions that identify the various artforms in terms of their characteristic *media*. Thus, sound is said to be the medium of music, pigment the medium of painting, and of course words or language the medium of poetry. The corollary formula—X (artwork) represents Y (object of imitation) in Z (medium)—has created more problems than it has illuminated, most conspicuously, perhaps, in regard to music, where art theorists, under the presumed obligation to locate the object that music imitates, have come up with an amazing assortment of chimeras, from shapes of feeling to states of being. It is another problem, however, that concerns us here. The plastic materials that are presumably the media of the visual arts—pigment, stone, metal, and so forth—do not have an expressive function independent of the artworks into which they are fashioned. These materials, moreover, do not in themselves resemble the objects and scenes that they represent. A block of marble is a very different thing from a human figure. The corresponding medium of poetry, however, *language*, is not a "raw" material, but itself a symbolic system with expressive functions independent of its use in artworks. For this reason, it has been difficult to conceive of language as both the medium of an artwork and also what is represented by it.

The difficulty here, however, is really the traditional concept of the art medium itself, particularly its implicit dualism of form and matter. This dualism—the notion of the art medium as formless matter—not only creates problems with regard to poetry (for language is obviously not formless matter), but it also obscures the nature of other artforms. We could just as readily and, I think, more fruitfully, think of the medium of the visual arts not as pigment and stone but as the visually perceived properties of matter or, indeed, as the elements and dynamics of visual perception itself. And, if we must have a corresponding "medium" for poetry, we would do better to locate it not simply in words or language conceived abstractly, but in the whole dynamic complex of verbal behavior and verbal experience.

But if we are content to do without the traditional notion of the

26

art medium altogether, we may be better able to appreciate the essential nature of poetic representation and its relation to artistic *mimesis* generally. As I suggested above, we may conceive of an artwork not as the imitation, in some different "matter," of the "form" of particular objects or events already existing in nature, but as the creation of a fictive member of a certain class of natural objects or events. Thus, paintings are fictive instances of what, in nature, are visually perceived objects. Musical compositions are fictive instances of acoustically perceived events, in other words *designed* sounds as distinguished from sounds simply occurring in nature. And poems are fictive utterances. The kinds of natural events represented in poetry are, of course, quite special: utterances are themselves human constructions, and in that sense "artificial." This should not, however, obscure the sense in which utterances are nevertheless *natural events*, like the flight of birds, the falling of leaves, and all the particular actions of individual men moving about in, and being moved about by, the natural universe.

We can, I think, readily conceive of a-man-walking as a natural event and should be able to conceive of a-man-talking as such; for, as I have already suggested, there is no real discontinuity between verbal and nonverbal events. A painting can represent, through a visual configuration of line and color, a man walking or a child sleeping, because such events are ordinarily perceived primarily as visual events. And although a visual artist can also represent a man talking (one may think, for example, of some of Daumier's prints of lawyers in animated conversation), he cannot represent pictorially the utterance itself, for speech is not perceived as a visual event—except of course, when it is in written form, a matter to which I will return later. But for now let us pursue the example of Daumier a bit further. As a visual artist, he was of course extraordinarily sensitive to the expressive and otherwise interesting qualities of the *appearances* of his fellow creatures: the way they stood and grouped themselves together, the "expressions" on their faces, the gestures of their hands, and so forth. Had he also been, as some people are, extraordinarily sensitive to the expressive and otherwise interesting qualities of the *speech* of his fellow creatures, he might have sought to represent that too. But how could he do so? The answer I am

27

suggesting here is that he could fashion a fictive representation of speech, that is, a poem—something, perhaps, like Browning's "The Bishop Orders His Tomb," which I think we might recognize as a verbal counterpart of a satiric Daumier print: *ut pictura poesis*.

The relation of "dramatic monologues" to dramatic poetry proper is, of course, readily appreciated, and we can see how either could be regarded as mimetic discourse. My claim here, however, is more general, for what is central to the concept of the poem as a fictive utterance is not that the "character" or "persona" is distinct from the poet, or that the audience purportedly addressed, the emotions expressed, and the events alluded to are fictional, but that *the speaking, addressing, expressing, and alluding are themselves fictive verbal acts*. To be sure, a fictive utterance will often resemble a possible natural utterance very closely, for the distinction is not primarily one of linguistic form. Moreover, although certain formal features—verse, most notably—often do mark and indeed identify for the reader the fictiveness of an utterance, the presence of such features are not themselves the crux of the distinction. The distinction lies, rather, in a set of conventions shared by poet and reader, according to which certain identifiable linguistic structures are *taken* to be not the verbal acts they resemble, but representations of such acts. By this convention, Keat's ode "To Autumn" and Shakespeare's sonnets are precisely as fictive as "The Bishop Orders His Tomb" or Tennyson's "Ulysses." The statements in a poem may, of course, resemble quite closely statements that the poet *might* have truly and truthfully uttered as a historical creature in the historical world. Nevertheless, insofar as they are offered and recognized as statements in a poem, they are fictive. To the objection, "But I know Wordsworth meant what he says in that poem," we must reply, "You mean he *would have* meant them if he *had* said them, but he is not saying them." As I shall explain later, we may choose to regard the composition not as a poem but as a historical utterance, but then the conventions by virtue of which its fictiveness is understood and has its appropriate effects are no longer in operation.

Another matter should, however, be clarified at this point. I have said that novels and tales, as well as lyrics, epics, and dramatic poems are also fictive representations of discourse. The fictiveness of prose fiction is, of course, commonly acknowledged, but it is more radical than is sometimes supposed. For not only are the characters and events narrated in a novel fictional, and not only is the narrator whose voice relates the events fictional, but most significantly, so also is the entire structure of discourse through which the narration is presented. Indeed, as we all know, many novels such as *War and Peace* allude to quite real persons and events, a consideration that has created theoretical problems for many literary theorists. The essential fictiveness of novels, however, is not to be discovered in the unreality of the characters, objects, and events alluded to, but in the unreality of the *alludings* themselves. In other words, in a novel or tale, it is the *act* of reporting events, the *act* of describing persons and referring to places, that is fictive. The novel *represents* the verbal action of a man reporting, describing, and referring.

Consider the following two passages:

> He was a gentleman of good family in Buckinghamshire, and born to a fair fortune, and of a most civil and affable deportment. In his entrance into the world, he indulged himself all the license in sports and exercises and company which was used by men of the most jolly conversation; afterwards he retired to a more reserved and melancholy society.

> He had been a member of the Court of Justice, and died at the age of forty-five. His father had been an official who, after serving in various ministries and departments in Petersburg, had made the sort of career which brings men to positions from which by reason of long service they cannot be dismissed.

The first is from the description of John Hampden in Clarendon's *History of the Rebellion*; the second is from Tolstoy's *Death of Ivan Ilyich*. (In both, we might note, allusions are made to real places, Buckinghamshire and Petersburg.) I am suggesting here that the relation between the two passages is that the second is a representation of the kind of thing the first really is, namely a biography. *The Death of Ivan Ilyich* is not the biography of a fictional character, but rather a fictive biography. The fiction attaches no more to the narrated facts of Ilyitch's life than to the fact of someone's narrating them. Tolstoy is, if you like, pretending to be *writing* a biography while actually *fabricating* one.

If we consider literature from the point of view I am developing here, it becomes evident that the various genres of literary art—for example, tales, classical odes, and lyrics—can often be distinguished from each other according to what types of natural discourse they represent: here, respectively, anecdotal reports of past events, public speeches, and more or less private or personal utterance.[5] Poetry itself, as distinct now from novels and stories, traditionally represents various kinds of *spoken* discourse. Certain types of discourse, however, are themselves typically textual inscriptions: that is, they exist characteristically in written and often in printed form—for example, chronicles, journals, letters, memoirs, and biographies. And certain genres of literary art, roughly what we refer to as "prose fiction," characteristically represent such varieties of *inscribed* discourse. Novels, for example, a distinctively post-Gutenberg genre, have typically been representations of chronicles, journals, letters, memoirs, and biographies. This aspect of prose fiction has some interesting implications for the nature of novels as *texts*, but they will be better appreciated after we have given some attention to literary texts generally.

A fictive utterance consists entirely of a linguistic structure, unlike a natural utterance, which consists of a linguistic event occurring in a historical context. In a nonliterate culture, for example, among Northwest American Indian tribes, the linguistic structure that would be identified as *that* song or story is preserved and duplicated, if at all, only in being remembered and recited. But in a literate culture, the identity of the poem may be preserved and reproduced through a standard notational system, that is, in a written text. The text of a poem, however, bears a quite special relation to the utterance of which it is presumably an inscribed counterpart. For it is neither a transcription of an utterance that actually occurred at some specific prior time, like Elizabeth's first speech to Parliament, nor is it a natural utterance in written form, like a personal letter. It is, rather, like the score of a musical composition or the script of a play, that is, formal specifications for the physical production of certain events. The text of the poem tells us, in other words, how to produce the verbal act it represents. This is evident enough for a playscript, which directs the performer's *verbal* actions along with other more obviously physical actions: for example, "enter," "exit," "is stabbed," "falls," *says* "I am dead, Horatio; wretched Queen, adieu." But this is true of any poetic text, that is, the text of any verbal artwork that represents spoken rather than written discourse. The text of a novel must be regarded somewhat differently, as I will explain below. But, allowing for this exception, the text of any poem is to be interpreted, in the first instance, as, in effect, a score or stage directions for the performance of a purely verbal act that exists only in being thus performed. A poem is never spoken, not even by the poet himself. It is always re-cited; for whatever its relation to words the poet *could* have spoken, it has, as a poem, no initial historical occurrence. What the poet composes as a text is not a verbal act but rather a linguistic structure that becomes, through being read or recited, the *representation* of a verbal act.

As I pointed out above, works of prose fiction are characteristically representations not of spoken but of inscribed utterances, and for this reason the texts of novels are, interestingly enough, closer to pictures than to musical scores. What the text of Richardson's *Clarissa* represents is not the speech of certain characters but a collection of their letters; what *David Copperfield* represents is not the spoken reminiscenses of a man, but his autobiography. Each novel itself, that is, the marks printed on its pages and, if you like, the pages themselves, plus covers and binding, is a depiction of—a fictive instance of—a kind of book. Indeed, in view of its three-dimensionality, the copy of the novel we hold in our hands could be conceived of as a sculpture, where the sculptor has not satisfied himself in representing the gross physical and visual qualities of a book, but has sought to represent the very text of one. But, rather than complicate matters, we may at least agree that what the text of a novel represents is, precisely, a *text*.

In what follows, I shall be speaking again of poetry in the narrower sense, that is, as representations of spoken discourse, usually in verse. Some of the points I shall be making would require a somewhat different or additional formulation with respect to novels or representations of *written* discourse, but I shall not develop them here.

Although a poem, unlike a natural utterance, consists entirely of a linguistic struture, we obviously do not respond to poems as pure forms or merely as organizations of sound, any more than we respond to plays as purely formal structures of movement or to traditional paintings as pure configurations of line and color. For each of these is understood to be a *representational* artform, and the spectator readily infers a meaning or context—though a fictional one—for the objects, actions, and events represented. The curtain rises on *Hamlet*, and we see a human figure blowing his fingers and stamping his feet on a dimly lit stage. Before a word is uttered, we have already inferred at least a cold night as the context for his speech. We read or hear recited a sonnet by Shakespeare: "To me, fair friend, you never can be old . . . ," and no matter how little we know about William Shakespeare of Stratford and the various earls with whom he may have been intimate, we immediately begin to create for those words a plausible and appropriate context: at the minimum, a speaker addressing some other person whom he regards as fair and, in some sense, as his friend. All our experiences with language and the contexts in which men speak not only enable us to make this inference but really *oblige* us to make it.

Throughout our lives as verbal creatures, we have learned to respond to linguistic structures in a certain way: namely to interpret their meanings, to infer their contexts from their forms. Many of the characteristic and valued effects of poetry as a representational artform depend on the strength of our habitual tendency to infer contexts from verbal structures. We should note that Milton, in *Paradise Lost*, does not create Eve or Eden; what he creates, rather, are statements about "Eve" and "Eden" that lead the *reader* to create a woman and a place—in order, as it were, to provide referents or "meanings" for those statements. Other representational artforms depend for their effects on comparable tendencies in the spectator: illusionist painting, for example, depends on fundamental habits of visual perception to transform a configuration of lines and colors on a flat surface into the appearance of a three-dimensional scene or object. It is only because of perceptual conditioning produced by our experiences in the natural visual world that we *can* see, as a cow grazing in the distance, what is actually only a few brushstrokes of color on the upper part of a canvas. This process of interpretive filling-in or perceptual inference is very similar to the process by which we infer, from a few lines in a poem, a rich context of motives, feelings, and situations. "To me, fair friend, you never can be old. . . ." Nine small words that summon up for us a man, his consciousness of the pathos of mutability, and his impulse to deny its hold on his friend.

Thus, although a poem is a fictive utterance without a particular historical context, its characteristic effect is to create its own context or, more accurately, to invite and enable the reader to create a plausible context for it. And what we mean when we speak of *interpreting* a poem is, in large measure, precisely this process of inference, conjecture, and indeed creation of contexts.[6] But these contexts—"meanings"—that we half create and half perceive can be no *more* than "plausible," for the poem is a *fictive* utterance and its contexts can be neither discovered nor verified in nature or history. As we saw earlier, when we interpret a *natural* utterance, we usually seek to ascertain its historical determinants, the context that did in fact occasion its occurrence and form. However complex and elusive that context, it is nevertheless understood to be historically determinate and particular. The context of a fictive utterance, however, is understood to be *historically indeterminate*. This is not to say that we regard the poem as an anonymous gift dropped from the empyrean or ignore the fact that it was *composed* by a real man at a particular time and place. It is to say, rather, that we may distinguish between the poet's act of composing the poem and the verbal act that the poem represents, just as we would distinguish William Shakespeare's act in composing *Hamlet* and the acts of the Prince of Denmark represented in the play. Shakespeare composed the play, let us say, in 1603, but in what year did Hamlet kill Claudius? In one sense, he kills Claudius every time the play is performed, whether in 1603 or 1970; but in another sense the slaying of Claudius is an act that never did, never will, and never can occur *in the historical world*. It can only be represented as occurring. The composition of the play, then, was a historically determinate event, but the events represented in the play are historically indeterminate. This means, among other things, that when we ask why Hamlet abuses Ophelia in the nunnery scene, we do not expect to find the answer in any historical particulars of the life of William Shakespeare or of the circumstances that occasioned his composition of the play. Knowledge of these particulars and circumstances may, of course, help us account for why Shakespeare *wrote* a play in which a character named Hamlet abuses a character named Ophelia, but that is an altogether different question. To understand *why Hamlet abuses Ophelia*, the reader must infer from, on the one hand, the linguistic structure of the play and, on the other hand, everything he knows about the world of men and the relation of their acts to their situations and motives, a plausible set of motives and situations for *that* act.

Similarly for a sonnet by Shakespeare, say 87, which begins: "Farewell, thou art too dear for my possessing,/And like enough thou knowst thy estimate...." To interpret it as a poem, to understand why the speaker is saying "farewell" in such apparently bitter tones to someone on whom he thought to have some claims of love, the reader will not require any particulars concerning Shakespeare's private life: the identity and moral character of whatever young men he knew at the time, the specific incidents of personal betrayal from which he may have suffered, or his opinion of himself as a lover. What the reader does require is the capacity to conceive of the *kind* of situation that *might* lead a man to feel thus and speak thus, and the reader can develop that capacity only out of his own experiences with men, their situations, their feelings, and especially their language.

The interpretation of a poem as a *historical* utterance may serve the special purposes of the literary historian or biographer, but it is likely to appear shallow, reductive, or "literal-minded" precisely to the degree that it restricts the context of the poem to historical particulars and suggests that the meanings of the poem are to be located exclusively in a historically determinate context. For example, a recent editor of Shakespeare's *Sonnets* prefixes the following note to Sonnet 107 as part of his running commentary on what was happening in Shakespeare's personal life at the very moment he was writing the poems: "Shakespeare had just escaped from the danger of his Company's involvement with the Essex rebellion and ... the Queen, furious with Pembroke for fathering Mary Fitton's child and refusing to marry her, had sent Pembroke to jail...."[7] Then comes the sonnet:

> Not mine own fears, nor the prophetic soul
> Of the wide world dreaming on things to come,
> Can yet the lease of my true love control,
> Supposed as forfeit to a confined doom....

Forfeit, indeed, to a confined doom, if interpreted as this editor suggests. But for the reader who values the sonnet as a verbal artwork, this sort of interpretation is absurd not only because its foundations in history are, in fact, quite dubious, but because the invocation of particulars of this kind—even if they were accurate— have no greater claim to constituting the "meaning" of the poem than an interpretation that infers from it and provides for it an appropriate and coherent context of circumstances and motives, quite independent of Pembroke, Mary Fitton, particular jails, and particular rebellions.

I pointed out earlier that personal letters often exhibit characteristics that we associate with poetic discourse, a "literariness" that is produced, for example, by unusually well-controlled syntax, precision of diction, elaborateness or specificity of descriptions, imagery, allusion, and metaphor. Since a letter will be read in a context both temporally and spatially remote from that in which it was composed, the writer must provide exclusively *through* its linguistic structure the sort of supplementary information that is otherwise, in spoken utterance, provided by the physical context shared by speaker and listener and also by the speaker's intonation and gestures. The letter writer, in other words, must exploit all the expressive possibilities of language itself to enable his reader to infer and reconstruct properly the meanings and context of his original utterance.

The poet is obviously operating under the same limitations, but even more so. He must convey to his readers not only a context remote from them in space and time, but one that may never have existed in history or nature, that may consist entirely of what the reader will be enabled to construct (rather than reconstruct) from the verbal form of the poem. Moreover, the poet must suggest, exclusively through a linguistic structure, the experiences, attitudes, and feelings—and, indeed, the identity—of a speaker of whom the reader has no other knowledge. Finally, especially since the text of the poem will function as the script for its future performance (and by reciters other than the poet), it must specify or direct its own vocal realization, including its pacing and other intonational features.

The poet will, therefore, in the verbal structure he composes, be straining to the limit all the expressive resources of language. And, beyond that limit, he will sometimes devise new ones. But what are sometimes spoken of as "poetic devices" (and we may include here rhythm or meter) are really the potentially expressive features of *natural* discourse. Tropes and figures, distortions of idiomatic syntax, departures from idiomatic diction, imagery and allusion— all these are certainly not restricted to poetic discourse; nor can they be taken as the distinctive characteristics of poetic language. They are not what defines poetry but are, rather, entailed by what does define it, namely its fictiveness.

Because a poem does not reflect but *create* the context in which its meanings are located, its linguistic structure must carry an extraordinary burden. Poetic language seems—and indeed *is*—richer, more "suggestive" and "evocative" than the language of natural discourse precisely because and to the extent that it requires the reader to participate in the creation of its meanings. In our efforts to interpret the poem, to construct the context of human situations and motives it demands in order that its meanings be realized, we will draw on all our experiences of the world and words of men. Indeed, the activity of interpreting poetry often becomes the occasion for our recognition and acknowledgment of otherwise inaccessible feelings and, in a sense, our own otherwise unknowable knowledge. The richer and more extensive our experiences and feelings—or as we say, "the

36

more we *bring to* the poem"—the more significance it can have for us, which is why, of course, subsequent readings of a poem "reveal" more meanings. The language of a poem seems characteristically "concentrated" because it allows for such an extraordinary and continuous expansiveness of meaning, not confined to finite and particular determinants, but drawing on all we know that we can relate to it. The language of the poem continues to mean as long as we have meanings to provide for it. Its meanings are exhausted only at the limits of the reader's own experience and imagination.

In speaking of the contexts created or projected by the reader, I have repeatedly used the term *plausible*; and although I have seemed to be saying, "If the meaning fits, wear it," I have also implied that the meaning must fit. This fitness and plausibility relate to significant constraints on interpretation that are themselves among the conventions of fictive discourse. Though these constraints differ in many respects from those involved in our interpretations of natural discourse, they are nevertheless substantial; and although there are inevitably grounds for argument in determining them for individual poems, they are nevertheless relatively determinate.

The poet, in composing the poem, will have made certain assumptions regarding his audience, specifically that they are members of a shared linguistic and cultural community, and thus able and willing to abide by relevant linguistic, cultural, and indeed literary conventions. Although a poem is a representation of discourse, we can understand it, infer meanings for it, only through our prior experiences with the sort of thing it does represent, namely natural utterances in historical contexts. The poet assumes, therefore, that his reader has a knowledge of the language represented by the poem and the linguistic conventions that govern the relation of an utterance to its meanings in that language. However, as we all know, linguistic convention can hardly be separated from cultural convention. An appropriately informed reader who encounters the word *God* in a poem by a seventeenth-century Englishman is not likely to interpret it as the deity of the Muslims or Hopi Indians, any more than he is likely to interpret a painting of the coronation of Elizabeth as the crowning of the Queen of Siam. Furthermore, the poet will

37

assume that his readers are capable of identifying his composition as one of a kind—a *genre*—of artwork, and therefore of interpreting it in relation to those generic and artistic conventions that operated for him in composing it. Thus the reader who is quite unfamiliar with the forms and traditional functions of the masque, and mistakes *Comus* for the script of an ordinary theatrical comedy, will obviously be interpreting it inappropriately.[8] We should note here that the poet's assumptions are not to be confused with his intentions. Whereas the latter—his intentions—are specific, personal, and can usually only be surmised, the former—his assumptions—are general, communal, and are therefore more likely to be recoverable.

The linguistic, cultural, and generic constraints on interpretation alluded to here are, of course, what much professional criticism (or "philology" in the broad sense) is directed toward establishing. And to the extent that it is engaged in determining the existence and nature of such assumptions and conventions on the basis of historical and publicly accessible data, criticism is a cognitively respectable enterprise issuing in at least theoretically "verifiable" and indeed cumulative knowledge (granting the probabilistic nature of verifiability in regard to historical facts and the inevitable grounds for uncertainty and controversy regarding their relevance to individual poems). It would be well, however, to recognize the distinction between this enterprise, which is more or less continuous with that of the cultural historian, and the aspect of professional criticism mentioned in footnote 6, that is, the public articulation and elaboration of the critic's experience as the audience of an artwork. Both are commonly spoken of as "interpretation" and, of course, both frequently appear in conjunction, but claims that may be made for the one cannot be made for the other, and their functions and value are distinctively different. The meanings of a work that a philological "interpretation" seeks to establish are those that the poem bears in relation to the historical universe in which it was composed, and are themselves historical and determinate; but the meanings that the poem has by virtue of its characteristics as a fictive utterance are historically indeterminate and thus cannot be the object of objective or cumulative knowledge, though we may for various reasons find their "interpretation" by individual readers interesting and valuable. It might be added that each of these types of interpretation may, in turn, be distinguished from those interpretations briefly alluded to below as the reader's (and, when publicly elaborated, the critic's) hypotheses and inferences concerning the poet's governing artistic design. The meanings of "interpretation" are no less multiple than the meanings of "meaning."

A final observation should be made here regarding the view of interpretation I have been developing. To recognize a poem as fictive rather than natural discourse, as a verbal artwork rather than an event in nature, is to acknowledge it as the product of a human design in accord with certain valued effects. I have not discussed here the very crucial question of the distinction between the effects or functions of fictive and natural discourse because it is a question that involves substantial problems in linguistic as well as poetic theory, and could not be dealt with briefly.[9] We should, however, at least acknowledge the fact that part of the effect of a poem, as distinct from a natural utterance, derives from the reader's awareness of the poet standing, as it were, behind the poem as its creator and artificer. This awareness is also commonly reflected in our interpretations, for among the meanings we seek for and infer from a poem are those that, in Aristotelian terms, might be called its *final* causes: that is, the motives or intentions, the governing design, of the poet as an artist, distinct from either a natural speaker or the fictive speaker of a poem. Thus, we can interpret Hamlet's abuse of Ophelia both in terms of a plausible set of human motives projected for Hamlet *and* in terms of a plausible set of artistic motives projected for Shakespeare; and the same sort of double interpretation could be offered for any poem.

This double aspect of interpretation reflects a more fundamental doubleness in the nature of poetry, indeed the duplicity of art itself. As we view the canvas, the myriad spots of paint assume the guise of natural objects in the visual world, but we are nevertheless always half-conscious of them as spots of paint. As we watch the play, the stage recedes and the personal identities of the actors yield to those of the fictions whom they portray, but when, at the final curtain, we clap our hands, it is not Hamlet whom we are applauding, but the performers and the playwright himself. The illusions of art are never *del*usions. The artwork interests, impresses, and moves us both as the thing represented and as the *representing* itself: as the actions and passions of Prince Hamlet and as the achievement of William Shakespeare, as the speech of men—and as the poet's fictions.

3

ON THE MARGINS OF DISCOURSE

I. DEFINITIONS AND CLASSIFICATIONS

What a Disease is, almost every Physician defines.

The Anatomy of Melancholy, I.i.2

Asked (or challenged) to define poetry, one is likely to reply with a sigh, a shrug, a look of exasperation or even one of contempt, indicating not only that the question is oppressive but that anyone who asks it must be something of a fool, a pest, or a vulgarian. Though these uncongenial reactions may be interpreted as the signs of intellectual embarrassment, they are, I think, quite justified. For the nature of definition and the particular historical fortunes of the term *poetry* conjoin to this effect: that a definition of the term will either be a total chronicle of those fortunes or will constitute merely one more episode in them. In other words, a definition of *poetry* is bound to be either inadequate to the job or, if adequate, then both unmanageable and uninteresting for any other purpose.

Problems of definition have attended literary theory almost from the beginning, which is to say, Aristotle. An obsessive and scrupulous classifier, he notes in the *Poetics* that while the term *poet* (ποιητης) is applied indiscriminately to all those who compose in meter, even if the composition is a treatise on medicine or physics, there is no term to distinguish and label what he evidently believes is the more significant class, namely, mimetic verbal compositions,

41

whether in meter or not. The same problem bemuses Sidney and Ben Jonson (the observation of it becomes, in fact, a commonplace of Renaissance criticism), and it is hardly solved by Coleridge who, in the space of three pages in the *Biographia Literaria*, offers a series of five definitions of poetry: poetry in the lowest sense, a legitimate poem, poetry of the highest kind, and poetry in the strictest use of the word, all of which are set aside in favor of a definition of the poet, which turns out to be a definition of the Imagination.

The difficulties are understandable and are still with us. A descriptive definition of a term such as *poetry* is primarily responsible to a history of usage: it attempts to specify the conditions governing the conventionally sanctioned use of the term in a given linguistic community. But the conditions governing the use of the term *poetry* have expanded, contracted, and shifted many times over in the history of its occurrence in actual utterances; and the presumable extension or denotation of the term—that is, poems, or the actual practices of "poets"—is itself a historical set of phenomena, with characteristics that develop and often change radically without particular regard for, or sense of obligation to, traditional definitions.

The difficulties are increased, moreover, by the very fact that the term *poetry* has been subjected to such a long history of explicit and self-conscious defining, so that any proposed definition must pay due respects not only to ordinary usage but also to what is, in effect, a series of independent and often conflicting traditions of usage and normative definition in the hands of critics, manifesto writers, and other theorists. One other tradition—implied, for example, when we speak of "poetry in the *broad* sense"—has arisen partly from that same dissatisfaction that Aristotle felt: the suspicion or conviction that there exists an interesting and significant class of verbal compositions, the distinctive nature of which is obscured by the conventional association of the term *poetry* with verse. I will return to that point later, but for the moment we might note that it would certainly be easier to define poetry if it had not been defined so much already.

Complicating the enterprise even further is the fact that the English word *poetry* has put in long service as a translation of presumably equivalent wordforms in other languages, and has thereby acquired intensions and extensions carried over from significantly different cultures and linguistic communities, with histories of usage that may conflict in fundamental ways with the history of the term's usage in English. Finally, the definition becomes even more problematic as a result of our increasing interest in and knowledge of the "poetry" of remote and primitive cultures. For although it is understandable that we should appropriate that term to refer to compositions that share so patently some of the characteristic features of our own verbal artworks, we inevitably discover in them other features, functional as well as formal, of a quite different sort; and these discrepancies in turn threaten to obscure or muddle whatever coherence and continuity of reference may be claimed for the term in our own culture and linguistic community. Thus we ask whether Hopi creation myths are really poems, and whether poetry really includes or should include anonymous communal chants.

The difficulties described here are reflected in those classic problems of classification that, even in the most sophisticated circles, are forever raised, repeated, and reinvented: problems arising either from intractably divergent views of how poetry *should* be defined or from the pressure of borderline cases on inherently feeble borders. Thus we open the gates between verse and prose in order to allow in such desirable immigrants as novels or "imaginative" essays, only to discover that we then have no way to keep out their undesirable relatives, such as vivid journalism or elegantly written philosophical papers. Or we establish more stringent criteria for admission in order to keep out the riffraff, only to find that we have thereby also excluded some natural-born citizens. Pope's *Essay on Man* and "Thirty Days Hath September" may, we say, be verse (or poetry in the formal sense, or in the loose sense, or in *your* sense), but they certainly are not poetry (or not poetry in the real sense, or in the most emphatic sense, or in *my* sense); and Plato's *Dialogues*, the sermons of Jeremy Taylor, and *Moby Dick* may not be verse (or poems in the formal sense, and so on) but they certainly are poetry (or poetry of the highest kind, or in the most universal sense, and so on). Disputes over such claims cannot be resolved nor conclusive answers given to comparable questions of classification created by

43

the innovative productions of poets, the discoveries of anthropologists, or the formulations of new generations of literary critics. For, as these disputes and questions themselves bear witness, the actual practices of the English linguistic community with regard to the wordform *poetry* have been and remain so divergent and inconsistent that any resolution or answer would constitute merely one more ad hoc and essentially arbitrary definition of the term, with no greater claim than any other to descriptive accuracy. It would not, then, be at all unreasonable or frivolous to conclude that *poetry* simply cannot be usefully defined.[1]

To observe that the term *poetry* cannot be usefully defined, or that there is a constantly shifting and dissolving borderline between what we usually call *poetry* and all the other things from which we might like to distinguish it, does not oblige us to deny the possibility of any relevant distinction between classes of verbal composition. It merely suggests that the distinctiveness of those classes is not reflected in the consistency of our labels for them. Their distinctiveness may, however, be reflected in something else at least as significant, namely, the distinctiveness of our actual behavior and experiences with respect to them. It seems clear, for example, that no matter how vague or naive our literary theories, or how problematic our explicit definitions, we do make *functional* discriminations between, say, biographies and novels, and between the transcriptions of actual utterances and the scripts of plays, through the very manner in which we experience and interpret them, and the sort of value and implications they have for us. In other words, we take them as different *kinds* of things and, accordingly, *take* them differently.

Most children learn at a relatively early age that some of the things we tell them are "really true" and others are "just stories" or, more generally, that sometimes we are saying things to them and at other times using language in a rather different spirit and with a different force. They learn to make this distinction quite in ignorance of, and independent of, categories such as fact and fiction or chronicle and tale. Nor do they make the distinction on the basis of the inherent credibility or "imaginativeness" of a narration: for many contemporary storybooks narrate banal events about banal characters hardly distinguishable from events and persons in their own lives, while many things we tell children truly must seem inherently incredible in terms of a child's own experiences. (How believable, for example, can a child of four find our statement that men have traveled to and walked on the moon? Yet the child will appreciate the difference between our telling him that and our telling him a story about a boy with a red balloon.) The distinction between, on the one hand, things that are *said* and, on the other hand, things such as stories, nursery rhymes, songs, and verbal games is learned, rather, on the basis of the child's own differential experiences with respect to each: the different contexts in which they occur, the different vocal tones in which they are delivered, the different stylistic features they may exhibit, but most significantly, the different force—implications and consequences—they have as verbal structures.[2]

The point I wish to emphasize here is not merely that children learn to make that sort of discrimination before they have terms for it, but that even when, as adults, the more sophisticated distinctions and labels are known, we continue to make functional discriminations of a comparable sort and on comparable grounds, producing, experiencing, and responding to various verbal structures differentially, in terms of what might be called "covert" categories, that is, categories implicitly acknowledged and respected in the culture, and learned by its members, but cutting through and across the explicit distinctions presumably reflected in traditional terms such as *poetry, prose, literature, fiction,* and *nonfiction.*

If the reality and significance of such covert functional categories can be recognized, then one may cheerfully abandon the thankless enterprise of stalking definitions for such terms and direct one's attention instead to how we do, in fact, differentially produce and experience various kinds of verbal events and compositions.

The distinction I draw between "natural" and "fictive" discourse is offered as an approach to such an alternative enterprise.[3] It is not intended to serve as a solution to the problems of definition mentioned earlier but, rather, as a diversion from them. "Fictive discourse" is not another name for "poetry" or "imaginative literature"; nor is "natural discourse" an equivalent of "prose," "propositions," or "ordinary language." Neither, in fact, is quite an equivalent of anything else for which we have a name. "Natural" and "fictive" are labels I have chosen to designate what I believe are functional categories in the sense described above. I also believe that exploring the nature of these categories, and the rather special nature of their distinction, may yield an interesting perspective on much that we do speak of as poetry or literature and on its relation to all our experiences of language.

It would not be unreasonable, of course, to ask whether the distinction between fictive and natural discourse developed here does not itself give rise to problems of classification: ambiguous and borderline cases comparable to those associated with traditional distinctions between poetry and whatever it may be distinguished from. Can every existing or conceivable verbal composition be assigned to one or the other of these categories without difficulty, ambiguity, or occasion for controversy? Do these classes, in effect, represent an absolute distinction? The suggestion that they do is likely to arouse skepticism in tempermental monists or those who have learned from intellectual history to be suspicious of all dualities, polarities, and starkly drawn boundary lines. In recent years, moreover, a number of influential literary theorists, having observed the repeated failure and apparent futility of every traditional attempt to establish a watertight definition of poetry or literature, have maintained that there *cannot* be any distinction drawn between poetic and nonpoetic discourse.[4] In view of such skepticism, the alternative concept of a "continuum" may seem more attractive and inherently plausible here. Thus, one might be inclined to argue that the differences between natural and fictive utterances are fundamentally relative and quantitative, and that what are described here as discrete kinds are really only distant points on a spectrum of some sort, a spectrum of degree of stylization, for example, or of personal expressiveness. I would not deny that verbal compositions *could* be arranged on continua of various kinds (though not without difficulty, as has been demonstrated many times over by attempts to do just that) but, as it happens, the principles according to which the items could be thus aligned have nothing to do with the basis of the distinction between fictive and natural discourse. To put this another way, there is no principle of relative differentiation that could allow us to speak of any given composition as "more" or "less" fictive or natural and thereby to assign it its proper place on the continuum.

To give due weight to skepticism, however, the distinction we are concerned with here may be thought of as relatively absolute. The apparent paradox arises from the fact that, although, for reasons to be discussed below, the status of a given composition as either fictive or natural may be problematic and, indeed, may switch under various circumstances, nevertheless on any given occasion that conposition must be taken as one or the other. Natural discourse was defined earlier as all utterances, spoken or inscribed, that can be taken as someone's saying something, sometime, somewhere: all utterances, that is, that are understood to be the verbal acts of particular persons on, and in response to, particular occasions. What is to be emphasized here is the significance of those phrases "taken as" and "understood to be." The distinction between natural and fictive discourse is absolute, as absolute as the distinction between being married or single, or between being Canadian or American; but, like these, it is equally a matter of convention. The Roman Catholic Church may refuse to recognize the civil divorce of communicants, and the chief of an Amazonian tribe may refuse to grant one the privileges afforded by one's American citizenship; for both these classifications depend on assumptions and conventions that have meaning and consequence only insofar as they are recognized and honored within some community. Similarly, the classification of any particular verbal composition as natural or fictive has meaning and consequence only insofar as those concerned with it share certain assumptions regarding how it is to be identified and interpreted, how it is to be taken.

Since the conventions in question here must be learned, it may happen that they are imperfectly mastered or, on some occasion, improperly used or inadequately signaled. Consequently, the appropriate classification of a given composition may be mistaken or doubtful. In quoting a line of verse allusively, we may be mistaken by our listener to have spoken in our own right. When the comedian in a nightclub act suddenly exclaims, with good reason, "Sorry, folks, we're being raided by the police," the audience may laugh, having mistaken the remark as part of the act, and thus fictive. Moreover, since these conventions *are* conventions, they may, like the rules of a game, be switched by the agreement of all the players—in this case usually a tacit agreement signaled in various ways—and what is properly taken to be a natural utterance on one occasion may, with equal propriety, be taken as fictive on another, or vice versa. It may happen, of course, that controversy will arise in connection with individual works, particularly those exhibiting internally contradictory or ambiguous features. For example, we may disagree as to whether Wordsworth's *Prelude* is to be taken as versified autobiography, and thus natural discourse, or the representation of a possible autobiography, and thus fictive; and we may also disagree about how to determine the answer. Similarly, reasons might be urged for taking Boswell's *Life of Johnson* as fictive and Emily Dickinson's verse as natural. In each case, however, the classification one chooses will differentially direct, or be directed by, one's experience of the work and the manner in which one interprets it.

Propriety of classification here is not merely an academic or philosophic concern. As numerous and now familiar psychological experiments have demonstrated, one's perception of and/or response to an event not only determine but are determined *by* how one classifies it: what we "see," and how we subsequently behave toward it, will depend on what we see something *as*. Moreover, since how we classify an event usually depends on our prior experiences with events having similar properties, and an event is likely to share properties with events in a number of other classes, quite practical problems of classification may arise accordingly: our prior experiences may be relatively limited, and conflicting possibilities of appropriate classification may present themselves. The guest who must ask his hostess if he may deposit cigarette ashes in a certain ceramic dish may have been understandably unsure of whether to "take" the dish as an ashtray, a saucer, or an *objet d'art* because it seemed to share distinctive properties with all three.

The fundamental perceptual or cognitive processes that are involved in what we call "generalization" (or, by some, "concept formation"), and by virtue of which prior experiences enable us to classify and thus deal more effectively with relatively novel situa-

tions, may also have personally or socially "dysfunctional" consequences, ranging from simple errors and perplexities to prejudice,
superstition, and what Gilbert Ryle calls "category-mistakes." [5] The
latter, broadly interpreted, would include all those instances in
which the classification of an event or object (or person) made on the
basis of certain of its properties yielded inappropriate assumptions,
expectations, and responses. With respect to discourse, this suggests
that, for us to behave appropriately in response to a given utterance,
we must classify it as, among other things, either fictive or natural.
We must know if a certain narrated anecdote is to be, as we say,
"taken literally" or taken as a joke, and if a certain rather
sensational piece of literature is to be understood as the reflection of
the author's personal history or as the representation of a "confession." Since it is usually to the advantage of the speaker as well as
his listener, or of the poet as well as his reader, that the proper
classification be made, identifying cues or signals, either formal or
contextual, are usually presented: the "joke" is related in a distinctive style and/or with distinctive vocal intonations; the representation of a confession is offered among a group of compositions
labeled or otherwise identifiable as "poems." In each case, the
classification of the utterance as fictive or natural will entail certain
distinctive assumptions, expectations, and responses. How we take
an utterance, or what we understand it to be, will determine the
dynamics of our experience of it, the nature and process of our
interpretation of its meanings, and the kind of consequences and
value it has for us.

It should be noted, however, that we always have the option of
behaving *inappropriately* in response to a given verbal structure, not
merely mistaking a natural for a fictive utterance or vice versa, but
knowingly taking it as something other than what it was "given" as.
Thus, the guest, in our analogy above, lacking a suitable receptacle
for his cigarette, may appropriate a "saucer" for the purpose or,
finding that the "ashtray" lends itself to aesthetic observation, may
choose to regard it as an *objet d'art*. Similarly, correspondence of
intention and reception is not required for a given verbal structure to
function as either natural or fictive discourse on any particular
occasion. We may say that, in taking a verbal structure as something

other than what it was given as, in some way other than its original constructor intended or expected it to be taken, we have in effect regiven it to ourselves.[6]

II. Fictive Illustrations and Examples

Not all fictive utterances are artworks. We fabricate verbal structures for a variety of purposes, including many quite remote from aesthetic ends or effects, and there are numerous kinds of verbal compositions which no one would speak of as poetry in any sense but which are, nevertheless, not natural utterances. There are, for example, those beguiling propositions constructed by logicians to illustrate a point or a problem: *All swans are white. Some swans are white. No swans are white.* This series could, no doubt, be taken as a minimalist poem, but it is certainly not offered as such by the logician, and it is not, in any case, natural discourse. For although the logician has constructed and presented these sentences, he is not, and will not be taken to be, *saying* them—nor is anyone saying them, for they are not being said at all. There are other kinds of fictive utterances that verge, in interesting ways, on poetry, and yet other compositions that verge on, or rather totter between, both fictive *and* natural discourse. These linguistic curiosities include such heterogeneous verbal structures as greeting-card messages, commercial advertisements, quotations, and proverbs. What relates them to each other is the fact that they all either stand beyond or straddle the border that separates natural from fictive discourse. It will be useful to consider these marginal cases here for a number of reasons: first, in order to clarify the nature and suggest the significance and interest of that borderline itself; second, in order to illustrate the range and variety of *non*aesthetic fictive utterances; and finally, in order to indicate both the relation and the distinction between poetry and its compatriots beyond the border.[7]

We may begin by considering the kind of verbal structure that consists of illustrative or exemplary utterances such as the logician's swan song or the propositions and sentences constructed by philosophers, linguists, and the authors of foreign-language textbooks to illustrate a lesson or exemplify a point. A vocabulary list in a Latin textbook, for example, *me, nihil, non, amare, terrere,* is followed by a series of sentences exhibiting those words: *Me non amat, Nihil me terret,* and so on. These sentences are not natural utterances; they are not being said by anyone, including the author of the textbook. He is not thought to be making revelations about his social life or asserting anything about his own character. Nor are they the transcriptions of utterances actually said by any particular person on a particular occasion. Of course, utterances having that form *could* be and no doubt *have* been said, but so could and have the individual words on the vocabulary list: *Me? Non!* Like the individual words, these sentences are verbal forms but not verbal acts or events. Both can be, or become, natural utterances, but only when they occur as the verbal responses of specific people to historically specific sets of circumstances. As textbook examples, they are not natural utterances and do not have meanings in the sense that natural utterances do. For the meanings of the latter are located in the historical universe, confined by and to the *particular* circumstances that actually occasioned them. But the meanings of both the individual words on the vocabulary list and the sentences that exemplify them consist of a *range* of possibilities, the possible circumstances in which those forms *would* be appropriate, the contexts in which they *could*, given the conventions of the linguistic community, plausibly and properly occur.

The logician's exemplary sentences can be regarded in similar terms. When we encounter, in a philosophic article, such structures as *All swans are white* or *The cat is on the mat,* we understand that, although they have the form of propositions, no one is proposing them; that, although they are in some sense statements, no one is stating them. They are not natural utterances, but fictive ones: verbal structures fabricated, constructed, created by someone, but not asserted by him.

The same is understood of those often grotesque, if grammatically "correct," sentences devised by linguists: *John and Harvey like the play and are disappointed by it respectively; John is easy to please; John is eager to please; The carpenter struck the nail with the hammer.* Again, one observes that utterances having these forms *could* occur—some of them, anyway. Philosophers and linguists are marvelously adept at devising sentences that evoke a surrealistic society where conversation consists of the exchange of limp, gratuitous, and otherwise improbable declarations. I will return to that later, but for the moment we are noting that although these sentences *could* be said, they are not, in these instances, *being* said. It would be absurd to ask Professor Chomsky for an introduction to this fellow John who is so easy and eager to please.

It would be no less absurd, of course, to inquire after the historical identity of the young woman to whom Christopher Marlowe's passionate shepherd addresses his invitation to pastoral pleasures— *Come live with me and be my love*—or, indeed, to inquire after the historical identity of the shepherd himself. The poem, too, was never really said by anyone to anyone—though, as a fictive utterance, it is in a sense *being* said eternally. There are, as we shall see in a moment, significant respects in which the poet's lyric and the linguist's example differ, but both are fictive discourse: ahistorical, noncontextual verbal structures, *possible* utterances, but not actual ones.[8]

The nature of the differences between poems and the other fictive utterances we are considering here may be clarified by an analogy drawn from visual art. The sample sentences and propositions of the philosopher and grammarian are verbal *illustrations*; they stand to poems as certain pictorial illustrations stand to visual artworks. The drawing of a laurel oak in a botany text, for example, or of a balalaika in a treatise describing East European musical instruments, is a fictive visual structure. Such a depiction may obviously be distinguished from a particular oak tree or a particular balalaika, each of which is an object in nature and history, with a specific identity in time and space. The illustration of the laurel oak, appearing starkly on the white page of a textbook, surrounded by nothing but printed words, is, in effect, a noncontextual, ahistorical visual structure. As such, however, the illustration can also be distinguished from the representation of an oak tree in a painting. A painting of an oak tree is also a fictive visual structure, but the artist's depiction, unlike the illustrator's, is designed to evoke in the spectator a more or less vivid *impression* of the tree's substantiality, particularity, and historical identity. In other words, the painting suggests or *implies* a specific context in nature and history: the artist's oak tree, composed though it be of spots of pigment on a flat canvas, nevertheless appears to grow from tufts of grass, appears to cast a shadow, appears to be "seen" against the line of horizon, and so forth. Both the textbook illustration and the painting may be referred to as depictions, but only the painting is a fully mimetic representation. In the illustration, the expanse of white paper on which the highly generalized tree is depicted is seen as just that: white paper. In the painting, however—let us say it is a watercolor— that blank expanse is assimilated into the representation: it becomes the sky above the horizon or, indeed, the three-dimensional space which the tree appears to occupy. By implying a context, the painter creates the illusion of one, eliciting the spectator's imaginative projections and perceptual inferences.[9]

The verbal "illustrations" discussed above may be distinguished from verbal artworks—poems—in comparable terms. Both are ahistorical, noncontextual linguistic structures, but the philosopher's *The cat is on the mat* and the Latin textbook's *Me non amat* are not fully mimetic: they depict utterances, but not utterances-in-contexts. The natural context and physical substantiality that the painter implies by colors and lines suggesting shadows and horizons are implied by the poet only through the expressive resources of language; but these resources are formidable. The sentence *Odi et amo* could appear in a Latin text as an illustration of the first person singular in first- and fourth-conjugation verbs. As such, it would be serviceable but hardly more evocative than *I eat and I sleep*. As the opening phrase of a lyric by Catullus, however, it effectively summons into existence an individual speaker and a substantial context of feelings, motives, and circumstances. In interpreting the poem, we do not, as with the verbal illustration, merely acknowledge that there is a range of contexts in which such an utterance could occur; we infer or project or imagine a particular context for it, a world in which the speaker is heard to bite out the alternately bitter and melancholy words that reflect the ambivalent emotions aroused in him by his faithless lover. *"Odi et amo...."*

The expressive resources of the poet are formidable because they draw on all our prior experiences with natural utterances, particularly how we learn to interpret them, and even more particularly the very fact that we are *inclined* to interpret them. As we noted earlier in passing, the illustrative sentences constructed by philosophers and linguists evoke a rather peculiar world, the sort of world where people make observations such as "The cat is on the mat," or "The carpenter hit the nail with the hammer." They evoke this world, however, only when the reader yields to the impulse, carried over from his experiences with natural discourse, to infer historical contexts from what appear to be verbal events. The impulse is obviously misdirected in these instances. No world of cats, mats, carpenters, nails—or speakers with any reason for talking about them—stands behind these fictive utterances. They are designed to be regarded as noncontextual. A poem, however, is designed to evoke a context: it takes advantage of the very impulse that is inappropriate with respect to the philosopher's or linguist's example, that is, the impulse *to interpret*, to infer historically particular meanings from verbal structures.

To conclude this section, we may return to that series of propositions concerning the whiteness of swans. I suggested earlier that one might take the series as a minimalist poem; we may note now what happens if one does so. Titled "Disillusionment," for example, or "Disorder and Early Sorrow," it might suggest a speaker's mournful expression of his graduation from naive optimism, to rueful skepticism, to abject nihilism:

> All swans are white.
> Some swans are white.
> No swans are white.

Or, presented with other titles or without any title at all, it might suggest other sorts of interpretations: a comment on the decline of aristocratic values, for example, or a terse résumé of an anticolonialist *coup* in an African nation. What is sometimes called "found poetry" operates, of course, on the same principle. Any verbal structure—a set of newspaper headlines, an obituary notice, the list of ingredients on a box of packaged cereal—can be isolated from its original context and presented in such a way (lineated, for example, or read aloud in a studied manner) as to suggest poetry and to invite our response to it as such, that is, as a verbal artwork, the representation of a natural utterance in an implicit dramatic context, designed to invite and gratify the drawing of interpretive inferences.

Poems elicit from us the projection of particular speakers responding to more or less particular situations. Because we understand them to be *fictive* utterances, however, we recognize that the contexts we infer from them are also fictive: unfixable, unlocatable, in the natural universe—as unreal as the sky we seem to see above the painter's oak tree. No matter how vivid the speaker and his world may be, the poem remains but a possible utterance, and the meanings that we, as readers, infer from it remain essentially our own creation, unverifiable in fact and principle. Far from being a defect, this aspect of poetry is the source of many of its valued effects—a point to which we will return after we have considered a number of other nonpoetic but fictive compositions.

III. Exploiting the Margins

No one takes the philosopher or linguist to be speaking in his own right in the examples he presents, and the distinction between the utterances he constructs and those he utters is clear. Deliberately more ambiguous is the status of those statements in which commercial products are commended in the popular media, particularly radio and television. "Everybody knows," of course, that the vacuous housewives, earnest doctors, and wide-eyed toddlers who celebrate the virtues of various soaps, aspirins, and puddings are actually actors, their "sincerity" part of the performance, their words no necessary or even likely reflection of their personal feelings and motives. No one would call such actors liars, for there is a convention or understanding between advertisers and their audiences regarding what commercials are and how they are to be taken. Advertisers are disposed, however, to strain the convention and, in any case, always count on a certain degree of breakdown of that understanding: a blurring between act and enactment or at least a carry-over of our responses to natural discourse.

For our present purposes, several points are worth noting here. The first is the simple fact that many advertisements are, like poems and the illustrative sentences of linguists and philosophers discussed above, fictive verbal structures. They stand in relation to poems as their pictorial counterparts stand in relation to pictorial artworks. A landscape with milkmaid by Constable or a landscape with beer drinkers by Mr. X: both are fictive visual structures, though there are again significant differences between them in other respects. As with a poem or a philosopher's example, what is crucial to the fictiveness of an advertisement is not that the statements of which it is composed are false (a certain product *may* reduce cavities; another one *may* bring headache relief faster) but rather that they are not being *said* by those who "say" them. Such an advertisement is not a natural utterance, moreover, because it never occurs as a unique historical event on a particular occasion in, and in response to, a particular historical context: the same ad looms from the same electronic void hourly or on twenty consecutive days. Its repeated presentations are experienced by the viewer not as later re-assertions of statements asserted previously, but as the replay of the same ahistorical statements, just as the various performances of a poem are experienced as the same verbal structure re-cited, and the various performances of a play are experienced as the same set of ahistorical actions re-enacted.

A second point is that most audiences recognize that, in commercials, the conventions of natural discourse have been suspended and replaced by other conventions that govern the relation between what is "said" and what may be inferred therefrom. An ad is certainly not interpreted the same way a poem is; but neither is it interpreted as a natural utterance. The audience understands the pretense[10] and responds accordingly: we learn to ignore the apparent "imperative" force of all those enjoinders to buy, try, use, taste, and wear the various products mentioned; we learn to shut off what would otherwise be our reactions to a fellow creature's enthusiastic recommendations and tones of urgency.

As I suggested above, however, the effectiveness of modern advertising depends on a certain amount of breakdown of the conventions or leakage between the barriers: our unwitting carry-over of our assumptions regarding natural discourse, particularly our assumption that people usually mean what they say. The reverse can also occur: as a consequence of learning to steel ourselves against the daily blandishments of commercial advertising, we may become extremely sensitive to the possibility of both fictiveness and deception until eventually the assumption that people usually mean what they say is replaced by the assumption that they usually don't. That a skeptical or even cynical attitude toward discourse may carry over to natural utterances is only one of the ways in which language becomes a casualty of the advertising industry.

We might remark, in this connection, that the "understanding" presumably shared by advertisers and their audiences must be reinforced by law, sometimes quite explicitly, as when we are informed that "The following is a paid political announcement" lest we mistake the nature of a citizen's hearty and apparently ingenuous endorsement of a candidate. Indeed, FCC "rulings" in such instances can be regarded as the actions of a referee in the interest of what is quite literally "fair *play*." For ad viewing *is* a sort of contest: one in which the advertiser tries to compel belief by any means short of outright deception, and the viewer tries to maintain disbelief as far as possible short of losing whatever information is there to be gotten. (It is useful to know that there is a product that reduces cavities—*if* it reduces cavities.)

Finally, we can recognize that highly sophisticated audiences are often capable of something close to an "aesthetic" appreciation of commercials. Secure in their understanding of the conventions that operate, they respond not as listeners in a natural verbal transaction, where the interest of what is said lies in what it reveals of the speaker and the world to which he is responding, but as the spectators of a more or less entertaining performance, the skill, novelty, and wit of which can be appraised with respect to other works in the "genre" and, indeed, even enjoyed as such—"disinterestedly."

IV. PREFABRICATED DISCOURSE

The commercial possibilities of fictive discourse are not confined to "commercials" proper but extend to the literal selling of fictive utterances. Poems and novels are marketable, of course, but what I have in mind here are certain verbal structures on sale at one's local drugstore as well as bookstore, of which the following is a fair example:

To Mother, with Love from Both of Us
This world may change in many ways
But you just grow more dear
And closer, Mother, to our hearts
With every passing year.
So this message from the two of us
Is very fondly said—
Just keep on being your own sweet self
Through all the years ahead!

This is, to be sure, dreadful stuff. The crudeness of its rhythm, the triteness and bathos of its sentiments, the vacuousness of its diction; all this, plus another quality we might be inclined to call "insincerity," makes us wince or groan. Would it be proper to sum up our characterizations and reactions by saying that this is abysmal poetry? I think not; for it need not be regarded as poetry at all.

Greeting-card verse is *like* lyric poetry, of course, not only in its formal pretensions and personal mode but also because it is fictive discourse. The text printed above is obviously not a natural utterance nor is it the inscription of one (though it is significant that the typography in which the original was set was evidently designed to resemble cursive handwriting). Though the statement is personal, it is not the statement of the person who composed it: it does not spring from or reflect *his* emotions and sentiments; it is not *his* mother who grows more dear; and he could not very well be "the two of us" who are purportedly saying the fond message. In fact, no one is saying it, and it is not a message. Like a poem and like a linguist's verbal illustration, it is fictive discourse; unlike these, however, it is designed to *be* a message under appropriate circumstances.

Actually, there need not be any insincerity involved in the creation or use of greeting-card verse, for certain conventions obtain here and are presumably respected. No one will take the author of this verse to mean what it says, and those who purchase and subsequently send the verse as a personal message may very *well* mean what it says. As the author's composition, the message is fictive; but once it is signed "John and Mary" and sent to Mrs. Jones in Cincinnati, it *becomes* natural discourse and, the conventions having switched, will be taken, perhaps quite properly, to affirm their sentiments.

As a fictive utterance, the meaning of the message is indeed vacuous: like the meaning of the linguist's or philosopher's examples, it consists only of a range of *possible* conditions (or contexts) in which it *could* be an appropriate response. As a natural utterance, however, it acquires particular meaning with respect to a specific context: it *means* what John and Mary feel and want to say. As they might have put it themselves: "We chose this card because it was so fitting."

Greeting-card messages are not poems. What they are is something we may call *prefabricated* utterances: verbal structures preassembled for later use as natural utterances. Indeed, it is precisely because the greeting-card message must meet the expressive needs of so many people that its language is so vague and general: the more precise and specific the diction and allusions, the narrower the range of possible contexts and thus the fewer potential sayers and, of course, buyers. Had the message included some reference to Mother's blue eyes or apple pies, it would have eliminated as potential customers all those whose mothers had brown eyes and were bad cooks. Greeting-card verse is like American canned (that is, prefabricated) soup, with its characteristically undistinctive seasoning designed to accommodate as wide as possible a range of tastes. In a sense, there is no poetry more "universal" than greeting-card verse.

This last point, concerning generality and universality, has some bearing on the distinction between greeting-card messages and poetry proper, that is, verbal artworks. The precision of diction and specificity of allusion that are so conspicuously lacking in these messages are, in poetry, highly valued qualities. In poems also, the more precise the language and specific the allusions, the more restricted and particular becomes the context in which the utterance would be appropriate. But in poetry, that restriction and specificity serve the characteristic effects noted before, that is, the vividness and force with which poems do evoke particular contexts and enable us to project individualized speakers with distinctive and subtly defined emotions. The world of imaginable circumstances and feelings that a poem implies, the response to such a world that the poem *represents*, are what interest and move us in it. A greeting-card message, though fictive, is not as mimetically "replete" as a poem. Its function is not to *represent* a natural utterance but rather to *become* one. It need not, *must* not, evoke a particular fictive context because it will acquire a particular real one.

As we shall see later on, poems can and often do serve a function quite comparable to greeting-card messages, that is, they are appropriated for use as natural utterances. Before turning to that possibility, however, I should like to pursue a bit further the notion of prefabricated discourse in general. The fact that greeting-card messages are prefabricated does not make them any the less sincere (or, of course, "natural") when they serve as the messages of real people. Natural discourse does not mean unique or original discourse and, indeed, the concepts of uniqueness and originality must always be rather strained in connection with language. A very large proportion of natural discourse consists of verbal formulas—conventional phrases, idiomatic "expressions," even whole sentences—that we have heard and used many times before. In spite of the much-vaunted creativity of speech and theoretical infinity of possible sentences, it is clear that most of our informal utterances are composed of a distinctly finite number of verbal structures: phrases and formulas that we learn along with individual words and rules of syntax.

As Albert Lord has demonstrated in his study of contemporary oral epics, the bard or "singer of tales" can recite lengthy heroic poems on demand, not because he has memorized those poems, but because he can simultaneously compose and recite them, just as we all simultaneously compose and *speak* in natural discourse.[12] The oral poet learns a large but finite number of traditional verbal formulas which, in conjunction with a store of suitable variants, form a substantial repertoire of what are, in effect, prefabricated lines of verse; and this repertoire can be drawn on instantaneously to serve a practically infinite number of compositional occasions, that is, to suit any narrative, thematic, syntactic, or metrical context. For example, in traditional Yugoslav poetry, most of the characters apparently have horses and are frequently described as mounting them. The phrase translated "mounted their horses" is a metrical unit (specifically, a half line), and it may appear numerous times at various points in the composition of a singer, each time with suitable variants:

> All the horsemen *mounted their horses* ...
> And the wedding-guests *mounted their horses* ...
> Then they leaped up and *mounted their horses* ...

Moreover, each of the variants here is itself a formula that may appear in other lines combined with yet other formulaic units:

> *All the horsemen* rode into Baghdad ...
> *And the wedding-guests* toasted the bridegroom ...
> *Then they leaped up and* called for their saddles ...[13]

Each line of the poem may be unique, but each one is composed of preassembled sections, like an automobile or prefabricated building. As Lord points out, these bards are none the less original poets, and each poem reflects continuous creative activity. But originality and creativity here are evidently not to be equated with absolutely unique combinations of words.

The generation of speech in natural discourse occurs in a directly comparable way: in speaking and writing, we draw on a repertoire of verbal patterns or formulas we have learned and used before, substituting, as the occasion requires, the variants that are appropriate to the particular needs of the moment. In the sentences written above, for example, there occur a number of phrases quite common to expository discourse: *As I suggested earlier, what I have in mind, something we may call, as Lord points out.* These expressions are clearly prefabricated, and *as X points out* is clearly a verbal formula where *X* is replaced by a suitable name depending on the immediate context. In composing these phrases I did not, as it were, start from scratch. *As it were, start from scratch*—it is really very hard to be verbally creative.

Whenever economies of time, space, or energy become significant, and subtlety or the marks of originality matter little, we are likely to employ those conspicuously prefabricated verbal structures we call clichés. In composing telegrams, for example, or interoffice memos, or impersonal business letters, most of us readily make use of formulas of expression which are nevertheless meaningful and sincere enough for the purpose at hand: *Congratulations on the new arrival and best wishes to both of you; Thank you for your letter of X.... I look forward to having your reply,* and so forth. We avoid

61

clichés, of course, when we do not wish to appear perfunctory, impersonal, or uncreative; and young writers and others who take too seriously the notion that original minds generate continuously original utterances often become so self-conscious in their search for unique combinations of words that they can hardly write at all. Even when we are not using clichés, however, we must still employ a great number of conventional or formulaic expressions simply in order to speak with the rapidity and fluency required for natural verbal transactions; and most of us do take advantage of those preassembled structures that the linguistic community has evolved, structures that exhibit a clarity, economy, and euphony of expression that recommend themselves to most native speakers.

We should notice, moreover, that if one breaks it down into small enough units, any utterance consists wholly of what are, in truth, prefabricated verbal structures—not merely idiomatic phrases and conventional formulas but individual words themselves, which we need not buy or borrow because they are freely donated to us for our immediate use by the linguistic community—all nicely preassembled from constituent speech-sounds. But it may be asked here: if phrases and individual words are to be regarded as prefabricated verbal structures, does this mean that they are also instances of fictive discourse? And if they are, then what can't be?

The answer to the first question is, of course, "it depends." Word-forms (lexemes) or phrases conceived of abstractly (for example, "the word *fire*," "the phrase *law and order*") are not natural utterances. Nor are they fictive utterances. They are simply something else altogether: verbal *forms*, types or classes of events, but neither events themselves nor the representation of events.

An individual wordform may be not merely *conceived of*, however, but produced vocally or in writing: typed, for example, by a lexicographer on a file card for the dictionary he is compiling, or dictated by an instructor at a spelling examination, or jotted down by a poet as a euphonious or otherwise interesting and potentially useful linguistic item. In such cases (and many others can be thought of), although the wordform is being typed, voiced, or written by a particular person on a particular occasion, it is nevertheless not being *said* (or inscribed) as natural discourse and would not properly be taken or interpreted as such by a listener or reader. If our lexicographer, spelling instructor, or poet had produced the word *conflagration*, for example, it would have been as a response, not to a fire experienced, recalled, or imagined at that moment, but simply to the verbal form *conflagration* itself. (The significance of the distinction becomes obvious if one thinks of the difference between the spelling instructor dictating *conflagration* and his *saying* "Fire!") Here, too, however, it would be improper to speak of the verbal structures thus produced as fictive utterances. For the term *fictive*, as used in this study, suggests representation of some kind, even if not always fully mimetic representation: the philosopher's and linguist's illustrations, the commercial ads, and the greeting-card messages discussed earlier, and the quotations and proverbs to be discussed below—all are representations, either of possible utterances, or kinds of utterances, or past utterances. In other words, fictive discourse always bears some relation to natural discourse other than mere distinction from it. Moreover, fictive discourse suggests the product of fabrication or construction, that is, a verbal composition presumably consisting of more than a single linguistic unit and exhibiting at least a rudimentary sort of structure. Thus it would seem to make sense to reserve the terms *fictive utterance* and *fictive discourse* for representational verbal structures with at least the minimal degree of length and syntactic organization that we usually associate with the terms *utterance* and *discourse*.

It must be emphasized, however (in answer to the second question raised above), that there is in principle *no* minimum length or degree of syntactic organization required for a verbal structure to function as an utterance and thus, in effect, *nothing* (that is, no verbal form) that cannot be, on some occasion, used and taken as fictive discourse. Many verbal exchanges consist of brief, syntactically detached phrases, and many consist of single words:

"Where are the keys?" "*In the car.*"
"How's the family?" "*Fine.*"
"Can I speak to Mrs. Smith?" "Wait, I'll call her. *Mother!*"

In the situations suggested by these examples (if one takes them for the moment as being real), the italicized words and phrases are complete linguistic events. But if an isolated phrase or single word can be a natural utterance, then it *can* also be a fictive one. For, to turn the tables now, the very examples I just used to illustrate the possible brevity of natural utterances are, of course, not natural utterances at all, but verbal illustrations like those of the linguist and philosopher discussed earlier; and I have therefore just constructed fictive utterances consisting of one word. I might add that there can be and are poems, or at least verbal artworks, consisting of one word: for example, Pedro Xisto's *"logograma"* entitled "Epithalamium II" and consisting of the word *She* (printed, to be sure, in an interesting way).[14]

v. Quotations

Although poems are not, like greeting-card messages, designed to become natural utterances, they are often appropriated for that purpose. We may recall here all those occasions, sometimes trivial, sometimes not, when phrases, lines, or even longer passages from literary works come to our lips and pens not in the course of our specifically citing or referring to them but, rather, as the borrowed containers for our own meanings. Those with bookish lives are ever ready to appropriate the words of others, and literature professors and graduate students are notably inclined to sprinkle even their casual utterances with literary locutions such as "Thereby hangs a tale," or to leave parties saying things like "Good night, sweet ladies, good night," or "When shall we three meet again?" The containers are often borrowed at least partly for the sake of the residual taste of the original contents. When T. S. Eliot dedicated *The Waste Land* to "Ezra Pound, *il miglior fabbro*," the borrowed phrase from Dante's *Purgatorio* now carried Eliot's compliment to Pound and no longer, as in the original, the poet Guinizelli's praise of *his* mentor, Arnaut Daniel; but it may be supposed that Eliot still wished to retain some of the flavor and resonance of the gracious allusion as it occurs in the original context. Nevertheless, Eliot was not simply *quoting* the phrase from Dante in the sense of citing it; he was *saying* it, making it his own by meaning it, though in an altogether different context and with a totally different referent.

64

There is a crucial distinction between speaking *of* and *speaking* the words of others.

We often use the term *quotation* in yet another sense, with reference not to a citation or a borrowing but rather to a *reporting* of someone else's words. In the course of telling an anecdote, for example, I may quote another person directly: "Well, John was pretty angry at that. *'I've had enough,'* he said, and slammed his fist on the table." Here a verbal action, what John said, is being reported or described along with other nonverbal actions, what he did. I can describe John's words more precisely than his other actions because I am describing them *in words* and thus, we may say, iconically. I am not, however, reproducing his verbal act exactly, since the original utterance must have included, among other things, vocal idiosyncrasies and intonational features that are inevitably lost or distorted when thus duplicated. Nevertheless, I am not simply *referring to* John's words as I refer to his slamming his fist on the table; I am, rather, *depicting* them, adequately enough for the purposes of the anecdote.

If we recall the discussion of verbal depictions in section III above and the analogy drawn there to visual depictions, it becomes evident that a quotation of the sort just described is also a verbal picture. Here, however, the representation is not of a possible utterance or an imaginary one, but of a real and particular one—drawn, we might say, from life. Indeed, we could regard a quotation as a sort of verbal photograph (or pretechnological *phono*graph) of a natural utterance, neither more nor less iconic than a snapshot or home movie of John's slamming his fist on the table. The analogies here are, in every sense, diverting; the significant point is that, in quoting John's words, I am understood not actually to be *saying* them but rather to be presenting a facsimile of them, and thus a fictive utterance.

The distinctions among *referring to, depicting,* and *saying* the words of others obtain, we should note, whether the original source is itself fictive or natural. We may refer to or cite passages of poetry without affirming them, and we may appropriate the words of real people as readily as those of characters in plays or novels. We may remark, "As Iago says, *What you know, you know,*" or "As Dr.

Johnson said, *To a poet nothing can be useless.*" In both cases the implication is: as he said, *so I am saying.* We will say what others have said, be they characters or historical persons, if we can make it mean or take it to mean what *we* mean—and are inclined to say.[15]

When we appropriate someone else's words, we confer on them our own context of meanings, often quite remote from that of the original. In such cases, we are using their words in a sense metaphorically, taking what was originally a reference to one state of affairs and applying it to a different but comparable or analogous state of affairs. It is not the individual words, however, but the utterance as a whole that becomes metaphoric. An illustration may clarify the point. A chapter of I. A. Richards' *Principles of Literary Criticism*, entitled "The Chaos of Critical Theories," bears as an ironic epigraph the following passage from *Henry IV*, part I: *O monstrous! But one half-pennyworth of bread to this intolerable deal of sack.*[16] In the play, this occurs as Prince Hal's exclamation on seeing Falstaff's bill at the Boarshead tavern, the point being that the proportion of wholesome food to wine in Falstaff's diet is appallingly meager. As the epigraph to Richards' chapter, it implies that critical theories exhibit a comparable disproportion between nourishing and merely heady stuff. What originally referred "literally" to Falstaff's habits of consumption now refers figuratively to the quality of critical theories.

We should note, however, that the line from *Henry IV* never really referred literally to anything; it was a wholly fictive utterance, not said on a particular occasion by a historical Prince Hal but constructed by William Shakespeare to be recited by any number of future actors in any number of future performances of the play. Metaphoric quotations need not, of course, originate in literary works: numerous epigraphs that function in a way similar to Richards' consist of passages quoted from *natural* utterances— letters, for example, or public speeches. Nevertheless, passages from poems, novels, plays, and songs do lend themselves more readily to metaphoric extension of this sort because they *are* fictive and we understand that, being so, they are in themselves essentially free of historically specific "literal" meaning.

The reverse can also occur, that is, we can take what were originally natural utterances and make them fictive, thus setting them loose from their historical moorings and specific meanings and opening them to metaphoric interpretation. In Donald Finkel's poem, "Angel Hair," for example, there occurs the following passage:

> Most Angels are uneducated. Only one Angel in
> 10 has steady work.[17]

The passage originally appeared in a magazine article about motorcycle gangs (such as "Hell's Angels") and was written without apparent irony. The fact and effects of its metaphoric extension in Finkel's poem are obvious. The poem itself, it might be added, is but a step away from "found poetry," the marginal aspects of which were considered above. Here we can note that when we take a natural utterance—an obituary notice, for example, from the columns of a newspaper—and present it *in* or *as* a poem, we are inviting the reader to interpret it metaphorically or parabolically, not with respect to its original context, but as implying some other, perhaps more general, significance:[18]

> Albert Molesworth
> Eighty-seven years old,
> Owner of the nation's largest
> And most prosperous potato farm,
> Died yesterday
> At his home in Idaho
> He left
>   no
>   survivors.

The implication becomes a sort of bathetic *sic transit gloria mundi.* One may be reminded of Shelley's "Ozymandias."

Some imagination and wit are involved in the finding of found poems, but certain natural utterances obviously lend themselves more readily than others to fictive transformation. Conversely, certain *fictive* utterances seem especially suitable for appropriation as natural discourse—eminently *quotable*, in other words, or likely to appear in the pages of an anthology such as Bartlett's. Among the qualities that make them so is something we commonly refer to as "universality" but which often amounts simply to generality. The listings in one anthology of quotations contain, for example, numerous passages like the following, culled from various poems and plays: *He that sleeps feels not the toothache; Whoever loved that loved not at first sight; Everyone can master a grief but he that has it. He that ..., whoever ..., everyone....* These lines have that sweep of reference that we associate with proverbs: *One man's meat is another's poison; He that fears you present will hate you absent*, and so on. The pronouns here, *he* and *you*, are essentially vacuous or indeterminate in meaning: like *one* (*on* in French, *man* in German), they refer to no one in particular and everyone potentially. What is interesting in such passages, as well as in the proverbs cited, is the fact that, when thus extracted, they do *not* evoke particular contexts: they do not imply individualized speakers responding to historically specific circumstances. On the contrary, they are very much like greeting-card messages in that they are so readily utterable in such a wide variety of contexts by speakers quite different from the original sayers and in circumstances quite remote from theirs. They are so amenable to repeated utterance because they are so repeatedly *meanable*. Recalling our earlier distinction, then, it would seem that the most universally quotable passages of poetry are the least poetic ones: the most general and therefore the least mimetic and evocative. It would be more to our purpose, however, to observe that in isolating passages of poetry from their original fictive contexts and pressing them into service as the "containers" of our own historically determinate meanings, we are re-authoring them as *natural* utterances, inviting and expecting from *our* listeners a response to them different from that which was presumably invited and expected by their original authors.

Consider, for example, Shakespeare's Sonnet 94, the one which begins "They that have power to hurt and will do none ..." and concludes with the strikingly proverbial line, "Lilies that fester smell far worse than weeds." Excerpted as a proverb, this line will suggest, as it does in the poem, something like: noble creatures, when corrupted, are more offensive than merely base creatures. We may have occasion to "quote" the line, that is, to appropriate it and assert it "meaningfully" in a particular set of historical circumstances. Experienced in the context of the poem, however, the line will be interpreted as the fictive speaker's assertion (or his own "pointed" application of a proverb); and what interests and moves us in the line is not its dubious wisdom or its excerptibility for later quotation but, rather, its expressive quality with respect to that speaker's feelings and motives, and the personal circumstances they appear to reflect.

My point here has not been to malign quoters or to suggest that the quotation of poetry is morally or aesthetically baleful; as we all know, it can be done subtly, imaginatively, and quite creatively (for example, by Keats in his letters). I have been concerned, rather, to use the various practices we call "quotation" to clarify the relation between fictive and natural discourse, especially the conditions under which a given verbal structure can shift from one to the other, and the consequences of such a shift for our experience of the structure. We will return to the specific relation of proverbs to poems, touched on just above, after we have looked more closely at the nature of proverbs themselves.

VI. SAYING AND SAYINGS

Proverbs are often referred to as "sayings." A *saying*, we note, is neither a *said* nor a *says*: the gerundive form identifies neither person nor tense. It suggests speech without a speaker, a self-sufficient verbal object rather than a verbal act, an utterance that asserts itself independently of any utterer—continuously, as it were, or indeed eternally. The proverbs cited earlier, and others such as *Misery loves company* and *All's fair in love and war*, are anonymous: not only are the original sayers of these sayings unknown, but no trace remains of the occasions on which they were originally said. They seem, in fact, never to have been initially said at all but rather to have arisen in toto from the race, culture, or verbal community as a sort of eternal verbal response to an eternal state of affairs. All proverbs do, of course, have particular origins even if they are no more readily traceable than the origins of individual words or inventions such as the wheel. But, like the latter, they have become cultural artifacts; they are no man's or, rather, all men's property, as much a part of the lexicon of a linguistic community as individual words or those idiomatic expressions they obviously resemble.

69

Taken as verbal structures, proverbs are, of course, fictive utterances; but, like greeting-card messages, they become natural utterances under certain circumstances. It is one thing to speak *of* a proverb:

> My mother's favorite proverb is "Live and let live." My father's is "Business is business."

and another thing to *say* it:

> She's always nagging him that he drinks too much or smokes too much. I [or, "I say"] live and let live.

> Yes, our families *are* old friends, but you know [or, "like they say"] business is business.

When it is not actually being said in (or, as we sometimes express it, *applied to*) a particular situation, a proverb is simply a verbal form, like an individual word. As such, it is noncontextual and its *meaning* (like that of a wordform, or a linguist's example, or a greeting-card message) is historically indeterminate; that is, it consists only of a range of *possible* contexts in which the proverb *could* be said, possible conditions under which it *could* be a natural utterance. But when we *say* a saying (as when we sign and dispatch a greeting-card message), we confer a *particular* context on it; we transform it from a verbal form to a verbal act.

It is often said that proverbs embody timeless wisdom or universal truth. It would be more accurate to say that the range of contexts in which they could be appropriately affirmed is unusually broad and recurrent. One reason for that is a characteristic which many proverbs share with greeting-card messages, namely, generality and indeed vacuity of language and sentiment. Although proverbs are not, like greeting-card messages, designed to serve as prefabricated utterances, they achieve that status by virtue of comparable qualities. By a sort of natural selection, those proverbs that survive are literally the *fittest*; that is, they fit the widest variety of circumstances or adapt most readily to emergent environments. And that is because their meanings are indeterminate enough to cover almost all human, natural, and historical exigencies. If the conditions in which a proverb could be affirmed disappear, it loses authority and the proverb itself disappears.

70

Proverbs also achieve "universality" by virtue of another quality that we have encountered before, namely, the readiness with which they lend themselves to metaphoric or parabolic application. When we apply a metaphoric proverb (such as *One swallow doesn't make a summer*, which is rarely said in connection with swallows or summers), we are in a sense interpreting it, but no single application exhausts its meanings:

JOHN: Are you still fixing that salad dressing?
BILL: Rome wasn't built in a day.
JOHN: I think I'm getting somewhere with Alice. She smiled at me this morning.
BILL: One swallow doesn't make a summer.
JOHN: Rome wasn't built in a day.

There are, of course, some limits to the range of meanings of such proverbs, usually maintained through a continuous history of interpretation and application. If, however, we are not familiar with the tradition of application, the metaphoric value (and limits) of a proverb may be impossible to determine. A certain Ashanti proverb, for example, goes *The okra does not show its seeds through its skin*. It is by no means evident that this botanical observation, which does not show *its* seeds through its skin, means "You can't tell what a man is thinking from the expression on his face." Archer Taylor, in his interesting study of the genre,[19] mentions a number of proverbs that have come down to us altogether without a tradition of application and are thus virtually limitless in meaning. My favorite, I think, is this one from the Old High German: *When it blows, the trees shake*. Very true, of course, and very proverbial sounding, but what does it mean? Well, we can *take* it to mean almost anything, from "Persons in subordinate positions become anxious when their superiors are in a bad humor," to "Certain events are inevitably produced by other events." It is, in effect, an all-purpose utterance, an unimpeachable truth for all seasons.

It was observed earlier that a proverb will lose authority and eventually disappear if the conditions in which it could be affirmed no longer hold. Presumably "extinction" of that sort has been the fate of numerous proverbs that appear in collections but are no longer actually heard, for example, *A woman hath no weapon but her tongue.* It should also be recognized, however, that since a proverb seems to derive its authority from eternal transcendent truth, it will often be affirmed in the face of immediately contradictory circumstances—sometimes with the implication that, if we sit the moment out, the reality that the proverb asserts will return and restore the force of its truth. Because the "saying" has no known original sayer, it appears uncontaminated by ordinary human error or bias, and thus oracular. This accounts, we may suppose, for the exceptional durability of some manifestly foolish bits of "wisdom." It also suggests why it can be so maddening to argue with someone who utters proverbs in reply to one's carefully thought-out proposals or empirically verified observations:

> "Women make up 40% of the labor force. One third of all women with children are employed. Government-sponsored child-care is available in every enlightened nation in Europe...."
>
> *"A woman's place is in the home."*

It is like waging battle with an adversary who is both immovable and immortal.[20]

The very anonymity or oracular nature of proverbs often recommends their citation to speakers who would not, for various reasons, wish or be able quite to *say* them. As Taylor observes, for example (speaking of proverbs as distinguished from formal religious doctrine), "A sound skepticism pervades proverbial wisdom and ventures to show itself in assertions which no member of the folk would dare utter on his own."[21]

Along with somewhat similar lines, Ruth Finnegan, discussing the Central African *sanza* (which means both proverb and circumlocutionary expression generally), writes:

> This hidden and oblique form of speech, then, with its overtones of playing safe and avoiding direct commitment, is one developed to a high degree among the Azande. However, it seems to be an element in all use of proverbs, one which comes out particularly in situations of conflict or

uneasy social relationships and where depths of hidden meaning are implied.[22]

More generally, we may say that the citer of proverbs manages to get something said without having to take the responsibility for having said it. (Often, the speaker cites the proverb as if he must concede its sorry wisdom although he would himself wish matters otherwise.) In saying only what "they" say, the speaker disclaims responsibility for the utterance but does not wholly dissociate himself from either its general "truth" or its applicability to the particular situation at hand. He attempts, in other words, to have it both ways. We touch here on a matter which, though it cannot be pursued on this occasion, is of considerable interest: namely, what might be called the ethics of verbal transactions.[23] For our present purposes, it is sufficient to observe that the assumptions governing the mutual claims and responsibilities of speakers and listeners in natural discourse are, in fictive discourse, evidently suspended or substantially qualified. And we might notice, in this connection, that poetry as well as proverbs may allow a speaker to utter what he could not or would not *say*. The poet himself may offer in a poem sentiments which he would not otherwise wish attributed to him; and, in quoting a poem written by someone else, we may present sentiments that we are not quite willing to assert. (A variation of this possibility is familiar to those who live with—or remember being—adolescents, for whom the singing of pop lyrics often seems to serve as something between the occasion for and the evasion of self-expression.)

Proverbs are obviously related to poems in a number of other ways. Many proverbs have originated or been preserved in works of literature and, as has often been observed, the formal characteristics of each are in many respects similar: cohesiveness, euphony, a high incidence of phonemic repetition, alliteration, parallelism, figurative language, and so forth. Both proverbs and poems are verbal structures identifiable exclusively in terms of their linguistic forms. Both are, or can be taken as, fictive discourse, possible utterances with possible contexts. And, most significantly for our concerns here, both are for that reason especially amenable to being interpreted (or "applied") metaphorically or parabolically. We do not, however, characteristically regard proverbs in the same way as we do poems, that is, as mimetically replete representations of discourse; nor do we characteristically experience or "interpret" them as such.

There is, as it happens, an eighteenth-century Japanese poem—a haiku—that resembles quite closely the Old High German proverb mentioned above (*When it blows, the trees shake*). The poem, literally translated, goes: "When the west wind blows, fallen leaves gather in the east."[24] The similarities are evident, but there is a crucial difference in our experience of and response to each: whereas the proverb, *cited as such*, independent of any particular occasion of application, stands as a vacuous truism, the eternally sayable saying said by no one, the haiku is read and in effect "heard" as a human utterance, occasioned by and referring to the experiences and feelings of a single speaker. Explicit interpretations of the poem will vary among readers depending on the richness, subtlety, and specificity of the inferences they are inclined to draw and articulate. One could, for example, read it as the speaker's bemused observation of the simultaneous ferocity and frailty of nature, or as his elegiac reflection on the inevitability of seasonal change and of mortality in nature and man. The point, however, is that inferences of that sort *will* be drawn from the poem—but not from the proverb. The poem invites and allows the construing of such motives and sentiments for two reasons: partly because of the relatively greater specificity and vividness of its diction and allusions, but primarily because we *take* it to be a poem and respond to it accordingly, that is, by interpreting it.

Interpretation—the construing of a particular set of conditions, a context, that could plausibly occasion an utterance of that form—is not merely a possible response to poetry but a characteristic one. In effect, to take a verbal structure as poetry is implicitly to acknowledge it as a fictive utterance designed (or, in the case of "found poetry," presented) to invite and reward precisely that kind of activity.[25] It should be emphasized that "interpretation" in this sense is an activity that differs from both the interpretation of natural discourse and the interpretation of other forms of fictive discourse. When we speak of interpreting a natural utterance, we refer not to the construction of a possible context but to the reconstruction of an actual one: the attempt to identify or infer the particular set of conditions that did in fact occasion the occurrence of that verbal event. The other forms of fictive discourse examined here (textbook illustrations, logicians' paradigms, greeting-card messages, proverbs) are, like poems, understood to be not verbal events but verbal structures. Such structures, to serve their characteristic functions or purposes (exemplification, illustration, subsequent employment as natural utterances, and so on), must be, in a sense, "meaningful," but only in the sense that there must be some range of contexts in which utterances of that form could appropriately occur. The activity of "interpreting" a verbal structure such as the textbook's *Me non amat* or the philosopher's *The cat is on the mat* is complete when that range of possible contexts has been identified or even just acknowledged to exist. With respect to these nonpoetic forms of fictive discourse, richer or more particularized interpretation is, as we have seen, uninvited and quite gratuitous: occasionally distracting, sometimes amusing, but, strictly speaking, not to the purpose. With respect to a structure we take as a poem, however, interpretation is not thus limited and certainly not gratuitous. Here, the activity of construing—imagining, projecting, elaborating—a particular plausible context *is* invited; and we accept the invitation on the assumption and with the expectation that the structure has been designed to make that activity an engaging and gratifying one. In short, with respect to what we take to be poetry, interpretation is understood to *be* the purpose.

II

EXCHANGING WORDS: ON THE ECONOMICS AND ETHICS OF VERBAL TRANSACTIONS

The Witter Bynner Lectures in Poetry
1977

4

IN THE LINGUISTIC
MARKETPLACE

My pleasure in being invited to offer The Witter Bynner Lectures in Poetry was pure, but attended by some bemusement. For none of these lectures, I realized, would be *in* poetry, and you would have reason to wonder, especially from the first of them, if they were ever going to be even *on* poetry. I can assure you that they shall be, though the route may appear, at times, a bit oblique. The obliquity arises from the fact that the question that concerns me here is what poetry *is* or, more precisely, what relation it bears to language and what that relation implies about the experience and value of poetry; and, for reasons I shall explain shortly, answering that question requires paying a good bit of attention to what poetry *isn't*.

The most fundamental problem of literary theory appears to be the location of its own subject, that is, "literature" or, as we sometimes call it (already locked into battle with the problem), "poetry in the broad sense." The attempt to solve that problem is not new; and it is not now, and never has been, merely an "academic" question. But I shall not rehearse here the history of its proposed solutions and what they have been taken to imply about how poetry is—or should be—experienced and valued. I shall instead, by way of reminding you of the nature of the problem and also introducing my own views, speak of some more or less contemporary solutions.

You may recall one solution as the distinction between "denotative" and "connotative" meanings, and the related one that distinguished between "referential" and "emotive" uses of language. Those distinctions have, for good reason I think, been abandoned, and nothing appears more dated than the once-confident contrast between "referential statements" and "pseudo-statements." One might, however, sense the ghost or reincarnation of that contrast in a number of more sophisticated formulations offered in recent years by literary theorists and linguistic philosophers of various persuasions: the distinction drawn, for example, between "judgments" and "quasi-judgments," or the one between "reality language" and "mimetic language"; or the contrasts made between texts with "engaged-designative meanings" and those with "disengaged-gestural meanings"; we have heard, and still hear, of the difference between "illocutionary utterances" and "imitation illocutionary utterances" and, most recently, have been presented with the difference between "serious speech acts" and "nondeceptive pretended speech acts."[1]

Now, it must be granted that there is something vainglorious-sounding in such a list when the entries are thus lined up. For one notes a certain similarity of structure in both the categories themselves and the basis of the contrasts: on the one side, the referential, the real, the engaged, the serious; on the other side, the pseudo, the quasi, the imitated, the pretended. Moreover, the very repetitiveness of that structure may suggest obsession and defeat, as if one hopeful champion after another had set out to capture a certain beast, and had returned to say he had done so, only to find that the beast had meanwhile escaped and was still at large. And, of course, it might also be suspected that the reason he so repeatedly eludes capture is not that he is so wily or protean but that he does not exist at all, that the champions have not simply been inadequate to the challenge but that their conviction that there *was* a beast to be apprehended was a contagious delusion.

And so it has been suspected, and so it has been maintained. For in addition to those who have, by one set of terms or another, sought to formulate a distinction between literary and nonliterary language, there are also those who insist that there is no distinction to be drawn: that *all* statements are real and *all* speech-acts serious—or, in the most recent and beguiling twist of skeptical monism, that *no* statements are real because *nothing* is real.

Now, I should say immediately that my own views on this question neither mediate nor synthesize the array of positions just outlined. Moreover, I do not propose to reestablish some traditional or commonsense view. There *is* no single traditional view: not only is the question itself ancient, but so also is the array of conflicting and unstable answers to it; and what we may think of as the common-sense view is likely to be only some version of one or another of those answers, recommended by early exposure and sustained by personal or institutional inertia. As for the most recent attempts to draw or erase distinctions, while I appreciate the force of some arguments that might press one toward a position of monism (either sober monism or nihilistic monism) I am nevertheless persuaded that, with respect to the question at hand, distinctions *can* be made and will continue to be made.

In that connection, we may return to the list that I presented a moment ago, those sets of "real vs. quasi" or "serious vs. pretended," that seemed so familiar and perhaps so dubious. It should be noted that, insofar as those contrastive categories have been developed to distinguish literary from nonliterary discourse, they all reflect a conviction, which I share, that the basis of the distinction cannot be grounded on any characteristic difference of linguistic *form*: in other words, that literary works do not always or necessarily look or sound any different from nonliterary works, that the identity of a text as "a work of literature"—or even as "a poem"—cannot always or necessarily be established by any surface inspection or even deep analysis of the text itself, and, in fact, that the same text may change its identity not only *in* time but at *any* time under different circumstances. The basis of the distinction is not linguistic form, then, but something closer to linguistic *function*, which (in the formulations I have mentioned) is variously identified as *purpose* or *intention* (what the author was up to) or as *value, attitude,* or *response* (what the reader is up to), or as some combination of the two: how the author intended the reader to respond, or how the reader assumes the author intended him to respond, or what each assumes and expects the other to do or to have done. All of which brings us very rapidly to a central concept in contemporary literary theory, namely *convention*.

These two concepts, function and convention, are, I believe, indispensable for any discussion of the distinctive character of literary discourse, but the mere invocation of them does not answer all questions: it tells us only what sorts of questions we might now try to answer. It will not do, moreover, to replace the question of the distinctive *forms* of literary discourse with the question of its distinctive *functions* without recognizing that the latter question entails answering—or presupposing the answer to—another question, namely the functions of nonliterary discourse. Indeed, it seems clear that the long history of attempts to formulate a functional definition of literature or poetry (that history, of course, extends over more than two thousand years) reflects the long history of our attempts to understand the nature and functions of language itself. Moreover, the fact that every attempt to formulate such a definition has proved imperfect or unstable does not reflect successive defeat or essential futility but is, rather, the necessary and salutary consequence of the fact that our understanding of language (among other things) continues to enlarge and refine itself. An altogether perfect, in the sense of eternally stable, theory of the relation of literature to language is, then, not to be looked for. What we can do, however, is recognize the problems in successive theories and seek to adjust those theories accordingly—expecting, of course, to have our own adjustments adjusted in turn.

To turn, then, to the adjustments to be proposed in the present series of lectures, I would begin by pointing out that a persistent problem among earlier theories of the distinctive functions of literary discourse was a tendency to regard certain types of utterances—"objective" assertions of fact, for example, or scientific statements—as the paradigm forms of nonliterary discourse. To take scientific statements, however (or any specialized type of utterance, especially one designed to reach its audience as inscription or through publication), as exemplifying nonliterary discourse at its purest, is surely to load, if not to beg, the question of what the functions of language are. Moreover, even among those who do

82

recognize that nonliterary discourse embraces a wide variety of utterances—vocal as well as inscribed, ephemeral as well as preserved, commands, promises, excuses and, of course, "emotive" speech—there remains a tendency to describe language as essentially a medium or channel through which a speaker encodes and transmits information to a receiving and decoding listener. This telegraphic model of communication is, however, unduly impoverished: not because it is so mechanical but because, unlike that which it describes, it is a machine without a casement and without a motor. For discourse is not the transmission of information between two minds located at opposite ends of a channel but, rather, a series of complex transactions between two persons who are located in a rich world of objects, events, experiences, and motives, including *reasons* for speaking and listening to each other.

It is important that we recognize not only that discourse is a transaction, but also that it is an *economic* transaction, and one in which the functions or value of an utterance differ significantly for the speaker and the listener. It is especially important for literary theory, because the dynamics of that transaction, and the value of an utterance for both "speaker" and "listener" can, under certain conditions, change radically; and we can begin to identify the characteristic functions of language in poetry or literature only when the nature of those conditions and the consequences of those changes are appreciated.

In the first of these lectures, I shall be concerned with the economics of that transaction, that is, the conventions—and, with them, the claims, responsibilities, and liabilities—that govern the behavior of speakers and listeners in the linguistic marketplace. In the second lecture, I shall consider how language functions *outside* that marketplace, why we sometimes license the unspeakable, how we learn to do so, and what difference it makes. In the third lecture, which is the most polemical of the three, I shall argue that the difference is a crucial one for the experience and value of literary works, and crucial for what might be called the ethics of interpretation.

Before I turn to the substance of this evening's lecture, however, it will be necessary to say a word about two terms that will figure throughout this series and are central to my observations here, namely *natural discourse* and *fictive discourse*. Since I have developed the distinction between them at some length elsewhere, and wish now to pursue some of its implications, I shall not take the time here to repeat its precise derivation. I shall, however, present an initial outline of it and trust that its more specific lineaments will emerge in the course of the lectures themselves.

Briefly, then, by "natural discourse" I mean all utterances that are performed as historical acts and taken as historical events. If one asks what other kind of discourse there is, the answer is simple: there is no other kind; natural discourse *is* discourse. There are, however, verbal structures which constitute, in themselves, neither historical acts nor historical events, but rather *representations* of them and, as such, are understood not to be governed by the same conventions that obtain for natural utterances: and these verbal structures I refer to as *fictive* utterances. Thus, when the French instructor illustrates a point of grammar by uttering the words *Je m'appelle Jacques*, it is understood that these words represent, but do not constitute, the verbal act of giving one's name in French, and do not have the force—make the claims, require the response, or entail the responsibilities—that they would have in a natural verbal transaction.

As you will have suspected, fictive discourse includes such verbal structures as poems, novels, and the scripts of plays—in other words, much that we speak of as "literature" or "poetry in the broad sense"—but clearly not *only* and not *always*. There are many varieties of fictive discourse, serving many functions, from the verbal playacting of children ("I'm a wicked witch, and I'm going to put you in a dungeon") to the exemplary sentences of linguists and logicians (*Je m'appelle Jacques*, "The cat is on the mat"). Fictive discourse can be handy or diverting, and it can also be constructed for specifically aesthetic ends, that is, as verbal artworks. But just as not all fictive discourse is literary, not everything that we might call "literature" is constructed or regarded as fictive. The essays of Bacon and the letters of Keats would, at this moment, for certain members of this culture, be regarded as "literature"; and although both of them *can* be read as fictive discourse, neither was designed to be read as such and neither is only read as such.

In short, "fictive discourse" is not a substitute label for "literature" or "fiction" or "poetry," and I am not engaged in *defining* these or any other traditional terms or concepts. Natural and fictive discourse refer to functional categories which, I believe, are fundamental to our use and experience of language. I also believe that the nature of the distinction between them illuminates a number of problems associated with those traditional terms or concepts, but precisely because it cuts across the distinctions on which they have traditionally been based.

I shall have more to say about the nature of fictive discourse in the second lecture, at which time many of the questions inevitably provoked by this brief outline will, I trust, be answered. This evening, however, I shall be concerned almost exclusively with natural discourse, which—as I emphasized earlier—is a transaction in which the functions of language differ significantly for speakers and listeners. I shall consider each party to the transaction in turn, and then put the parties together.

1. The Speaker: Utterances as Acts

We begin, then, with the speaker, with respect to whom utterances are, to be sure, acts but which, like most other acts—such as pushing doors open, lifting books off shelves, or hammering nails into walls—we perform because they enable us to obtain and achieve things that are of value to us. We perform verbal acts as well as other acts, that is, in order to extend our control over a world that is not naturally disposed to serve our interests. If utterances are recognized as sharing this basic motive with all other acts, we must regard with some suspicion the common view that the basic function or purpose of speech for the speaker is to communicate information to the listener; for, in the absence of further qualification, that view implicitly attributes to our verbal actions a uniquely altruistic set of motives.

This is not to deny that information *is* communicated by speech; indeed, it is communicated by all our overt actions, at least to the extent that any action is potentially expressive, leaving marks and presenting signs and evidence of the performer's state and circumstances which, in turn, could be correctly inferred by a sufficiently alert and interested observer. In other words, any overt act or action, whether voluntary or involuntary, from sleeping to sneezing, from shifting in one's chair to rubbing a mosquito bite, will "say" things about us to other people if they have reason to take note of them. Thus, observing that my friend holds an unlit cigarette in his hand and that, after reaching into all his pockets, he is scanning surfaces and lifting objects, I may readily infer his state from his behavior and, being amiably disposed toward him, may offer him a pack of my own matches—without a word on the subject having been exchanged between us.

Though all actions are potentially expressive, it is also true that our *verbal* actions are highly specialized to be expressive, that is, to make manifest to those who observe them the most subtle features of our states and circumstances. That is not, however, because we have a wholly disinterested desire to make such information about ourselves or our world available to others. What is distinctive about *verbal* actions is not the selflessness of our motives in performing them but, on the contrary, their radical dependence on social dynamics and, indeed, social economics, for their effect. For it is in the very nature of verbal actions that they can have appropriate consequences for the performer—that is, can serve his interests and enable him to obtain and achieve what he desires—only to the extent that they affect and control the behavior of other people.

Nonverbal actions—such as pushing doors open—characteristically have consequences for the performer through their direct physical impact on his environment. As we move through the world, we move things (including our own bodies) around in it, performing an almost continuous succession of actions—placing, pushing, pulling, and so on—that have the effect of arranging our environments more to our liking. A verbal act, however, has only trivial physical consequences. The marks it leaves on air or paper can raise armies, topple empires, and secure our hearts' desires only through the effect those marks have on other people. The enormous disproportion between the direct physical impact of a verbal act and its

86

ultimate force in modifying the speaker's environment is related to the point mentioned above: that whereas all overt acts are potentially expressive, verbal acts are *specialized* to be so. In that respect, verbal acts must be considered in relation not to acts in general but to that particular class of acts which we may term *symbolic*.

Since this class has been given other names (for example, "communicative" or "semiotic") and since all these terms—including *expressive* and *verbal*—are used in many and overlapping senses, a full-dress definition will be useful at this point. In the sense of the term used here, then, an act is symbolic *when* and *to the extent that*:

1. the relation between (*a*) the performance of an act of that form and (*b*) the set of conditions in response to which it is performed is governed by a set of regularities or system of conventions, *and*
2. the act can have appropriate consequences for the performer only through its effects on other members of a community, specifically those who have learned those regularities or share those conventions and who are thus able to infer (*b*) from (*a*), that is, who are able to infer the conditions in response to which it was performed from the fact and form of its occurrence.

It is clearly not the physical form of an act that gives it symbolic force, for the "same" act can be performed either symbolically or nonsymbolically, and a single act can have both symbolic and nonsymbolic force at the same time. Thus, when a door is sticking and will not close properly otherwise, my slamming it shut will be a nonsymbolic act; the slamming will be symbolic, however, when I want a family member to appreciate the energy of my indignation at his recent words. Or, when I press the button of a doorbell, my act is nonsymbolic to the extent that its appropriate effect is to operate an electrical mechanism, and symbolic to the extent that its appropriate effect is to summon the inhabitants to the door. In each case, the act is symbolic when it can have appropriate consequences for me only through its effect on someone else, someone who interprets it correctly, inferring from it the motives and circumstances to which it was a response.

Ringing doorbells and slamming doors shut are not *verbal* actions but, like utterances, as *symbolic* acts they can be interpreted correctly only by those who have learned the regularities that govern the relation of their forms to their motives or who share the conventions that can give them symbolic force. The same is true of numerous other forms of behavior that are not, strictly speaking, verbal or linguistic, but which are nevertheless symbolic in this sense: gestures such as winking or shrugging; the wearing of certain items of apparel, such as crowns or tweed jackets; the display of certain objects, such as badges or fine china—in short, the whole array of actions that are increasingly recognized as having at least some specialized expressive or semiotic functions. (I might note that some of these actions and displays obviously have nonsymbolic as well as symbolic functions. Moreover, the *forms* of some of them obviously have their origins in biological, historical, or other *non-arbitrary* connections to what they conventionally imply. That does not, however, make them any less conventional when they occur *as* symbolic acts, for to say that an act is governed by convention is not to say that it has no basis in nature or history, but that its effectiveness does not depend on that basis.)

Although the definition of symbolic action proposed here is not altogether novel, I should like to acknowledge and emphasize some aspects of it that are a bit unusual and will be of importance to our general concerns here. First, due acknowledgment must be given to the fact that two terms, *meaning* and *intention*, do not appear in it. That is because one of them, *intention*, is superfluous here, its usual function in distinguishing symbolic from nonsymbolic acts having been covered here by specifying the distinctive way in which symbolic acts have consequences for the performer. The other term, *meaning*, does not appear because invoking it at this point would obscure rather than clarify the distinctions I am attempting to draw here.

I shall not, for the moment, speak further of *intention*, though I shall return to it in the final lecture, in connection with authorial intentions. I do want to say more about *meaning*, however. First, I would point out that what is usually covered by the term *meaning* in discussions of verbal or symbolic acts appears in this definition as 1(*b*): that is, "the conditions in response to which an act is performed," and which can be inferred from the act only by those who have learned the set of regularities or system of conventions governing the relation between acts of that form and some range of conditions. Thus, in the example used earlier, to the extent that my ringing the doorbell was a symbolic act, its "meaning" can be crudely described as the set of conditions consisting of my wanting, for some reason, to summon the inhabitants of the house to the door. In short, the meaning of my act is equivalent to its causes or why I performed it. The relevant set of regularities or conventions here can be crudely described as follows: it is regularly the case and conventionally understood that people ring doorbells when, for some reason, they want to summon the inhabitants to the door. In our culture, children learn that regularity or convention very early, but they are not born knowing it and those who have not yet learned it do not ring doorbells when they want to summon the inhabitants and do not go to doors when doorbells are rung.

For our immediate purposes here, in considering the relation of verbal acts to other acts, the translation of *meaning* just offered will suffice, that is, the conditions in response to which an act is performed. It is obviously not an adequate translation for all purposes, however, and when we turn, later, to the *listener*, for whom utterances are not acts but *events*, a richer and more comprehensive translation will be both possible and necessary. In the third lecture, I shall expand the translation even further in connection with the meanings of literary works. We may now, however, return to the speaker and to the characterization of utterances as highly specialized acts which have consequences for the performer in a quite distinctive manner.

The child discovers fairly early in infancy how extraordinary may be the consequences of certain sounds he makes. Sometimes, when he has done no more than emitted a syllable, powerful creatures will enter his presence and do things that minister to his needs and desires, things that he could not do himself. The child also learns that by shaping and combining those sounds in certain ways, he can have an increasingly strong and specific effect on those around him and thus on his environment. Of course, the child would not learn to speak as rapidly as he does if he were merely exposed to the verbal behavior of others or merely rewarded with praise for producing or imitating linguistic sounds. It is, rather, the very specific services and attentions he can elicit from other people by producing those sounds that recommend their rapid acquisition and increasingly "correct" formation and combination.[2]

The instrumental functions of language for the speaker are obvious enough when he is issuing commands, making requests, and asking questions ("Leave the keys on the table, please." "What time is it?"). It may be thought, however, that when he is making statements about the external world or about himself ("The movie starts at 7:30." "My feet hurt."), he is using language essentially to inform and express, not to affect other people or to direct their actions. We may still ask, however, why we *should* tell people things they do not know, either about the world around us or about our own ideas and feelings. Since we obviously *know* more than we ever affirm and have more feelings and ideas than we ever express, the question is why we affirm or express anything to particular listeners or on particular occasions. When we consider the actual circumstances under which we speak, the evident answer is, I think, that what we communicate, when we do so and to whom, are always determined at least in part by the likelihood of advantage we thereby derive for ourselves. Information is a commodity of some value, and we do not normally squander it or donate it *gratis* to whoever happens to be around. Rather, we *exchange* it for specific services, or invest it for long-term yield. In other words, we are disposed to provide our listeners with information when our doing so will dispose *them* to act in ways that serve our own interests; and our enlightenment of our fellow creatures is always tainted by ulterior motives.

It should be emphasized here, in view of the cynical sound of that formulation, that the personal interests served by language need not be grossly selfish and may range as widely in, say, *moral* terms as the interests served by any of our acts. Thus, we often give information to our friends and family members out of an independently motivated concern for their welfare. Our "interests," moreover, are not always a matter of the immediate satisfaction of specific needs and desires; and it is usually to our general advantage that our fellow creatures, whose actions may ultimately affect us directly or affect the world we inhabit, know what we would have them know about ourselves and that world.

There are two further aspects to the value of language for the speaker that require particular attention here, for they are closely related to the functions and effects of fictive discourse. First, we may consider that significant but rather obscure set of motives that impels us, as we say, to "share our experiences" with other people. Of course, as I suggested a moment ago, we may be inclined to inform other people of our personal experiences, including our sensations and feelings, when our doing so will secure their sympathetic attitudes and perhaps practical assistance. Moreover, when we exclaim to a companion, "Look at this interesting photo," or urge someone to taste what we are tasting or listen to what we are hearing, or when we narrate personal anecdotes ("Say, do you want to hear something funny ..., awful ..., wonderful ...," and so on), we are, no doubt, partly engaged in verbal gift giving, and thus in seeking to please those whose pleasure and goodwill are of general value to us. When all this is granted, however, there does seem to remain another aspect to our motives when we attempt, sometimes straining language to its furthest reaches, to make known to our companions the most subtle features of our experiences. It might seem, in fact, that there is an irreducible satisfaction to be gained from the sense that there are people around us who not only occupy the same gross physical environment as we do, but who also to some extent share the same experiential environment, seeing what we see, tasting what we taste, feeling what we feel.

The notion of a fundamental human desire for experiential companionship is appealing, and it might even be thought that such a need is innate in our psychological construction, evolving perhaps through natural selection as a condition for our development as social creatures and thus our enhanced ability to survive. On the other hand, it may not be so irreducible a satisfaction after all; for, by making our experiential environment available to others, we may not only secure their sympathy, assistance, and gratitude, but also their very important services as sources of cognitive feedback, that is, the responses of other people to *our* experiences can serve us as an external testing, and either confirmation or qualification, of our own most elusive perceptions.

The other point to be mentioned here is the fact that we are almost continuously "saying" things to that most intimate, congenial and attentive listener whom we carry within our own skins. Interior speech or verbal thinking is evidently a derived capacity that could not arise prior to, or independent of, one's participation, as both speaker and listener, in a linguistic community. But the functions and value of language are significantly extended by our ability to speak (and listen) to ourselves. For one thing, since one's "self" is always part of one's most immediate physical environment (as philosophers with toothaches have had occasion to observe) and also, in a sense, part of one's social environment as well (we are always our own companions) we have considerable interest in controlling and modifying its behavior; and so we take great care to feed ourselves information. Second, when we command, question, warn, and instruct the listener within, we can be, well, *fairly* confident of his inclination to act appropriately in serving our interests. Also, perhaps most importantly, by assuming the dual roles of speaker and listener, we are able to internalize the feedback functions of language mentioned just above, that is, to appraise our own perceptions and responses, to expose, test, compare, and confirm or correct them. It seems clear that our capacity for interior articulation also increases our ability to discriminate and classify our experiences, and therefore enables us to make more effective use of *prior* experiences in solving problems, making plans, and generally dealing with the world as we encounter it. Interior speech certainly comprises a major part of the "activity" of all human beings, and it is likely that our sense of personal identity and, to a large extent, "consciousness" itself are products of our internalization of the linguistic transaction. But we must now consider the other side of that transaction, or the functions of language for the listener.

II. THE LISTENER: UTTERANCES AS EVENTS

The child who discovers that the sounds he makes can marvelously extend his own powers also discovers that the sounds made by *other* people may be of great interest and consequence to him. As he learns more extensively and precisely those conventions that govern the relation between the sounds people make and the circumstances in which they make them, he is better able to predict and deal effectively with his world, including the behavior of the people who make those sounds.

Whereas an utterance can be properly regarded as an *act* from the speaker's point of view, it is, from the listener's point of view, an *event*, that is, an occurrence in the natural world that affects or interests him insofar as it provokes or demands an immediate response from him or provides him with potentially valuable information. I shall consider the peculiarly "provocative" aspects of verbal events below. For the moment, concentrating on their function as sources of information, we might observe (bending J. L. Austin's terms a bit) that while we are always using our own words "to do things," and that all verbal acts are therefore "performative" *for the speaker*, we are also always using the words of other people to discover things, and that all verbal events are therefore to some extent *informative* for the listener.

Any natural utterance does bear and can communicate information, no matter what its syntactic or modal form, whether assertion, question, command, or counterfactual conditional, and whether emotive, metaphysical, or verifiable in fact or in principle. Certainly when someone asks a question or makes a vow, extends a greeting or asserts the existence of a supreme being, the listener thereby learns something about the world, even if it is only something about the state of the speaker's needs, attitudes, or beliefs; but of course these may be things very useful for the listener to know.

We *speak* so that our listener will infer the conditions that caused us to speak, specifically so that he will infer that which it is in our interest that he know or believe about those conditions. And we *heed* the speech of others, take notice of their commands, promises, and threats as well as their announcements and declarations, because we can always expect to infer some of the conditions that caused those utterances and therefore something perhaps important to know and otherwise unknowable. It is true, of course, that the quantity of information we receive from the speaker may be quite minimal, either because we already know it from other sources or because it is of no inherent interest to us. In such cases, we may resist serving as a listener; we grow bored, stop paying attention, change the subject, or flee. Unless, however, our interests are themselves unusually limited, we *do* tend to listen to what other people say, having learned that the circumstances and motives that occasion their utterances are part of a world that affects us, and that what they are saying just may be "news."[3] Moreover, although we do not depend exclusively on what people *say* to learn how they feel and what they think—for all of their actions are sources of information concerning their internal states, and we usually learn to check what they "do" verbally against what they do otherwise—we nevertheless recognize that *verbal* responses are sometimes the *only* perceptible responses a speaker can make to certain of his personal states or experiences, and that his speech is therefore the only available source of information we have as to them.

It is important, at this point, that we return to the matter of *meaning*, specifically to the relation and the distinction between the meanings of symbolic events and the meanings of events generally. I would suggest, first, that every event can be conceived of as the center of a causal nexus, that is, a set of causes and consequences, corollaries and entailments, both gross and subtle, that obtain at every level of potential organization; and that total set can be conceived of as the total meaning of the event. Obviously no mortal creature can ever determine the total meaning of an event; but then, no mortal creature is ever likely to be interested in doing so. What we usually mean by the meaning of an event is not that totality but some *subset* of it, that is, some *selection* from among all the conditions to which the event ever could be thought to have causal connections; and which subset we refer to, on a given occasion, as *the* meaning of an event will depend on which of its connections are, on that occasion, of interest to us and also the extent to which those causes, consequences, corollaries, and so on then appear to be inferrable. In other words, when we speak of, or inquire after, the *meanings* of an event, we usually do so with reference to some subset of its total meaning that is (*a*) of at least conceivable interest to someone, (*b*) not self-evident and therefore problematic or worth remarking, and (c) at least theoretically inferrable on some basis.

Let me make these abstractions more concrete. If we encounter, in a history textbook designed for high school students, a chapter entitled "The *Meaning* of the French Revolution," we will expect something, but of course not *everything*, to be said about the origins and implications of the French Revolution, that is, about its historical causes and historical consequences. Or, learning that the train is late, we may remark, "That probably means there was a tie-up at 30th Street," thereby speculating on some of its causes, or "That means we'll have to catch a cab to the airport," thereby observing some of its consequences of interest to us. Jane says: "Look, John, a falling star! What does it mean?" John replies: "Who knows?", meaning that no one—or at least not John—can ascertain its causal connections; or "Who cares?", meaning that no one—at least not John—is interested in those connections; or "It doesn't mean anything," meaning that no one—at least not John—can ascertain or is interested in those connections.

So far, I have been speaking of the meanings of events generally (the French Revolution, late trains, fallings stars). I should now like to turn to the meanings of symbolic events, which, of course, includes natural utterances (*utterances*, it must be emphasized, not *words*; verbal *events*, not verbal *forms*), and the first point to be made about verbal or symbolic events is that everything I have said up to this point applies equally well to them. That is, we can conceive of the total meaning of a symbolic event as all the conditions that ever were or ever will be seen as having some causal connection to it, whether or not, at some given time, anyone has determined or could determine them. And we can go on to observe that, as with all other events, what we usually mean by the meaning of a symbolic or verbal event is some subset of that totality, specifically a subset of conceivable interest to someone and theoretically ascertainable on some basis. Certain *additional* characteristics, however, distinguish what we usually mean by the "meaning" of symbolic or verbal events.[4]

The first is fairly trivial, namely that, in view of the radically ambiguous nature of the term *meaning*, we usually take special care, when we speak of the meaning of an utterance (or other symbolic event), to distinguish antecedent from subsequent conditions, often reserving the term *meaning* for the first and using some other term, such as *significance* or *import* for the second (and also for various noncausal relations). Thus, we may speak of the "meaning" of someone's remark as what caused him to say it and its "significance" as what effects it will have. The distinction of usage is by no means consistent, but because it is common in English and also because it has some contemporary currency with respect to works of literature, I will concentrate my observations in what follows on meanings-as-causes, though the expansion to meanings-as-consequences should be understood as possible in all cases. A further expansion to meanings in the sense of certain *noncausal* relations will be of particular interest to us in the third lecture.

The second characteristic is more important. One of the ways in which symbolic events differ from nonsymbolic events is that they are always understood to have occurred by virtue of some personal agency—usually, though not necessarily, the agency of some human being. Nonsymbolic events may be—and many of them are—the products of personal action, but symbolic events, by definition, must be regarded as such. Because a symbolic event is always seen as the product of someone's act, we can conceive of *its* total meaning as all the conditions that caused that act to be performed, whether or not the performer or anyone else, at some given time, knows or can know them. With respect to a natural utterance, its total meaning is therefore *everything* that made the speaker speak it.

The third point to be made about the meanings of a symbolic event is that, although many of those meanings can be inferred on *other* bases, to the extent that it *is* symbolic, some of its meanings can be inferred *only* by reference to a set of learned regularities or a system of arbitrary conventions. And, of course, with respect to *verbal* events, that set or system is everything that we mean—or should mean—by a *language*, that is, all the regularities and arbitrary conventions that govern the relation between the occurrence of verbal acts or events of some form and the range of conditions in response to which they are performed.

The fourth and final characteristic of the meanings of symbolic events follows from the fact that, by definition, at least two persons are interested in it: the person by whose agency it occurred and the person for whom it *is* an event:[5] in the case of natural utterances, the speaker and listener respectively. And what follows is that which particular subset of its total meaning we refer to, on any particular occasion, *as* its "meaning" will depend in part on *whose* interests are of interest to us.

An example will be useful here. One evening, in a bar, after a couple of drinks, John leans over and says to Jane, "You know, I think you're really a wonderful person." We can say that the meaning of John's utterance, in the broadest sense, consists of the total set of conditions, circumstantial and psychological, to which that utterance was a response: in short, everything that made John say it, whether or not he or anyone else then knows it. We can also specify various subsets of that totality, *each* of which might be referred to as "*the* meaning" of his utterance.

Thus, we can say that its meaning consists of all the conditions that are potentially inferrable by any interested listener—including some eavesdropper—on the basis of that listener's knowledge of various matters. First, there is the listener's knowledge of *linguistic convention*, that is, the general regularities or conventions governing the relation between the occurrence of utterances of that form and the conditions under which they characteristically occur. Second, there is the listener's knowledge of *the particular context* of that utterance, including the physical and social circumstances in which it occurred, the character of John and his relationship to Jane, what the conversation between them was like up to that point, and so forth. Third, there is *everything else* the listener knows that might enrich or constrain the inferences he draws on the basis of linguistic convention and the context. *All* of the listener's inferences made on all these bases, however, will be *less* than the total set of conditions that did obtain, and *different* from the inferences made by some other listener whose knowledge was more or less extensive or subtle, and whose interests in John's utterance were different.

We can also speak of the meanings of John's utterance as those conditions that it was in *John's* interest that *Jane* infer from it, which will again be less than the total set though probably more, and possibly less, than what would be implied by linguistic convention alone. (We may imagine John leaning over even closer and saying, "You know what I mean?")

Finally, we can speak of the meaning of John's utterance as all those conditions that it was in *Jane's* interest that she infer, or all those that she did in fact infer—again, in each case, less than total set and probably different from the set that it was in John's interest that she infer. (We may imagine Jane as replying, "Yes, I *do* know what you mean," or "Yeah, I know what you mean.")

The implications of this analysis of meaning for our general concerns here will become clear if we return to the discussion of the value of natural discourse to the listener and particularly to its value as a source of information. If, as I have been suggesting, we regard the meanings of any historical event as the total set of conditions that determined its occurrence, it follows that no natural utterance is "meaningless," for the very fact that it occurred is evidence that something determined it and therefore that it has some potentially inferrable meaning. Even the gibberish uttered by an idiot or a psychotic has meaning in the sense that it has causes. Of course, to the extent that linguistic convention does not operate for such a speaker and that the determinants of his speech cannot *thereby* be reliably inferred from its form, his utterance becomes, from the point of view of the listener, in effect a *nonverbal event*. As such, however, it still has meanings, and a listener might arrive at some of them on the same basis as he would the meanings of any event: through inferences based on his general knowledge and on his prior experiences with more or less similar events in more or less similar circumstances.

Indeed, it is important to recognize that the bases on which we "interpret" the meanings of a verbal event are fundamentally the same as those on which we interpret or infer the meanings of *any* event. In an upstairs room, I hear a variety of noises—shufflings, slidings, bangings—and infer, on the basis of all my prior experiences with (among other things) sounds of these sorts, what their source is and what has caused them to occur: namely, that my daughter, while preparing to go to bed, is moving around in her room, opening and closing closet doors and bureau drawers. Later, as another recognizable sort of clattering sound grows louder, I infer that she is coming downstairs. A minute later, when she pops her head into my study and says, "Hey, my alarm's broke—don't forget to wake me up at seven tomorrow," once again I make inferences as to the source and cause of *those* very subtly and precisely formed sounds. It would be accurate to say that I have, in each case, interpreted the meaning of a set of sounds on the basis of my prior experiences with sounds of those sorts occurring in similar circumstances, and that, in each case, what I interpret them to mean will be sharpened, enriched, and perhaps modified by other things I know or believe, including things about those *particular* circumstances.

Having said what is the same about verbal and nonverbal events, we may now say what is different. First, we note that whereas the actions my daughter performs in opening and closing closet doors and walking down a staircase have appropriate consequences for her that are quite independent of my inferences concerning the sounds they incidentally produce, that is not the case for her verbal actions, which will have an effect only through my proper interpretation of them. Second, the relation between the *form* of the verbal sounds she produced and the circumstances that produced them (her discovery of a broken alarm, her concern lest she be late for school, her need to secure my services, and so on) is not a matter of direct physical consequences, as when a slammed door produces a slamming sound, but is governed by a highly complex, largely arbitrary, and extremely subtle set of social conventions.

As I have sought to emphasize, the conventionality of verbal events does not distinguish them from other events with respect to the process by which, or basis on which, one draws inferences from them. One learns the system of rules that governs the relation between verbal events and their causes in the same way as one learns the nonarbitrary regularities that obtain in the world of nonverbal events, that is, by generalizing from prior experiences with events of that kind. The fact that the rules or regularities governing verbal events are largely arbitrary and *conventional* does, however, have a very important corollary for both the speaker and the listener: for an arbitrary convention is something that, by its nature, must be shared if it is to be effective. Consequently, it is not enough to say that the listener can draw inferences from a verbal event only with reference to a system of conventions; we must add that the inferences he draws will be correct only if the form of the speaker's act has been governed by that system. In other words, a listener can take the form of a verbal event as a reliable index of its determinants *only on the assumption that those determinants are implied by it and are expected to be inferred from it in accord with the relevant rules and conventions.* That assumption—that a speaker means, and expects to be taken to mean, what he says—is the fundamental convention on which all natural verbal transactions are based.

This basic assumption of the linguistic marketplace operates very much like the one shared by both buyers and sellers that paper or metal currency has a specific economic value exchangeable, according to a relatively stable system of equivalences, for valued goods and services. When this assumption is violated by the speaker in natural discourse—when he palms off counterfeit linguistic currency—we say that he is lying; and lying is a social transgression of the first order precisely because it undermines the community's confidence in that verbal medium of exchange so basic to social transactions. We do not have a simple term like *lying* for the converse violation of that assumption by the listener, though it is important to recognize its existence, and the situation is familiar enough in everyday transactions. One may think, for example, of listeners who refuse to credit what we say in the spirit in which we have said it, or of those who persist in interpreting latently what we offer patently, extracting the revelation of unflattering unconscious motives from our innocent casual remarks, or, generally, of those who take our utterances as implying something other than what their forms would, according to linguistic convention, reflect.

Of course, this lying-in-reverse (or what I shall refer to as "false listening") is only an extreme form of what all listeners do when they interpret our verbal acts as nonsymbolic events, inferring the conditions that caused us to perform them on some basis *other* than linguistic convention. We cannot restrict the inferences people draw from our acts only to those inferences which it is in our interest that they draw or only to those implied by linguistic convention—and, when *we* are listeners rather than speakers, we will do the same. Nevertheless, if we were never taken to mean what we say, if all our verbal actions were interpreted contrary to our interests and altogether without reference to linguistic convention, the linguistic marketplace would rapidly disappear to the loss of all listeners as well as all speakers.

In natural discourse, we do, of course, distinguish lies from erroneous statements and from linguistically improper or obscure utterances. Similarly, we recognize that listeners can "mis-take" or draw erroneous inferences from what we say, and that they may, for various reasons, find our utterances incomprehensible. In all such cases, however, the assumptions of the verbal transaction break down because the speaker's or listener's knowledge of the world or of linguistic convention itself is deficient, and such breakdowns are accepted by the community as understandable accidents that do not seriously damage the health of the verbal economy. As we shall see, however, the assumptions of natural discourse may, also without damage, be deliberately suspended or replaced by other conventions operating for both "speaker" and "listener." In such circumstances, "counterfeit"—that is, fictive—utterances will, like stage money, have a positive value, as will also the listener's *not* crediting the speaker's words or *not* taking what he "says" as meaning what made him "say" it.

I spoke earlier of the distinctively provocative aspects of language for the listener. Like other events in our experience, verbal events may not only provide information about the environment, but also require responses from us. Moreover, because every linguistic transaction is also a social transaction, it inevitably reflects and partakes of all the responsibilities and moral and psychological pressures that can characterize our relations with other people. A natural utterance constitutes, for the listener, not only an invitation and provocation, but ultimately an *obligation*, to respond to the speaker. When we "listen" to someone, as distinguished from merely noticing or overhearing what he says—in other words, when we identify ourselves as his audience—we implicitly agree to make ourselves available to that speaker as the instrument of his interests. We agree not only to hear

101

but to *heed* his promises, excuses, questions, and commands—and also, of course, his assertions. Most simply, but most significantly, we agree *to understand what he means*, that is, to infer the motives and circumstances that occasioned his utterance, and to act in accord with the information thereby obtained, or at least, to take it into account along with whatever else we know and however else we are inclined to act.

We are commonly conscious of the social risks that the *speaker* incurs when he speaks (or writes, or publishes): his increased vulnerability to other people; the exposure of his feelings, attitudes, and perhaps ignorance; the fact that he has made himself more knowable to others and that their knowledge may not be used to his advantage. *Hamlet* provides the classic image of a speaker attempting to avoid those dangers, particularly in the scene between the Prince and his prying schoolmates: ". . . Why do you go about to recover the wind of me, as if you would drive me into a toil? . . . You would play upon me, you would seek to know my stops, you would pluck out the heart of my mystery. . . ." But there is also risk involved for anyone who identifies himself as a *listener*, a fact apparently well-appreciated by children, servants, Army recruits, and others who, having been exploited as "captive audiences" in the past, either learn to avoid verbal encounters or develop functional deafness. Gertrude, in the closet scene, is often portrayed as putting her hands over her ears: "O Hamlet, speak no more . . . Oh, speak to me no more. These words like daggers enter in my ears." Sophocles' Jocasta, sensing the imminence of "unspeakable" revelations, urges Oedipus to ignore the messenger from Corinth, and flees rather than listen. Oedipus himself, however, never flinches: When the shepherd hesitates, "Ah, I am on the brink of dreadful speech," he replies, "And I of dreadful hearing. Yet I must hear." We might say that Oedipus was a heroic listener.

In spite of all these risks and liabilities, however, we are usually willing to accept the implicit responsibilities of listening, and we accept them primarily for two reasons (that is, aside from the fundamental reason, namely the chance that we will thereby obtain useful information): first, because the speaker himself—friend, guest, child, employer—may be someone whose interests we are independently disposed or constrained to serve; and second, because it is to our general advantage, as members of a shared linguistic community, to preserve the effectiveness of language *for the speaker.* For, as present and future listeners, we have a vested interest in our fellow creatures' continued disposition to speak and thus to provide us with information; moreover, since we will ourselves be speakers on other occasions and require the mediating services of those who are *our* listeners, we have a vested interest in maintaining the assumption of the listener's availability and responsiveness.

A final point should be made here concerning the conventions that govern natural verbal transactions, namely that those conventions are not confined to the contents of dictionaries and grammars, but include all those rules that govern the relation between the things people say and the conditions under which they say them, rules that we learn from our lifelong experiences with language in use. "Linguistic convention" thus includes what we learn to be the complementary obligations and responsibilities of speakers and listeners. For example, if a speaker says, "Dinner is ready" or "Sorry, I didn't catch your name," the listener will assume not only that certain facts obtain about the state of dinner or a failure of apprehension, but also that the speaker's affirming those facts at that moment reflects other implicit features of his circumstances and motives: presumably that he expects the listener to rise and enter the dining room, or that he desires a name to be repeated.

Ordinarily, the listener will take the occurrence of an utterance as a fairly reliable index of the speaker's situation, beliefs, and motives (with, of course, due or paranoid caution as to the possibility of lies and errors, depending on his prior experiences with that speaker and on what his sense of the immediate context dictates), and he will act accordingly; that is, the listener will act on the assumption that the speaker has taken responsibility not only for the "truth" and "sincerity" of his utterance—its correspondence to what he believes to be the case and to what he believes his motives are for saying it—but also for what might be called the "spirit" of what he says. Thus, having heard someone say, "I never want to see you again," or "Jane is wild about you," and having acted accordingly (that is, avoided the speaker, made a bold pass at Jane), the listener may justifiably feel that a trust had been betrayed if the speaker later tells him, "Oh, I was just *saying* that. You shouldn't have taken it seriously." Accused of making irresponsible or misleading statements, however, the speaker may defend himself, pointing out that he had obviously been "kidding" or "being ironic" or "speaking figuratively," and, perhaps with justice, accuse the *listener* of an insensitivity to linguistic convention or contextual cues ("Anyone else would have known what I meant," or "Yes, I said that, but that's not the *way* I said it"), or of being crudely "literal-minded."

The listener's problems and the speaker's excuses here reveal the significance and subtlety of certain aspects of the dynamics of language that have not, until quite recently, been recognized in formal linguistic theory[6]—though we are, of course, familiar enough with them from the hazards and disasters of our ordinary verbal dealings. Of particular significance to our concerns here is the fact that speakers and listeners depend on one another's knowledge of, and sensitivity to, various formal and contextual features that signal *how* a given utterance is to be taken: with what force, in what spirit—and, most important, *whether or not it is to be taken as a natural utterance at all*. Among the signals a speaker may use to indicate that what he says is *not* to be taken "seriously," or "straight," or "literally," are intonation (such as exaggerated stress), attendant gestures (such as a wink or a sidelong smile), and unidiomatic or personally uncharacteristic diction or phrasing. The speaker may also simply rely on the listener's appreciation of the total context of the utterance, or his recognition of the fact that what the speaker says is at odds with what the listener would otherwise expect, given his knowledge of the speaker's general situation, beliefs, and attitudes. In any case, such formal anomalies or contextual discrepancies would, when properly interpreted, have the effect of *qualifying* the conventions and assumptions that would otherwise be understood as governing the relation between what was said and what was so (or "meant"). If the signals are missed, so that the listener mistakes the spirit and force of the utterance, his interpretation of and response to it will be inappropriate; and although the consequences of his error may be nothing more than social embarrassment, the consequences are nevertheless quite real.[7]

At the beginning of this lecture, I suggested that the distinctions commonly drawn between literary and nonliterary language on the basis of their differing *functions* often suffer from an inadequate appreciation of the dynamics of discourse itself. The observations offered here hardly constitute, of course, a full description of those dynamics. They have been designed, however, to emphasize those aspects of *natural* discourse that are particularly significant for understanding the characteristic functions and value of *fictive* discourse, including poetry. It is important to recognize that natural discourse *is* a transaction, that it operates through a formidable and often fragile network of assumptions that extends beyond what we sometimes think of as linguistic convention—that is, the rules governing semantic and syntactic propriety—and that this transaction involves not only complementary advantages but also complementary responsibilities and risks, for both speaker and listener.

To understand the ethics of verbal transactions, we must appreciate its economics. That means we must appreciate that language *is* action, both speaking it and also listening to it, and that it always operates through the use and control of other people. Like all other economic markets, the linguistic market is never an altogether free one: it can be rigged, and it can be floated with counterfeit currency; the exchanges are not always conducted between those on an otherwise equal footing and, when attended by the machinery of political power, the control exerted and services exacted through language can be literally killing. We sometimes speak of language as a *game*—in the sense that, like games, it is a form of behavior governed by rules. But, in that sense, so is trade, so is politics, and so is war. If they are games, they are all games that are played for real.

Since I have not, in this first lecture "in poetry" so much as mentioned a poem, I'll conclude this evening by reciting a brief one that touches on this last point and suggests quite incisively the limits of metaphors of play. It was written by Sir Walter Raleigh, a man who played every game and fought every war that the period offered:

> What is our life? a play of passion;
> Our mirth, the music of division;
> Our mothers' wombs the tiring houses be
> Where we are dressed for this short comedy;

Heav'n the judicious sharp spectator is,
That sits and marks still who doth act amiss;
Our graves, that hide us from the searching sun,
Are like drawn curtains when the play is done.
Thus march we, playing, to our latest rest:
Only we die in earnest—that's no jest.

5

LICENSING THE UNSPEAKABLE

In the last lecture, natural discourse was described as an economic transaction between speaker and listener, typically an exchange of information for services. This evening, I shall be concerned with how we move *out* of the linguistic marketplace, why we do so, and what difference it makes. First, I shall consider some of the conditions that take us out, conditions that arise from the very nature of verbal transactions. For as we have seen, the conventions that make those transactions possible also control and constrain us as both speakers and listeners; and we would, and do, sometimes escape them. In the second part of the lecture, I shall be concerned with the potential aesthetic and ludic functions of language that are liberated by the removal of discourse from the marketplace, and shall consider briefly the relation of verbal art and verbal play. In the third section, I shall focus on the verbal licentiousness of children and consider how, even as they are learning to enter the marketplace, they also learn to find its exit gates. At the conclusion of the lecture, I shall have a few words to say about epistemological skepticism and what I have referred to as nihilistic monism.

I. CONSTRAINTS AND CONVENTIONS

You will recall the observation made last time that being a listener always involves a liability of some sort. We do not always want to

107

know the truth; we certainly don't always want to hear it. Though usually under circumstances less extreme than those suggested earlier—the verbal daggers against which Gertrude shields her ears, the "unspeakable" revelations that Jocasta truly would rather die than hear—the risks and burdens of serving as someone's audience are nevertheless familiar. One may think, for example, of the times one has found oneself the audience of a friend's irrepressible and unabridgeable report of a recent dream, or a child's rambling narrative of the plot of a television drama, or a lecture on the chemical composition of packaged foods delivered by a recently enlightened colleague. The excruciating boredom we may suffer under such circumstances arises from the fact that while general social propriety or our particular relationship to the speaker prevents us from simply taking flight or tuning out, the amount of interesting information we receive from such utterances is quite minimal—and thus out of proportion to, or insufficient payment for, the time and attention we have been constrained to donate.

We may also consider these poor market conditions from the point of view of the other party to the transaction, that is, the speaker, who may have something to sell for which there is no immediate buyer. Or, to drop the analogy for a moment, it appears that our impulse to speak is often strong even when there is no willing or otherwise appropriate listener.

No one has ever said everything he knew or felt. That is not, however, because we are secretive or, in the ordinary sense, inarticulate, but rather because the opportunities for speech are quite limited compared to the motives for it. Because of the various crucial and unique ways in which language serves us as speakers, we probably have a generalized tendency to respond verbally to almost all our experiences. Yet it is obvious that we do not talk continuously, at least not publicly. Of course, we can always indulge that tendency by talking to our*selves* (either covertly, as in verbal thinking, or overtly, as in muttering or writing diaries); but it is also obvious that there are severe limits to the satisfactions to be gained thereby, and also limits to the services that can be provided by the listener-within.

Of all the not strictly physical afflictions to which we may fall victim through such misfortunes as exile, imprisonment, illness, and old age, perhaps the one most acutely felt is loneliness—which means, among other things, the sheer unavailability of listeners. When there is "no one to talk to" (note that we far more rarely complain of there being "no one to listen to"), we are manifoldly deprived; for, lacking listeners, we lack not only the opportunity to affect others instrumentally, to secure their services in ministering to our physical needs and desires, but we also lack their services in providing what I referred to last time as cognitive feedback, that is, the occasion they offer for us to verbalize and thus to integrate, discriminate, appreciate, and indeed experience our own otherwise elusive perceptions. For we often come into possession of an idea or feeling precisely through the expression of it, the process required to make it intelligible to others. Prisoners, exiles, and suburban mothers often suffer, for what appears to be good reason, from the fear that they are becoming unresponsive, undiscriminating, torpid, or indeed not quite sane.

But we may hunger for an audience even in the midst of a feast of companions. For what we have to say may be too extensive, subtle, or specialized to be of interest to, or even comprehensible by, those around us. Or we may, in their company, be unable to select and organize our words in such a way as to control our listeners' attention or to insure that they do listen to what we are saying. To a great extent, the institution of "literature" supplies these needs by extending the domain of the linguistic marketplace. That is, we may *inscribe* what we cannot speak and put it up for general sale as, for example, an essay, article, or memoir. "Literature" in this sense, however, that is, as *inscribed natural discourse*, is still subject to the economics of the marketplace. Although no specific service or immediate response may be asked of the reader (who may be remote in time as well as otherwise from the author, and therefore under no pressure of personal or social obligation to him), it is still understood that the reader will take the inscribed composition as a direct reflection of the writer's sentiments, beliefs, and circumstances, and will find interest and value in it primarily as such.

Inscription and publication allow one to "speak" utterances that, because of essentially practical difficulties, would be otherwise unspeakable. Some utterances, however, are even more radically unspeakable. Most obviously, we can neither speak nor write what we would say when the "saying" of it—in either form—would make us vulnerable, when the revelation of our sentiments, situation, or even knowledge would expose us to contempt, hostility, or danger. Also, we may be moved to address a listener who, for some reason, cannot or will not heed us. Thus, we cannot really "speak" to dead friends, estranged lovers, sleeping babies, nightingales, or Grecian urns, although there may, in a sense, be things we wanted to say to them. And, of course, even when we do not require a particular listener, there are few occasions on which we can give unlimited expression to all of our attitudes, feelings, and recognitions. Not even lovers or psychoanalysts can be enlisted as continuous audiences. Finally, even granted endlessly attentive lovers and analysts, our public voices are always dependent on our public roles, qualified as well as constrained by our relationships to our listeners. Consequently, there are always sentiments we could express, knowledge we could display, ways we could speak—possible utterances, in other words—for which there are no occasions, no audiences, or no available style. The conventions and assumptions of fictive discourse, however, may allow us to define the occasion, enlist the audience, and create or discover the necessary style.

Fictive discourse allows us to speak the unspeakable—but only if we agree not to *say* it. This catch could be put in the terms of our economic analogy as the need for the seller either to lower his price or to throw in additional goods or otherwise valuable premiums. Indeed, the characteristic qualities of verbal art are often accounted for in such terms: meter or rhyme being seen as "additional goods" (or, as Wordsworth implies in the Preface to *Lyrical Ballads*, "superadded pleasure"), and enchanting stories and stylistic coloration being seen as superior (if slightly deceptive) packaging (as in the classical "sugar-pill" theory of didactic poetry and in some modern psychoanalytic theories). But these accounts miss the essential nature of the accommodation made in fictive discourse. For the "speaker" does not really cheapen, dress up, or disguise his goods when he offers them as poetry: he transforms them into something entirely different and, in effect, removes them from the common verbal marketplace to another kind of arena. What makes it worth the reader's while to heed the historically unspeakable utterance depends on the understanding that he shares with the "speaker" that it is not, in fact, historically spoken: that, insofar as it is being offered as fictive discourse, the reader and author have entered a special relationship, one that is governed by assumptions, claims, and responsibilities quite different from those that obtain between the speaker and listener of a natural utterance.

Produced in the theaters of language or displayed in its galleries, fictive discourse is not subject to the economics of the linguistic marketplace. Thus, the poet can use language and his audience can respond to it without the constraints that would otherwise shape and confine the behavior of each of them. Though this may appear to be a tendentious way of describing "poetic license," its implications are considerably more far-reaching than what the cliché suggests. For the licensing that I am speaking of here extends to the audience as well as to the poet, and it involves not merely formal or even thematic features of the utterance, but quite fundamental aspects of the linguistic transaction itself.

As we have seen, the basic assumption of natural verbal transactions, shared by both parties, is that the speaker means what he says and that the listener will take him to mean what he says. It is precisely the suspension of that assumption that defines fictive discourse. It is not, of course, that the poet is understood to be lying, but rather that he is understood not to be *saying* at all. The poet is not a speaker addressing a listener, but one who composes a verbal structure that *represents* a natural utterance. The poem may represent the poet himself addressing a dead friend or estranged lover, but the poet, as a historical creature, is not engaged in the historical act of addressing them—just as the language instructor, whose name really *may* be Jacques, is not engaged in the historical act of giving his name when, in illustrating the use of a verb, he represents that act by presenting the words *Je m'appelle Jacques.* Nor is the poet really "addressing" the audience who may at any time read his poem, except in the metaphoric (and for that reason often confusing) sense that any artist—painter, sculptor, or composer—"addresses" those whose interest and pleasure his work is designed to secure. Whatever *communication* may be taken to mean in regard to the dynamics of art, it is not the same as what it means in regard to the dynamics of natural discourse.

A representation, we note, does not have the same force as an event in nature, does not demand and also does not preclude the same response. We do not have the same attitude or reaction to the sculpted figure of a nude as we would to a naked person standing or reclining before us. To mention only a trivial—or perhaps not so trivial—difference, we cannot *stare* at persons (clothed or not) as we can at sculptures or portraits without feeling, as we might say, a bit voyeuristic. The actual presence of someone both requires certain social acknowledgments and also constrains our actions in various ways.

The exceptions here are particularly instructive. We can stare at naked persons—such as live models in a drawing class or actors on a stage—when they are in a sense "in our presence" but yet understood as not occupying the same ontological space as we do. In these circumstances, the conventions that require or preclude certain responses to other people are understood to be suspended. The model or actor is, under these conditions, no longer another person, but the representation of one: in short, a fictive person.

With respect to language, the point may be made concrete if we consider a situation in which the special assumptions governing fictive discourse are strained or come into conflict with those governing natural discourse. A close friend tells us that he has just composed a poem, and asks us to read it; in the "poem," we discover what appear to be allusions to his poor health or domestic troubles. Under such circumstances, something of a moral dilemma is likely to arise. On the one hand, in view of our concern for the writer and the apparent revelations of his griefs or problems, we may feel that it would be insensitive, an evasion of moral responsibility or of simple civility, to direct our comments to "aesthetic" matters: to observe that the metaphor in the third line is muddy, or that the rhythm toward the end is flat, or even that the poem is a splendid achievement. On the other hand, we may hesitate to take explicit notice of the personal allusions, hesitate to offer sympathy or press for further details, as we would had our friend spoken to us (or, of course, written us) about his misfortunes; for to do so would seem somehow indelicate, presumptuous, a violation of his privacy or, more significantly, a violation of an understanding that such a response is not expected and not appropriate.

We may give the ambiguities of the situation a further turn by supposing that we have good reason to suspect, on independent grounds, that our friend is in fact using the poem primarily as a way of informing us of his situation. In that case, although our sympathies may be genuinely aroused by the substance of the revelations, and we may appreciate the motives that led to this indirect means of revealing them, we are still likely to feel to a certain extent exploited. For, by presenting us with what he calls a "poem" and yet intimating that he wants us to take it as a reflection of his immediate circumstances, he has tried to have things both ways—or, more specifically, tried to say something while evading the responsibilities of having done so. Our sense of exploitation here is composed of a number of elements which we would find difficult to express to him, not only because they are subtle but because they involve those economic aspects of social transactions that we commonly hesitate to invoke or acknowledge explicitly.

For one thing, we are always inclined to resent, or experience as in some sense unjust, situations in which someone "lets us know" things without actually saying them: the barely articulated or subsequently denied mutter of annoyance; the pointed inflection that gives to an otherwise innocuous statement an edge of sarcasm; faint sighs, "loaded" silences, and a variety of "expressive" though not conventionalized acts and gestures, such as slamming a door or fluttering one's eyelashes. These paralinguistic and nonlinguistic forms of communication may, of course, be patently symbolic acts or be used patently to supplement or qualify natural utterances, and thus be incorporated into what *is* "said." The situation becomes uncomfortable, however, when acknowledgment of what they communicate and of the very fact that they communicate things, is evaded: "But I didn't *say* I minded your coming home late." "But I didn't *ask* for help with the dishes." What is evaded in such cases is the acknowledgment of an intention to affect or control the other person, and also acknowledgment of the usual understanding that the "listener" will and should act in accord with the information thus delivered. When a speaker does tell us his state or situation verbally, he implicitly acknowledges his interest in or need for our consequent response—and thus also acknowledges that he is to that extent in our debt and that we, in turn, have a counterclaim on him for a return of services. But the "speaker" who "lets us know" things without saying them may also be attempting to evade that acknowledgment, to obtain our services *gratis* under cover of not really asking for them.

The various moral derelictions described here obtain for all speakers who want to have it both ways. There is a special kind of culpability in the double-dealing of our friend, however, for to the extent that he indicates that he want the "poem" to affect us primarily as a revelation of his immediate circumstances, he has abused the conventions of fictive discourse and thereby contributed to their undermining. If we see his duplicity as a form of lying, we must also recognize the possibility of its converse on the part of the audience, just as we recognized the possibility of reverse lying or "false listening" in *natural* discourse. There is, here, an interesting double reversal that can be spelled out as follows: The basic assumption of *natural* verbal transactions is that the speaker means what he says and will be taken to mean what he says in accord with linguistic convention. Thus, in natural discourse, the lying speaker is one who *says* what he *does not mean*, and the false listener is one who interprets an utterance as *meaning* what the speaker *does not say*. But in *fictive* discourse, where that basic assumption is understood to be suspended, the "liar" and his counterpart "false listener" are those who do not acknowledge the suspension or who do not permit it to be in force. It would be as if the French instructor, whose real name is *Seymour* and was addressed that way by a student, were, for his own amusement, to comment curtly, "But I *told* you my name was Jacques"; or as if the student, out of malice or waggishness, were to address him as Jacques, saying, "But that's what you *said* your name was."

The implications of this double reversal will be explored in the third lecture, when we are concerned with the ethics of interpretation. For the moment, however, we may consider more generally how the dilemmas and difficulties discussed a moment ago illustrate the disparity between the poet's relation to his reader and what would otherwise be a speaker's relation to his listener.

Any utterance occurs in and presumes upon a social context, and, in natural discourse, that context is constituted in large part by a relationship between speaker and listener that has been established on prior or what might be called external grounds. In other words, we speak to each other as friend to friend, parent to child, teacher to student, master to servant, or, it may be, one twentieth-century intellectual to another. The nature of the utterance and also of the listener's response to it are always to some degree determined by the nature of that relationship: the claims and responsibilities that exist by virtue of it. The relationship between poet and reader, however, is established on internal grounds, that is, it is defined with respect to the particular poem, making neither concessions to nor acknowledgments of whatever external relation the poet may have to the reader. (This reader or audience, of course, is to be distinguished from whatever listener—mistress or nightingale—may be "addressed" in the fictive utterance itself and also from any audience addressed by the poem offered as a *natural* utterance.) The poet and reader do have a "relationship" and certain social responsibilities toward one another, but these derive from cultural assumptions regarding not personal relationships but the nature and value of artworks. In "personal" terms, there need be *no* relationship between the artist and his audience. Although this description may suggest a morally grim and socially chilly state of affairs, the "impersonality" that characterizes the relation between poet and reader reflects neither evasion nor abdication of social responsibility but, on the contrary, a most punctilious respect for it. Like the impersonality that obtains between painter and model, or between actor and audience, it is a highly moral state of affairs that serves each of them and preserves the conventions by virtue of which art can exist and have value. We shall return to that point also in the third lecture, where we shall be concerned with claims made for the ethical basis of certain constraints on literary interpretation, claims that depend, in part, on the obliteration of the sorts of distinctions just made.

ii. VERBAL ART AND COGNITIVE PLAY

I should like now to pursue further my earlier observation that "poetic license" extends to the listener or reader as well as to the poet. Put another way, we might say that, for both parties, the removal of the poem from the linguistic marketplace—or, more generally, the disengagement of any verbal structure from its functions in a marketplace transaction—liberates its potentiality to serve other functions which, in turn, replace its market value. Verbal artworks are structures presumably designed to be thus disengaged and designed accordingly to fulfill other functions. Any verbal structure, however, has the potentiality to fulfill multiple functions: just as the metal disc that once served Roman citizens as a coin of the realm may now be exhibited in a museum case as an archeological "find" or, duly set by a jeweler, be displayed as a body adornment, so a text that once was (and still could be) linguistic currency may serve other functions and thereby acquire a different sort of value. The discovery and demonstration of the archeological value of verbal structures is a characteristic occupation of the biographer or historian, who, in making "documents" of texts that originally functioned as natural utterances (or, for that matter, were originally designed as poems), thus actualizes another of their potential functions—though not, it might be noted, an originally intended one.[1] Similarly, compositions not originally designed to serve as verbal artworks may be "found" or "set" to do so, that is, discovered and exhibited to be the occasions for certain perceptual and cognitive activities that appear to be associated with what we sometimes speak of as "aesthetic experience."[2] It will be pertinent to our concerns here to consider briefly some aspects of those activities and their relation to the potential functions of fictive discourse.

As creatures who must know our world in order to survive in it, we are engaged in almost continuous cognitive activity, scanning and exploring the environment, searching out principles of regularity and patterns of conformity, classifying and reclassifying phenomena, testing present against past experiences, examining and adjusting the categories of our knowledge. Indeed, we are probably creatures who *have* survived because of our epistemic hunger and irritability, our itch to know and our capacity to learn. The possession of information is obviously a condition for survival, but so also is the continuous pursuit of it, and it would seem that we are conditioned by our individual histories—and, in a sense, "conditioned" by the history of our kind—not only to seek and value knowledge but to find fundamentally gratifying the very process of *coming to know*, that is, the activity of learning itself or the sheer exercise of our cognitive faculties.[3] As Aristotle observed, we are creatures for whom learning is the liveliest pleasure.

We are not commonly conscious, however, of the independent charms of epistemic activity. For one thing, most of our "learning experiences" occur in a context of practical concerns: our explorations of the environment are usually directed and constrained by more or less immediate needs and interests, and the value of our learning is usually recognized and measured by its instrumental consequences. Getting off the train in a strange city, we search for an exit, a restaurant, a taxi, an "information" booth. Picking up a newspaper, we scan the headlines for "news" that might interest us, focus on an article, flip the pages quickly to find the continuation of its text. When we are clearly intent on cognitive ends rather than cognitive processes, the processes themselves are likely to be attended by anxiety or irritation rather than that lively pleasure of which Aristotle speaks. Indeed, it would seem that the pleasures of learning are maximal when the pressure to know is minimal and the consequences of knowing are not of immediate concern.

The potential gratifications of learning are, moreover, enhanced or diminished by various conditions. Certain objects and events yield discoveries more readily than others to our search for patterns and principles. In a situation where structural relations are elusive or fragmentary, where we encounter mostly clutter and noise or discontinuity, unpredictability and irregularity, where the objects of perception resist classification and offer no readily graspable principles of order, either internal or in relation to prior experiences, learning will be continually frustrated. Under such circumstances, we will feel radical discomfort, disorientation, alienation, and perhaps panic as the categories by which we organize experience prove inadequate and our sense of control over the environment slips from us. It is not the unknown but the unknowable that we dread. On the other hand, if the patterns or principles are totally manifest and predictable or conform exactly to prior experiences, the conditions for learning are not really favorable, for there is nothing to learn. In the language of information theory, one approaches total redundancy and zero information; in more colloquial terms, there is no news, and the situation is experienced as boring, bland, unchallenging, uninteresting.

It would seem, then, that the optimal conditions for engaging in gratifying cognitive activity are characterized by, among other things, a combination—either a balance or a particular ratio—of novelty and familiarity, repetition and variation, conformity and disparity, redundancy and information. Learning is most graciously invited by a situation that appears to some extent unknown but that promises knowability. Moreover, the process of "coming to know" seems to be most rewarding when there is what might be called a gradient of reinforcement, that is, when each step into the blur or darkness yields increasing clarity and structure, where intuitions of order may be tested and either confirmed or disproved, and where local patterns and simple conformant elements are seen as coherent in relation both to one another and to more comprehensive or hierarchic principles of structure. The various characteristics described here, it should be emphasized, are not independently measurable "properties" or objectively describable "features" of a situation, and can be specified only relative to some perceiver. What is "familiar" and "redundant" to me may be novel and rich in information to someone else, depending on our individual personal histories, including our cultural experiences. Moreover, because there are individual, and to some extent innate, differences in our capacities to process information, a degree of novelty and unpredictability that is agreeably "interesting" to one perceiver may be experienced by another as intractably chaotic. Nevertheless, there will always be conditions that are more likely than others to invite and reward the very process of learning, that is, learning to no immediate end, or what we might call "cognitive play."

While the conditions described here are most conspicuously exemplified by situations or activities that we do, in fact, refer to as "games" or "play" (for example, doing jigsaw puzzles, solving cryptograms, playing solitaire), they are not confined to them; and, though the world is not naturally a cognitive playground, we do find, frame, or fashion *gymnasia* for the mind in the midst of its marketplaces and battlegrounds. Those conditions are perhaps just as conspicuously exemplified by what we refer to as "works of art" and by other objects and events that become the occasion for "aesthetic experiences," and also (though perhaps less conspicuously) by *aspects* of certain situations and activities which, while generally considered serious or elevated business, may nevertheless be recognized as potentially "playful" or "aesthetic", for example, religious ceremonies, sexual engagements, doing philosophy.

These observations can obviously be extended to our experiences with language. To survive in the verbal universe and to profit from the economics of the linguistic marketplace, we must scan and explore utterances as well as other visual and auditory structures and we must attend to the forms of verbal events at least as closely as to those of any other events. We characteristically obtain information from linguistic sights and sounds, however, in relation to the symbol systems by virtue of which they do bear most of their information, and "cognitive activity" with respect to verbal structures consists primarily of inferring their meanings from their forms in accord with the conventions of those systems; it consists, in other words, of *interpreting* them.

Two points must be added if we are to appreciate the potential "aesthetic" functions of fictive discourse. The first is that, with respect to verbal structures, the process of interpretation is typically energized and rewarded by the economics of the linguistic marketplace and both directed and constrained by contextual considerations: the possible instrumental value of the information thereby to be obtained and the possible responses thereby required of or provoked from us. In interpreting natural discourse as such, then, our cognitive activities are always in the service of more or less immediate cognitive ends. We do not, therefore, usually give ourselves over to the independent pleasures and interests of *merely* interpreting a natural utterance, nor do we usually infer or ascribe meanings that are irrelevant to its presumed context of origin or to the context of the transaction itself.

The second point is that although interpretation is the cognitive activity characteristically evoked by verbal structures, it is not the only one that is possible. For those structures are not only potential sources of conventionally coded information; they are also physical phenomena—shapes and sounds—and, as such, have formal properties that may become the subject of more or less independent perceptual and cognitive interest. That potential interest, however, is usually not actualized and is, in fact, commonly surpressed ("edited out" by speakers, "not noticed" by listeners) when we are engaged in marketplace transactions.

As we know, it sometimes happens that for some reason—for example, boredom, social alienation, high-spiritedness or inebriation—we will be "distanced" from the marketplace and find ourselves listening to (or reading) natural discourse with the sort of desultory concentration, "disinterested interest," that we associate with "aesthetic experience," attending to features of utterances that would otherwise distract us from the business of verbal transactions: for example, the intonational contours and rhythms of a dialogue; chance rhymes, parallelisms, and other formal patterns; evocative allusions, submerged metaphors, potential puns. Thus decontextualized, the ongoing natural discourse in which we have no "interest" will become quite *interesting* in another way—or, of course, amusing or absurd. Or, if we happen to find ourselves in the congenial company of others who are similarly distanced and disposed, we may engage in forms of verbal behavior and exchanges of words that have only limited market value: elaborate metaphors, chains of puns, jokes, verbal impersonations or self-parodies, teasing or mock arguments, in all of which we play not only with verbal forms and meanings but also with the very dynamics of natural verbal transactions and the linguistic and social conventions that govern them.

But of course we need not wait for such distancing conditions simply to "happen" or to arise casually; we can create them our-selves or seek out those already created by others. Poems, novels, plays, and other "works of literature" are, among other things, verbal structures that have been designed or discovered to constitute precisely such conditions, to invite and reward the sorts of activities I have been describing as "cognitive play": here, the exploration of the formal and symbolic properties of language, the contextually unrestricted interpretation of verbal structures—that is, the playing out of their potential "meanings"—and the playing with or playing at the conventions of linguistic transactions.

Clearly works of literature may and do serve other functions as well, and their potential function as occasions for cognitive play is not always actualized, not always dominant, and therefore not the only source of their interest and value. It is, moreover, proper and possible to distinguish between, on the one hand, verbal artworks and, on the other, those structures and forms of behavior that are more readily seen as verbal toys and games. While the distinction is not, I believe, an absolute one and can never be drawn with preci-sion, certain relative differences can be suggested.

First, to the extent that a verbal artwork exhibits greater struc-tural complexity or "relational richness" than a verbal toy, the range and variety of cognitive activities it evokes will be more extensive.[4] Compared to the solving of a cryptogram, the reading of a poem is an exercise that both requires and gives scope to more multileveled information processing and multiple patterning. Also, to the extent that its formal and thematic elements can be seen not only to enter into conformant and hierarchical relations with one another but also to enter into more relations with *other*—prior and subsequent—experiences, the poem will be more amenable to *re*patterning. As new principles of organization are recognized, different internal relationships and relations to different external experiences are per-ceived and new "meanings" are manifested. The rereading of a poem is thus more likely to be rewarding, and rewarding in new ways, than the resolving of a crossword puzzle, and the jokes and riddles exchanged in a community are likely to become stale for its members more quickly than its songs and stories. Conversely, to the extent that puzzles, jokes, and riddles do exhibit a relatively high degree of structural complexity and relational activities, we are more likely to think of them as works of art or literature (cf. *Finnegan's Wake*, which may be, among other things, the most complicated verbal toy ever devised).

Second, our consciousness of the artificer is likely to be of particular significance in our experience of a verbal artwork—as distinguished here not only from such verbal games as jokes and riddles (whose original "authors" are usually unknown and, in any case, of less interest in this respect than their *presenters* in the context of verbal play), but also from such "casual" occasions for the aesthetic experience of language as were described above. As I suggested earlier, among the conditions that invite our cognitive explorations of a structure is the assumption of an ultimate reward to those activities, that is, the promise of its ultimate knowability; and no matter how well that promise is actually made good, it will obviously be strengthened if the structure has presumably been *designed* to be thus explored and "known." Consequently, although we can engage as deeply with anonymous poems as with those whose authors are vivid figures for us, the presumption and/or projection of some author, and thus the presumption of the "designed" design of a work, is usually crucial to the nature of our cognitive engagement with it; and, among the cognitive processes that constitute our experience of a poem is the process of inferring or hypothesizing various aspects of that design. It should be noted here that in an orally transmitted folkloric work, such as a ballad or a tale, the successive acts of artifice of its various transmitters constitute a process of gradual "design" which is, in this respect, equivalent to the various acts of selection and revision that enter into the composition of a text by an individual author. What is crucial is that we may assume, in our experience of each, that the structure of the work has been shaped by either its anticipated or actual effectiveness in serving an aesthetic function for some audience.[5]

This brings us to the final and perhaps most significant distinction, namely our assumption that a verbal artwork, unlike a verbal toy or game, has been designed to be experienced as fictive *discourse*; for the presumption of its amenability to "interpretation" as such, that is, as the representation of an utterance, will be a major source of its interest and value. Whereas the riddle, cryptogram, or crossword puzzle characteristically promises knowability in the form of a "solution" to be found, the joke in the form of a "point" to be gotten, the poem promises knowability primarily in the form of "meanings" to be inferred, and the process of inferring those meanings is central to our cognitive engagement with it. Thus, that engagement is brought to a conclusion (comparable to the solving of a puzzle or getting the point of a joke) not only when we perceive the principles that allow the work to be experienced as a coherent formal structure, but also when we have the sense that we have "understood what it means": when, for example, we have been able to construe the identity of a "speaker" implied by the represented utterance and a plausible context of motives and circumstances that would account for his speaking thus, and/or when we have constructed various stable hypotheses of thematic design. The latter might range from our presumptive identification of various local and specific "meanings" (for example, an allusion to Queen Elizabeth, a pun on the word *lie*, an allegory of Christian redemption) to our inference of more general "meanings"—attitudes, sentiments, values, and so on—that the work appears intended to imply or exemplify (for example, that war is hell, that the love of money is the root of all evil, that death should be faced with courage).

As the examples here suggest, the material with which we play in our engagement with a poem is often sober stuff, but the concept of cognitive play entails neither triviality nor shallowness. When we watch the Prince of Denmark play with a jester's skull or hear the dying Mercutio play with "grave words," we are entertained, though we know that death is no jest. Indeed, part of what entertains us in these plays is the occasion, scope, and *license* they can provide for our entertaining thoughts of death: not only for imagining Hamlet's thoughts or for inferring Shakespeare's thoughts, but also for playing out our own thoughts of death—a playing out for which there would otherwise be no particular occasion or which, when there is one (for example, the death of a friend), would be colored

123

and controlled by the very particularity of the occasion and yet *not* "controlled"—fed, focused, and shaped—by the playwright's counter-play.

I shall develop this last point further in the next lecture, where I shall suggest that the "transaction" between the poet and his reader is indeed more a form of gamesmanship than one of commerce, and shall have a few more words to say about the nature of the cognitive activities described here. I should like to conclude the present discussion of those activities by pointing out that the various inferences, identifications, and hypotheses alluded to above are not to be confused with the overt and more or less formal "analyses," "readings," or "interpretations" of poems that are produced as academic exercises from either side of the professorial desk. Such exercises reflect an essentially arbitrary arresting, segmentation, and articulation of a process that is itself always fluid and dynamic and that may be quite "inarticulate." Moreover, that process is in certain respects endless. Although it is typically "concluded" when we have the sense that we understand what the poem means, we never "finally" understand a poem. To be sure, we never finally understand *any* structure or event, that is, never can (and rarely seek to) ascertain what was described in the first lecture as its "total meaning." Our efforts to understand a *natural* utterance are usually satisfied and terminated when we have inferred enough of its meanings to serve our own interests and those of the speaker in the context of the verbal transaction. To the extent, however, that a poem is removed from the marketplace and is not currency in such a transaction, there are no such interests to be served and there is thus no corresponding (or "natural") termination to the activity of inferring meanings from it. We can be repeatedly motivated, therefore, to "come to know" a poem, and repeatedly gratified by the sense that we have understood what it means: not understood "at last" what it "really" means, but understood *again* what it *might* mean.

III. Children at the Gates of the Marketplace
We may now turn to the third aspect of verbal licentiousness to be considered here, namely the linguistic behavior of children and,

thereby, not only the beginnings of verbal play and art but also the functional origins of the distinction between natural and fictive discourse.

In the first lecture, I alluded briefly to how children, from the time of infancy, are introduced to verbal economics, how they learn to extend their control over their environment though their own verbal actions, and also how they learn the significance—in all senses—of the verbal actions of others. It must be added, however, that from our earliest years, indeed from the very beginnings of our lives as verbal creatures, we find sources of fascination and pleasure in language that are largely (though probably not altogether) independent of its instrumental functions. Infants apparently find inherently gratifying their own imitation of the linguistic sounds they hear, and young children seem universally to take delight not only in storytelling, songs, and verbal impersonation, but also in producing and hearing rhythmic or repeated linguistic sounds and, later, in puns, riddles, paradoxes, and other kinds of formal and thematic wordplay. One may speculate on the developmental origins and functions of such wordplay, noting, for example, that it allows children to rehearse and exercise those skills required for the use of language in the marketplace: perceptual and cognitive, as well as motor, skills. It seems clear, however, that our interest and pleasure in exploring the properties of language, and also in exploring our own responses to it, do not disappear when we come of age, and that we continue throughout our lives to make excursions from the marketplaces to the playgrounds of language.

I shall not take the time here to develop the observation, increasingly supported in recent years, that play is a very serious matter for children.[6] It has not, however, always been thought so, and its relation to other serious matters is still often misunderstood and underestimated. We may recall here the words of Thomas Gradgrind, the arch-utilitarian of Dickens' novel *Hard Times*, on the occasion of his visit to the Coketown elementary school:

> Now, what I want is Facts. Teach these boys and girls nothing but Facts.... You can only form the minds of reasoning animals upon Facts; nothing else will ever be of service to them. This is the principle on which I bring up

my own children, and that is the principle on which I bring up these children. Stick to the Facts, sir!

There remain parents and educators who would banish fairy-tales from the nursery and schoolroom as pernicious sources of misinformation or as encouragements to what is taken to be the child's innate tendency to confuse fact and fiction. It is likely, however, that these ideological descendants of Gradgrind not only underestimate the child's ability to make the relevant distinctions, but also fail to recognize the nature and strength of the pressures that oblige him to do so. Children learn to discriminate at a quite early age—almost, indeed, from the time they begin to engage in anything we would call verbal behavior—between, on the one hand, things that are "said" by and to them and, on the other hand, such things as nursery rhymes, songs, and verbal play. They do so, moreover, not on the basis of explicit instructions or distinctive labels but, rather, on the basis of their own differential experiences with each, that is, with the relatively distinctive forms and the absolutely distinctive *consequences* of natural and fictive discourse.

Fictive verbal structures are commonly marked off from verbal acts and events by various features, both contextual and internal, that operate for the child as identifying cues or signals. We need not specifically instruct a child to regard as fictive any utterance that begins "Once upon a time . . ." and, indeed, traditional formulas of that sort are probably less crucial than is sometimes supposed, and not necessarily more effective than purely contextual signals of fictiveness.

We do not commonly recite a rhyme or begin telling a tale in the middle of a conversation. Fictive structures are not distributed haphazardly among natural verbal events but tend to occur in a specially marked, framed or self-enclosed context, a "storytime" or "playtime" that may be named as such, or identified in other ways. Moreover, even when they *are* imbedded in natural discourse, the imbedding itself is signaled. Intonational markers are common, as are distinctive body motions, and both are readily picked up by children. We begin a story, "There was once a wise king of England, and he was named King Arthur . . ." with a style of delivery that is appreciably different from the "matter-of-fact" manner in which we would say, perhaps in reply to a child's question, "Elizabeth the First? Oh, she was queen of England a long time ago, before the Pilgrims came to America. You remember who the Pilgrims were, don't you?" We commonly employ a distinctive vocal register when we narrate fictions or read them aloud; also the rise and fall of pitch and loudness are often exaggerated, the tempo is often slower or at least more studied, and even if the material is not itself metrical, we may be inclined to phrase more rhythmically.

Fictionality, in the sense of historical falsehood, is not, for the child, the defining quality of a "story." If he says, "Tell me a story," he may continue with "Tell me the one about Red Riding Hood" or "Tell me the one about how you got stuck in the sticky tar and Grandma had to wash you with gasoline." What was initially a family anecdote may be spoken of as a "story" even though the child knows and believes that the events really happened. Should the parent reply, "But you know what happened with the sticky tar; I *told* you about it just yesterday," the child may insist, "No, no, you have to *tell* it." The parent who himself appreciates that implicit distinction between *dicere* and *narrare* will construct the story accordingly, and will deliver it in proper storytelling fashion, "not speaking" (as Sir Philip Sidney put it) "table-talk fashion, words as they chanceably fall from the mouth," but employing the intonational markers and distinctive body motions mentioned a moment ago. Leaning back or forward, lifting or lowering his head, closing his eyes for a moment or looking into the distance, the teller will create the sense of a special space, his own entrance into a world apart from the immediate one: a bardic stage or magic circle, in short, a playground set off from the verbal marketplace. These distinctive tones and gestures may be themselves conventional, learned (or unconsciously imitated) from storytellers we have heard; they may also be universal, arising more or less naturally from the contexts and functions of storytelling. The origin of those features, however, is not at issue. The point is that, however they arise and whatever other functions they serve for the storyteller and his audience, such features also operate as signals of fictiveness that inform the listener how that discourse is (and is not) to be taken.

In the example just given, the family anecdote becomes a tale, a fictive "telling," relished now as much for its structure, rhythms, predictable details, and bits of quaint dialogue as it was initially, perhaps, for the amusing image of a once-young parent in a sorry predicament. An episode of domestic history has acquired the status of family lore somewhat as in a nonliterate community, a fragment of presumably true national history becomes part of the culture's lore as *told* by one or more local bards. In both, the thematic core of the narration may have been first heard or presented as part of a natural utterance in a context of *reportage*; but, in becoming a "tale," its identity and interest become independent of that context. The factuality of the subject does not compromise the fictiveness of the tale, for it is not the events told that are fictive but the *telling* of them. That telling is set apart from reports of past events and from such allusions to them as may occur in natural discourse. As we have seen, the listener's interest in a natural utterance lies primarily in the information it bears, what it reveals of the world or of the speaker. For this reason, the repetition of such reports is felt to be redundant. If someone who has just heard a radio broadcast bursts into the room and begins, "Say, did you know there was a terrible earthquake in Los Angeles?" we are not likely to reply, "Yes, I read it in the paper this morning, but tell it to me again," though we might say, "Yes, I know. Is there any more news about it?" "News," or information, is what the listener values in natural discourse. It is obviously not what he seeks or expects from the twice-told tale. Children are no less sensitive to redundancy than are adults, and they are often more openly and even brutally disdainful of it. ("Oh, I know that already. You don't have to tell me again.") But they are also more openly eager for the special pleasures of "redundancy" in fiction, and the refrain "Tell it again, tell it again," appears to be universal among them.

I mentioned earlier the contextual and paralinguistic features of a recitation that set it apart from natural discourse for the child. There are, of course, also internal or stylistic features that he will learn to associate with fictive discourse: most obviously, rhyme, meter, and other systematic repetitions, but also archaic diction and otherwise unidiomatic expressions, and various opening, closing, and transitional formulas. Like the intonational markers mentioned earlier, these stylistic features need not have been specifically or exclusively designed to function as signals of fictiveness, and most of them have other functions that are related to the valued effects of verbal artworks. Moreover, stylistic features of this sort do not define fictive discourse and are not altogether reliable signals of fictiveness: they occur in household maxims and cautionary homilies that are *said* to the child while they may not occur in naturalistic and crudely didactic storybooks that are nevertheless *story*books (for example, *John and Mary Visit the Airport*). However, when they *do* occur, they inform the child that he is probably being presented with something *other* than natural discourse.

It is, in fact, this negative definition of fictive discourse that is most significant for the child, that is, the fact that certain verbal structures are recognized as *not* being natural utterances. As I observed earlier, the child learns to distinguish between natural and fictive discourse on the basis of his differential experiences with each. These differential experiences, however, relate not merely to the more or less distinctive features of fictive utterances, features that signal them as different from natural utterances, but much more importantly, to the fact that *that difference itself* has consequences. If there were no differential consequences, there would be no reason for the child to learn the distinctive features, and he would not learn them! In effect, he learns the difference between natural and fictive discourse because it makes a difference, and his learning the difference consists basically of his learning the difference it makes.[7]

The child's earliest experiences with the adult use of fictive discourse usually involve verbal games, songs and lullabies, and nursery rhymes; later his experiences with fictive discourse involve not only the stories and tales told to him by adults, but also his own verbal make-believe, in which he may induce adults and other children to join. At the very simplest level, these events and activities introduce the child to a special class of verbal structures that do not function for him, either as speaker or listener, in the same way as do the natural utterances he otherwise hears and produces. "Patty-cake" does not occur in the presence of cakes and ovens; "This little piggy" is not a piggy, and does not go to market or eat roast beef.

Adults will allow the child to berate them as witches and revile them as monsters in terms and tones for which he would otherwise be scolded. Parents will accept, without murmur, his offers of invisible tea and his invitations to invisible castles, and will make allusions, without explanation, to such exotic objects as porridge and tuffets, and such anomalous events as talking animals and metamorphosed pumpkins.

Children learn, then, (1) that certain linguistic structures can and do occur outside the normal context of verbal transactions, and (2) that the linguistic conventions and social assumptions of the verbal community do not hold for those structures: specifically, those conventions that govern the relation of a verbal form to the speaker's motives and circumstances, and those assumptions that govern how the listener is expected to interpret and otherwise respond to an utterance.

When we consider how the child learns to recognize and respond to fictive discourse, we must remember that he is still in the process of learning the forms and effects of natural discourse. Even those language theorists who are persuaded of the extensiveness of innate linguistic capacities do not maintain that a child enters the world with a complete functional mastery of language. From his own incohate vocalizing and the initially undiscriminated sounds he hears, the child must learn to produce effective utterances and to interpret the verbal behavior of others in accord with the conventions of his linguistic community. For the adult, who has mastered the language, and whose verbal acts and experiences consist largely of natural utterances, fictive discourse is discriminated as a "special class" of linguistic structures. For the child, however, natural discourse *itself* gradually emerges as a "special class" of linguistic structures. For even after he has acquired a substantial repertory of well-formed words, phrases, and syntactic structures, a good deal of the child's verbal behavior still consists of what might be called "extranatural" discourse, that is, the production of verbal structures that are not governed by the conventions of either natural *or* fictive discourse: for example, his repetition, to no one in particular, of "funny" words, phrases, or phonemes; the semi-melodic and minimally verbal "songs" that he makes up himself; and long streams of essentially private—that is, nonsocial though overt—speech and verbal impersonation. A child may engage for hours in solitary activity, or even group play with other children, accompanied by almost continuous extranatural "speech" of this kind—which is, in effect, *interrupted* by occasional natural utterances: either his own ("Now you be the princess") or those of other people ("A little less noise, please").

My point here is that the child actually learns two sets of linguistic convention, that which governs natural and that which governs fictive discourse: the distinctive features, distinctive occasions, and distinctive consequences of each.

Since the child's earliest verbal behavior is "extranatural," and since a large portion of it continues to be such for a few years, it may be tempting to think of this as evidence for the notion that fictive discourse (or "poetry") is more natural than natural discourse, and to extrapolate the notion to a theory of the poetic origins of speech in primeval man. It must be emphasized, however, that the earliest extranatural speech of children is nonnatural or "poetic" only in the the sense that its forms and occurences *imperfectly* reflect the conventions of the linguistic community and are *not yet* governed appropriately by the assumptions of natural verbal transactions. It is nonconventional by default, not by design. Thus, we should not confuse the child's verbal play for the poet's verbal art any more than we should confuse his delightfully improper generalizations (for example, his pointing to the sun and saying "Lamp?") with the poet's artful metaphors (for example, alluding to the sun as "the bright eye of day"). As for extrapolating the child's verbal play to a theory of the origins of language, it must be emphasized that the verbal behavior of every child we observe arises within a functioning linguistic community and is shaped by its practices from the very beginning, whereas the "original" speech of primeval man presupposes, by definition, the absence of any such community. Although extranatural discourse is the first to occur in the child's own behavior, it nevertheless *follows* from the prior existence of natural discourse in the social world around him.

Granting these distinctions, however, we may still suppose that our tendency, as children, to explore the properties of verbal forms and verbal behavior is related to the pleasure we take, as adults, in creating and experiencing verbal art. Wherever we find a linguistic marketplace, we also find, just outside its gates, and adjacent to each other, a playground and a theater; wherever we exchange words, we also play with them and play—that is, *represent*—the exchange of them. Fictive discourse appears to be as universal as natural discourse and we may suppose it to be as ancient as language itself.

In concluding this evening, I should like to return very briefly to Thomas Gradgrind. Gradgrind, you recall, maintained that the Coketown children should be taught "nothing but facts." For philosophers and others who observe, on epistemological grounds, that there are no facts, that the universe is a structure of fictions, Gradgrind's absurdity lies in the fact that his facts are themselves fictions. Since nothing is really real, they argue, there can be nothing that is unreal—or nothing that is not unreal. I would reply that it doesn't quite follow. That is, while it may be that there are no ultimate realities, it does not follow that there are no distinctions among unrealities. The distinction is often in the kinds of consequences they have. We are at some peril if we fail to distinguish the unreality of dreams from the unreality of waking experiences or unreal representations of tigers from unreal tigers—a peril that I shall not call "real" but, as Sir Walter Raleigh put it, at least "in earnest." It may be argued that all natural utterances are themselves fictive. But the distinction between natural and fictive discourse does not thereby collapse: it simply, so to speak, moves over one ontological notch.

6

THE ETHICS OF
INTERPRETATION

The observations presented in the two previous lectures can be brought to bear on certain questions of literary theory. My topic this evening is their bearing on questions of literary interpretation. I shall, in a moment, be reading to you a passage from a recently published essay by Professor E. D. Hirsch. The volume in which it appears is entitled *The Aims of Interpretation*; the essay is entitled "Three Dimensions of Hermeneutics." Although I shall be taking issue with a number of points in it, my argument is not with Professor Hirsch specifically, but rather with the general and not uncommon practice—which the passage handily exemplifies—of enjoining certain forms of literary interpretation and interdicting others through an appeal to the ethical basis of verbal transactions. The passage reads as follows:

> Therefore, let me state what I consider to be a fundamental ethical maxim for interpretation, a maxim that claims no privileged sanction from metaphysics or analysis, but only from general ethical tenets, generally shared. *Unless there is a powerful overriding value in disregarding an author's intentions (i.e., original meaning), we who interpret as a vocation should not disregard it.* [Hirsch's italics] . . . When we simply use an author's words for our own purposes without respecting his intention, we trans-

gress what Charles Stevenson in another context called "the ethics of language," just as we transgress ethical norms when we use another person merely for our own ends. Kant held it to be a foundation of moral action that men should be conceived as ends in themselves, and not as instruments of other men. This imperative is transferable to the words of men because speech is an extension and expression of men in the social domain, and also because when we fail to conjoin a man's intentions to his words we lose the soul of speech, which is to convey meaning and to understand what is intended to be conveyed.

I am not impressed with the view that this ethical imperative of speech, to which we all submit in ordinary discourse, is not applicable to written speech or, in particular, to literary texts. No literary theorist from Coleridge to the present has succeeded in formulating a viable distinction between the nature of ordinary written speech and the nature of literary written speech. For reasons I shall not pause to detail in this place, I believe the distinction can never be successfully formulated, and the futility of attempting the distinction will come to be generally recognized. Moreover, if it is seen that there is no viable distinction between "literature" and other classifications of written speech, it will also come to be recognized that the ethics of language hold good in all uses of language, oral and written, in poetry as well as in philosophy. All are ethically governed by the intentions of the author.[1]

One may readily sympathize with the sort of impulse that produces so strong a statement as this, especially if one recalls various ignorant, inept, perverse, or preposterous interpretations of literary works; and one may appreciate the effort to devise an argument exposing the impropriety of such interpretations in principle. The grounds of this particular argument are nevertheless weak, for they consist primarily of begging the fundamental questions: *Are* there no relevant distinctions to be made between a man's "speech" and any literary work? *Do* the "ethical imperatives" that we acknowledge in ordinary discourse hold good in "all uses of language"? Those who, like Hirsch, argue for the reader's—or professional interpreter's—moral obligation to discover the "original meaning" of a work assume, assert, and insist that the answer to these questions is yes. The burden of the previous two lectures has obviously been to answer them otherwise.

Before turning to the substance of the disagreement, I should like to consider briefly the precise nature of what Hirsch alludes to as "the soul of speech," that is, "to convey meaning and to understand what is intended to be conveyed." So defined, this is clearly quite close to what I have been describing as the fundamental assumption governing natural verbal transactions, namely that the speaker means, and will be taken to mean, what he says in accord with linguistic convention. What follows, however, is that all uses of language are ethically governed not by the author's intentions but by the conventions of the linguistic community. In his formulation and discussion of this assumption, Hirsch introduces a gratuitous and ultimately obscurantist note of piety into the dynamics of an essentially pragmatic situation. It is true enough that when we fail to respect that assumption, "we lose the soul of speech"; like all categorical imperatives, however, those that govern verbal transactions derive their force from the fact that their transgression would make the universe we share with our fellow creatures a poorer place for all of us, in this case poorer for the loss of the benefits of language. We "submit" to these assumptions not because we conceive men as "ends in themselves" rather than as "instruments of other men," but because to violate them would be to reduce the effectiveness of language for all speakers and listeners, among whom we ourselves number. Indeed, it seems clear that to use language at all is inevitably to use other people as instruments, though there is no reason to regard speaking and listening as therefore any more unethical than, say, grabbing hold of someone's arm on an icy road without first asking his permission or consulting his interests. We graciously serve others as instruments because, in doing so, we contribute to, and preserve, the network of social assumptions that permits us to use *them* as instruments; and it is just as well for all of us that the vitality and effectiveness of language do not depend on anything so vagrant as the moral rectitude of any of us.

We may now turn to the more fundamental issues, which are (1) whether the assumptions (or, if one prefers, imperatives) governing natural verbal transactions do "hold good in all uses of languages, oral as well as written, in poetry as well as in philosophy," (2) whether there are no relevant and viable distinctions to be made in this regard, and (3) if they do *not* uniformly hold good, and there *are* distinctions to be made, what the ethics of interpretation are.

One would agree, of course, that the assumptions governing "ordinary speech" extend to "*written* speech" and to "literary *texts*" when, by these latter terms, we refer to *inscribed natural utterances*, which include not only notes to the milkman and love letters but also essays, memoirs, and works of philosophy—and thus many compositions that we do consider "literature." What I have been suggesting, however, is that there is a class of verbal structures to which the assumptions governing ordinary speech *cannot* be extended because the suspension of those assumptions is precisely what defines that class. For Hirsch to maintain his resounding generalization, "the ethics of language hold good in *all* uses of language," he would have to deny the existence of *any* verbal composition of the sort referred to here as fictive discourse. This would require him not merely to deny that such "literary texts" as poems, novels, and playscripts are distinguishable from "written speech," but also to deny that such uses of language as the presentation of sample sentences by linguists and logicians, the verbal play of children, the citation of proverbs, and the recitation of stories are, any of them, in any relevant way distinguishable from "ordinary speech."

That there *is* a relevant distinction to be drawn is obscured, in Hirsch's argument, by the shifting and otherwise problematic senses in which he uses certain expressions: among them, "ordinary discourse," which seems in some instances to mean specifically vocal or conversational speech but, in other instances, to mean any form of nonliterary discourse; and also "original meaning," "authorial meaning," and "the intentions of the author," all of which seem to be equivalent at some points, but not all points.

In the article under discussion, Hirsch is arguing for the reader's (or interpreter's)[2] obligation to identify and articulate "original meaning," primarily as opposed to what he calls "anachronistic" or "nonauthorial" meanings, that is, meanings which there is reason to believe (presumably on linguistic or historical grounds) that an author did not intend, or could not have intended, his work to convey. The opposition and preference may appear reasonable enough, but when they are examined more closely in connection with the nature of literary meaning and literary interpretation, the opposition becomes tenuous, the preference dubious, and the ethics of interpretation are seen to lie elsewhere.

i. Determinate and Indeterminate Meanings

I would begin by suggesting that Hirsch's tendency to equate meanings with authorial intentions, conjoined with his failure to distinguish between natural and fictive discourse, have made it impossible for him to recognize that *although the intentions of all authors are historically determinate, the meanings of all utterances are not.* I shall elaborate both halves of that observation, beginning with the meanings of utterances and proceeding to the nature of authorial intentions. It will be useful at this point, in order to clarify the distinction between determinate and indeterminate meanings in natural and fictive utterances, to draw together a number of observations made earlier in these lectures:

1. Because every natural utterance, from a conversational remark to a philosophical treatise, is a historical act and a historical event, some of its meanings are historically determinate. That is, the conditions that occasioned the utterance and shaped its form, the conditions to which it was a response, are understood to have occurred in the historical universe. Therefore, like the meanings of *any* historical event, from the explosion of a supernova to the falling of a leaf, some of the meanings of a natural utterance can be more or less validly inferred by an interested observer, and the validity of his inferences can be challenged or supported by, among other things, appeals to historical evidence.

2. Because a natural utterance is also a *verbal* act and event, some of its historically determinate meanings presumably can be and are expected to be inferred by the listener on the basis of linguistic convention, and the propriety of those inferences can be challenged or supported by appeals to those conventions.

3. Because the composition (N.B., *composition*) of a fictive utterance is a historical act and event, some of the meanings of *that*

137

act or event are historically determinate; that is, it is understood that the conditions that occasioned the composition of the utterance and shaped its form *as* a historical act occurred in the historical universe and that some of those conditions are at least theoretically ascertainable on some basis. If the fictive utterance is a literary work, such as a poem, play, or novel, the meanings of the work, *in this sense*, would be no different from the meanings of a nonliterary composition. They would include everything from the author's most intimate motives in composing it to all the social and intellectual circumstances that could be conceived of as having occasioned its composition or shaped its form; and inferences concerning such meanings could be supported or challenged by appeals to anything from personal diaries and theater records to the traces of an entire set of social and cultural conditions. Thus we have the efforts of (and the disputes among) literary scholars, biographers, and historians.

4. Because a fictive utterance is a *verbal* structure, some meanings can be assigned to it—and were presumably expected and intended by the author to *be* assigned to it—on the basis of linguistic convention, and assignments of meaning made on that basis can be supported or challenged by appeals to those conventions. Thus, if the utterance is a literary work, we have the efforts of (and disputes among) literary explicators. Of course, especially if the work was composed in a remote time, the establishment of those conventions *themselves* may require historical validation and therefore be supported and challenged by appeals to historical evidence. Thus we have efforts of (and disputes among) literary philologists.

5. *However*, because a fictive utterance is not itself a historical act or event, because it is understood that that verbal structure was not "performed" and did not "occur" in the historical universe, some of its meanings are *historically indeterminate* and therefore not even theoretically ascertainable on the basis of historical evidence. In other words, to speak of the meanings of a fictive utterance as historically indeterminate is not to override—ignore, mistake, or betray—something that is *there*, but to acknowledge the fact that something is *not* there.

These observations will be made more concrete if we consider the following two situations:

A. We discover, in an old attic trunk, the fragment of what appears to be a letter written by some unknown correspondent to some equally unknown recipient.

B. We encounter, in the current issue of a magazine, a verbal structure identical to that of the letter fragment, but labeled "poem." The author, let us say, is someone about whom we know nothing but his name.

In both the letter and the poem, there are an unidentified "I" and "you," and various objects, places, and events are alluded to in general terms: a "tree in the garden," the time "I saw you walking by the seashore."

As we read the letter, we will "interpret" it as an eavesdropper might interpret an overheard conversational remark; that is, we will infer meanings from it on the basis of linguistic convention and whatever general knowledge seems relevant. The writer appears to have been a woman; she was, it seems, rather imperiously demanding someone's return. We gather that she and the person addressed had lived together in a house by some seashore and that there had been a garden attached to it.

Of course, because the letter is an *inscribed* utterance, certain textually uncodable features of vocal speech—such as intonation—will be lacking, and we may find ourselves unsure of its precise tone. Perhaps it is not so much imperious as cold; and perhaps the coldness is a mask for self-doubt or pride. Thus, in interpreting the letter, we will inevitably be drawn into speculation about various conditions *not inferrable from it on the basis of linguistic convention*: all those conditions that would enrich or constrain the inferences drawn on that basis—for example, the character of the writer, her relationship to the person addressed, and the exact motives and circumstances that occasioned the letter. And we may also be drawn into speculation about the particular objects and places alluded to.

We would recognize, however, that our speculations were just that: hypotheses entertained in ignorance but at least theoretically falsifiable by further or more specific information ("Oh, it was written by Aunt Louise; and it was her daughter, not her lover, she was asking to return—she was very ill at the time, you see—and the house had been in California, not Maine," and so on). We would recognize, in short, that if the letter *was* a natural utterance, composed as a historical act and regarded as a historical event, some of its meanings were *historically determinate*, at least theoretically locatable in the historical universe.

As we read the *poem*, indistinguishable from the letter as a verbal structure, we will again ascribe meanings to it on the basis of linguistic convention and general knowledge. As with the letter, we may again be drawn into speculation about the tone of the utterance and about the circumstances and motives that occasioned it. And we may again supply particulars for the general allusions: the tree will be pictured as an oak, the seashore will be imagined as that of Maine, and the "I" and "you" will acquire personal features and personal histories as evoked by that verbal structure but also as supplied by our own projections, drawn from our own experiences. As with the letter, we will recognize (1) that the particulars we have supplied are not "in" the poem (that is, not inferrable from it on the basis of linguistic convention: "tree" does not imply oak any more than it implies birch, "seashore" does not imply Maine to the exclusion of California), (2) that these particulars may not correspond to those the author had in mind when composing it, and (3) that another reader would be likely to supply somewhat different particulars and also to imagine somewhat different circumstances and motives as occasioning such an utterance.

What *distinguishes* our speculations here is that *none* of them are falsifiable by subsequent information. An adequate or valid interpretation of the poem—an interpretation that served our interests as readers and the poet's interests as an artist—need not wait upon and does not depend upon our identifying the particular tree the poet had in mind. For the species of that tree and the location of that seashore will be understood by *both* the poet and the reader as being *historically indeterminate*—as will, also, the unspecified features and character of that "I" and "you," and the unspecified motives and occasion of that entire utterance. All of these meanings, to the extent that the poem is offered and taken as a fictive utterance, will be understood to be unfixable, unlocatable in the historical universe.

I have emphasized the condition "offered and taken as a fictive utterance" because that does, in fact, make all the difference. If the structure labeled "poem" was designed by its author to be taken as a natural utterance, the label was unfortunately chosen, for it would misdirect the assumptions of at least a large number of its readers. The same would be true had the structure been presented with a title or lineation or any other features suggestive of such structures as are commonly labeled "poem" and had not been otherwise distinguished from them. Conversely, the fragment that we took to be a letter may have been designed to be taken as a poem or fictive utterance but, lacking signals to that effect, have been misidentified. Errors of identification produce erroneous assumptions and bring into play inappropriate conventions. Conventions *are* conventions, however, and they may change over time and, under varying conditions, be altered. Since I have discussed both these matters elsewhere at some length,[3] I shall not elaborate them further here. We may now return to the interpretation of our poem, taken as a fictive utterance, and our letter, taken as a natural utterance.

Now, in addition to all the meanings we have considered up to this point, there is another set of meanings that may be attached to any utterance, natural or fictive, and indeed to any object or event. What I refer to here are all those relations, connections, or implications which, as I mentioned in the first lecture, are often distinguished from antecedent or causal meanings by some other term, such as *significance* or *import*. These other meanings include various *metaphoric or analogic implications*, as when a tree in a garden is said to "signify" nature, endurance, traditional family values, or the temptation of Adam and Eve. Objects and events "mean" or "signify" other objects or events in this way when they are *seen by someone* as belonging to the same class by virtue of what are perceived as shared properties. These other noncausal meanings also include those more or less general propositions that an event may be seen to *instantiate* or *exemplify*, for example that Russian landowners were oblivious to the condition of the peasants or that provincial life produces intellectual stultification or that suffering is inescapable. Events "mean" or "imply" such propositions when they are *seen by someone* as being instances or exemplifications of them.

It will be worth our while to focus here on the second type of noncausal meaning, that is, meaning as exemplification. If we return to our hypothetical poem and letter, what appears to be different about the poem in this respect is that it was *meant* to have meanings of that kind. The implication—or, as it is sometimes said, the "communication"—of such meanings, that is, more or less general propositions about the universe, would seem to be one of the primary motives for writing poems, and also plays and novels. The authors of such works, it seems, would have us know what they have been blessed or cursed to know: that love is ruthless or redeeming, that men are craven or heroic, that life is, after all, meaningful—or, after all, meaningless. To this extent, we may say not only that the line between didactic poetry and pure poetry is hazy, but that all poetry is didactic. We usually refer to a work as "didactic" when such propositions are explicitly formulated within them. But all works of literature may be seen to imply propositions, most of them not stated explicitly and many of them unstatable—unspeakable— in terms of the formulated wisdom of the culture. Indeed, every literary work may be regarded as the *fictive exemplification* of some set of propositions and, as Sir Philip Sidney observed, "a feigned example hath as much force to teach as [doth] a true." It is as if each novel opens with the invisible words, "For example": "[For example,] about thirty years ago, Miss Maria Ward, of Huntington, with only seven thousand pounds, had the good luck to captivate Sir Thomas Bertram, of Mansfield Park . . .;" and as if every play opens with an invisible prologuist who says "For example, events such as these could occur," and every lyric with the invisible words, "For example, I (or someone) could say. . . ."[4] Furthermore, it might be maintained that the interpretation of a literary work *should* be directed largely or most centrally to inferring its meanings in this sense, that is, to identifying and making explicit the propositions that it exemplifies, these propositions being seen as precisely the point, the significance, the import—in short, the *meaning*—of the work.

The difficulty with all this, however, is that every literary work, like every object or event in the universe, can imply—can be seen to exemplify—an infinite set of propositions and can correspond analogically to an infinite number of other objects and events. To be sure, when we are speaking of an object or event that exists by virtue of personal agency, such as an utterance or a poem, among that infinite set of propositions and correspondences may be some particular sets that it implied for the author and that the author intended it to imply for his audiences. The question, then, for the ethics of interpretation, is to what extent, and for what reason, the reader or interpreter of a literary work is obliged to identify and articulate those particular sets and obliged to infer no other sets. And an adequate answer would, I think, acknowledge the following: (a) that we cannot ever identify those sets, but only hypothesize them, (b) that while the provisional identification of those sets may be of interest for some purposes, it may also be the very process of hypothesizing them that, in our experience of the poem, is "interesting," (c) that the reader inevitably will infer sets of propositions and correspondences that are different from those the work implied for its author, for no two persons could infer exactly the same sets or, of course, articulate them exactly the same way, (d) that it is most unlikely that the work implied only one particular set for the author himself, even while he was composing it, and, finally, (e) that we are under no ethical obligation to do what cannot be done, or to refrain from doing not only what we inevitably *will* do but the doing of which may be a significant aspect of our engagement with a literary work and a central source of its interest and value for us.

Some of these points will be considered more fully when we turn to the matter of authorial intentions. One of them, however, can be considered immediately, and that is how the distinctive nature of literary interpretation contributes to the characteristic value of literary works. We may, one final time, compare our hypothetical poem and letter.

I referred earlier to the speculations we may entertain when we read each of them, speculations about such matters as the character of the "I" and "you," the nature of the relationship between them, and various particulars of place, circumstance, and motive. The difference that I should like to emphasize now is that, with respect to the poem, our speculations *constitute* our "interpretation." In other words, since these matters cannot be even theoretically determined, there is nothing we can do but endlessly hypothesize them. I would suggest, however, that in that very endlessness is a major source of the poem's vitality and a continuing source of its value for us. While we may transform the letter, originally designed to function in a natural verbal transaction, into an occasion for such speculative inferences (that is, into an occasion for "cognitive play"), we may have reason to suppose that the verbal structure labeled "poem" was designed (meant) to be interpreted in that way—and designed (constructed) accordingly. What I would add now, in view of the discussion of meaning as "import" or "significance" (that is, the infinite set of metaphoric correspondences and general propositions implied by the poem), is that here, also, it is precisely their endlessness that gives the poem its life.

A poem may be described as, among other things, a structure of parabolic meanings, "parabolic" in both senses, that is, displaying the infinitely open curve of a parabola, and forming parables for an infinite number of propositions. It is partly by virtue of the parabolic nature—or indeterminacy—of "meaning" in poetry, and the consequent difference in the process by which we arrive at that meaning, that poems acquire value for us. For they thereby become the occasion for the exercise of the reader's own imaginative powers, specifically as the occasion for unusually creative cognitive activity. Engaging in this activity is not the mark of the reader's solipsism, self-indulgence, or amorality; nor is it an incidental or gratuitous by-product of his experience of the poem; on the contrary, as I suggested in the last lecture, it can be quite central to that experience. I should now like to make a few observations on another aspect of that activity.

At every moment, throughout our lives, we are the subjects of potential "experiences," but we are not always aware of them as such. Given the practical demands of ordinary existence, we cannot give equal attention to all the events that impinge on us, either from the external world or from the world of our own feelings; nor do we recall them all with equal precision. Our perceptions are not only directed but selected by the demands of the immediate occasion, and our experiences are usually preserved in memory only to the extent that they continue to serve our cognitive needs. Thus, much

144

that is potentially knowable to us, because it is part of what has, in some sense, happened to us, slips by apparently unknown or at least unacknowledged.

For the same reason, however, some particular subsequent occasion can evoke those forgotten or unacknowledged experiences, causing us to remember what we did not even know we knew: a perception never before quite articulated, an emotion we had sustained on the periphery of consciousness, a sense—barely grasped before—of the "import" of some incident. Our memories are thus triggered; our knowledge is magnetized to a center, ordered by and organized around it; and those prior "experiences" become available to us because the present occasion presents us with some reason for acknowledging them. Thus we are put in full possession of what was always our property but kept in reserve, as it were, until we came of age and found some way to use it.

Poetry may be eminently an occasion of this kind for the reader. To the extent that the meanings of a poem are understood to be indeterminate, we must supply meanings for it; and by obliging us to do so, the poem creates a need and therefore a use for knowledge that might otherwise remain unavailable to us. This is not to say, however, that a poem is a springboard for daydreaming. On the contrary, its value lies not simply in provoking that activity but also in shaping and, indeed, resisting it. Even as certain possibilities of interpretation are opened, they are also directed, lured, and re-directed by the poet through the verbal structure he has designed.

I think we can see, in this description, the outlines of an engagement between the poet and reader that is very close to that of a game. Moreover, as in any game, there may be masters and amateurs on both sides of the board: readers who, less attentive than others to the poet's own moves, play a wilder but perhaps less gratifying game—and, for an observer, a less elegant one; "unimaginative" or "literal-minded" readers who, not taking advantage of the openings, play a tighter, more timid, and, for the observer, less interesting game.

Having mentioned possible observers, we might pursue the analogy a bit further, noting that literary interpretation can also be a spectator sport and, in fact, has been one for some time. The

145

"interpretation" of a literary work may be seen as the descriptive report or reenactment of a game that has already been played. And since there *can* be masters on both sides of the board—great readers as well as great poets, matches for each other in the boldness or subtlety of their moves—there can also be master games, as engaging for the spectator as those he plays himself, or even more engaging. Thus, to fill out an incomplete list presented earlier, we have the achievements not of literary historians or explicators as such but, precisely, of literary interpreters, those who offer not to *give* us the poem—which often means taking it away—but rather to *take it on* for us, as one plays a match with an opponent.

II. Authorial Intentions and Literary Ethics

But where, in all this, are the intentions of the author? Do we not, in making sport of him, in turning his words into cognitive toys, use him merely for our own ends and thus transgress ethical norms? I do not think so, and we have, in fact, been speaking of the intentions of the author all along.

I observed earlier that although the intentions of all authors are historically determinate, the meanings of all utterances are not. Having considered the second part of that statement, we may now consider the first and, finally, the implications of both for the ethics of interpretation.

The intentions of an author with respect to his composition, whether originally designed as fictive or natural discourse, can indeed be seen as historically *determinate*—and therefore at least theoretically ascertainable—but only in the sense in which the intentions of anyone, with respect to any act he performs, are historically determinate. Thus, if we see a boy throw a basketball toward a hoop, we may infer that he "intends" to get it through: in other words, that getting it through is, for him, the appropriate consequence of that act. Our inference may, of course, be incorrect: perhaps he was, in fact, mischievously intent on breaking the garage window just above the hoop. Whether or not we inferred them correctly, however, his intentions were historically determinate and someone who knew more about the thrower and the context of his throwing might have inferred them more accurately.

146

What is distinctive about a symbolic act, we recall, is that the performer's intentions can be realized, that is, his act can have appropriate consequences for him, only to the extent that the conditions in response to which he performed it—its meanings in that sense—are correctly inferred by someone. If the boy's act *was* to some extent symbolic—if he wanted it to "*say* something" to someone (about his hostility perhaps, toward the owner of the garage window)—then his intentions could be realized only if they *were* correctly inferred by an appropriate witness.

Consider, now, the situation in which a young girl announces meanacingly to her father, "I'm a wicked witch and I'm going to put you in a dungeon." Although she is, we assume, presenting a *fictive* utterance, and thus does not intend her father to believe that she is a witch or will put him in a dungeon, nevertheless, she does intend to have some effect on him—perhaps to amuse him, divert his attention or engage him in play—and that historically determinate intention may be correctly or incorrectly inferred. If, in the midst of play, she had directed her announcement to a much younger child and thereby "unintentionally" frightened him, we would say that the younger child had misinterpreted her intentions—but precisely, we should note, because he *had* taken her to mean what she said, had interpreted her words in accord with the conventions of natural discourse—or, in Hirsch's terms, in accord with the "imperatives" of "ordinary speech." Clearly, then, it may be among the historically determinate intentions of *some* "authors" that we *not* take them to mean what they "say."

In natural verbal transactions, the speaker's act has appropriate consequences, and his intentions are realized, only insofar as the listener correctly infers the motives, sentiments, and circumstances that occasioned his utterance and are implied by it in accord with linguistic convention. When my daughter remarks growlingly at breakfast, "Damn it, I didn't get a minute's sleep last night," I assume that she expects me to infer, from the fact and form of her utterance, that she spent a more or less sleepless night, that she is now in an irritable mood, and, furthermore, that, having inferred these things, I will behave accordingly, that is, offer commiseration and make few demands on her energy. Had I not made those inferences, her act in speaking would have failed of its intentions, which were primarily to secure my services in her behalf.

The "appropriate consequences" of an author's act in composing and offering a poem or play or novel are not, however, usually a matter of securing our services or affecting our behavior in that sense. Indeed, the composition of such a work is not, in that sense, a symbolic act at all. The author may have found satisfaction in anticipating (and thus would have "intended") his readers' recognition of certain allusions, their appreciation of certain experiences and illuminations, and their inference of certain "propositions" (perhaps otherwise unspeakable and inaudible) that the work could be seen to exemplify. It also would have been his intention, we assume, to produce a work which, in engaging our interest and providing for us the pleasures of verbal art, would secure our admiration for his artistry. None of these intentions, however, depend for their realization on the reader's identifying the particular historical determinants of his composition, the personal motives and the specific sentiments, states, and circumstances that occasioned its creation; nor are those meanings implied by or "expressed" in the poem.

It may be presumed, for example, that when Keats wrote his sonnet "To Sleep," not only did he not expect Sleep or anyone else to *act* in response to the imperatives of which it consists—

> O soothest Sleep! if it so please thee, close,
> In midst of this thine hymn, my willing eyes ...

—but he also did not expect anyone to *infer* anything from the poem concerning his wakefulness on any particular night or, indeed, anything in particular concerning him as a historical person. His act in composing the sonnet did, of course, have particular historical determinants (which may have included the insomnia produced by his nascent tuberculosis, or his current fascination with Shakespeare's sonnets), and we may, for various purposes, seek to identify some of them on the basis of biographical and other historical evidence. It is most doubtful, however, that such determinants were what the poem was designed to "express," or that the inference of them is required for the poet's act in composing it to have "appropriate consequences." On the contrary, it is more likely that in designing his poem as a verbal artwork, Keats would have expected and intended his readers *not* to infer those determinants, not to direct their interpretations and certainly not to confine them to ascertaining the particular conditions that occasioned its composition. Indeed, the crudest violation of a poet's artistic intentions, depriving his work of its potential effectiveness in providing the particular pleasures and interests he did design it to afford, would be to insist on interpreting it as a natural utterance. It would, we might note, be the converse violation of linguistic convention alluded to in the last lecture as reverse lying or "false listening."

Let us turn now to the general question of authorial intentions as raised by Professor Hirsch's argument. As we have seen, "authorial intention" can be taken to mean many things, among them the sort of *effect* that any author or speaker designs his words to have on his audience. These effects may range from such specific and local ones as "eliciting information on the time of day" or "evoking the passage in Canto V of the *Inferno* concerning Paolo and Francesca" to such general and comprehensive effects as "being instructive" or "being amusing." If that is, at least in part, what Hirsch means by it, we could agree that a listener or reader who missed or misconstrued such authorial intentions would, to that extent, have misinterpreted the utterance. We could also agree that the misinterpretation would be, if not quite unethical, then at least unfortunate, the degree of the misfortune depending on the nature of the author's intention and the consequences for both him and his listener entailed by its correct or incorrect interpretation. If a stranger asks us for directions to Times Square and we reply by telling him how to get to Grand Central Station we have, in so misconstruing his intentions, behaved rather stupidly, to his distress. Or if someone shouts a well-intentioned warning to us in traffic, and we mistake it for an obscene call, we may put ourselves in otherwise avoidable physical jeopardy. Normally, however, we take care as speakers and listeners to make intentions readily inferrable and to identify them as best we can, since it is usually to the advantage of both parties in natural verbal transactions that a speaker's intentions be correctly inferred.

To a certain extent we may, as Hirsch suggests, extend these observations to poems, plays, and other literary works, noting, for example, that it is always unfortunate for a reader when, through ignorance or incompetence, he misses out on whatever delight or interest the author designed his work to provide, and that, if the ignorance or incompetence is grave enough (for example, leading him to mistake a parody for the real thing), it may effectively deprive him of the work altogether. Moreover, although in the case of dead poets it is hard to say what misfortune they suffer from a misidentification of their intentions, it could certainly be maintained that the effectiveness and thus continued production of all art depends on the existence of competent and informed audiences who can experience the effects that individual artists designed their works to produce.

This much said, however, there are a number of further points that may be made if we consider our actual practices and what might seem, in the terms of Hirsch's formulation, to be our morally unregenerate behavior with respect to literary works. For one thing, we may always choose, for aesthetic or other ends, for example in book titles (*For Whom the Bell Tolls*), epigraph quotations (*Il miglior fabbro*), and "found poetry," to decontextualize a verbal composition, detaching it from its original moorings and exhibiting it in a new context that evokes interpretations that may be quite remote from those presumably, or even certifiably, intended by its author. I do not, however, believe that we need think of ourselves as violating authorial intentions when we do so; for, in knowingly and candidly appropriating for one purpose (and to evoke one set of meanings) a verbal structure originally designed for another purpose (and, as such, designed to evoke other meanings), we have in effect regiven it to ourselves and thus reauthored it. The composer of a verbal structure does not, and presumably does not expect to, retain eternal proprietary rights to the manner of its employment.

Second, it seems obvious that much of the canon of "literature" consists of works that have been pressed into services they were not designed to perform, works that attain the status of literature and have value as such largely to the extent that we *do* "disregard" or "fail to respect" their author's original intentions. Thus we read for "entertainment" what was intended for instruction or inspiration, and now find aesthetically engaging what was originally meant to rouse us to political action or convert us to pious practices, or to warn, accuse, blandish, or seduce the readers to whom they were originally addressed.

Finally, if we consult the literary history of any culture, we find that the works that survive—the plays that continue to be produced, the poems and novels that continue to be read, the proverbs that continue to be cited, the tales that continue to be *recited*—are those that evoke and exemplify *emergent* meanings. It is true that literary works may engage our interest and touch our spirits as records and images of an otherwise irrecoverable past; but to endure as something other than vivid historical artifacts, they must also be able to serve as metaphors and parables of an unpredictable future. They must, in short, continue to have meanings independent of the particular context that occasioned their composition, which will inevitably include meanings that the author did not intend and could not have intended to convey.

I may seem to be maintaining that there are no ethical considerations in literary interpretation. That is not the case. There *is* an ethics of interpretation; what it governs, however, is not the behavior of interpreters toward authors but rather of interpreters toward their own audiences. For the interpreter, if he speaks, presumably speaks natural discourse. His utterances are therefore governed by the ethics of the linguistic marketplace, where the fundamental imperative for all speakers is that they mean what they say and take responsibility for having said it. For professional exegetes, this means, among other things, that they should acknowledge the nature, limits, motives, and consequences of their activities; specifically, they should recognize and acknowledge that the publicly articulated "interpretation" of literary works (for example, in classrooms and in the pages of professional journals) is a highly specialized activity, the forms of which reflect the particular historical and cultural conditions in which it arose and in which it is now pursued, and the pursuit of which serves particular social and institutional functions.

To the extent that interpreters claim to have identified the historically determinate meanings of a work, their claims may, as I pointed out earlier, be supported or challenged by appeals to historical evidence and the proprieties of evidentiary logic. An interpretation can be demonstrably "wrong," however, only to the extent that it claims to be demonstrably "right," and it is clear that there are forms of "interpretation" that need not and *should not* make such claims: those, for example, that I alluded to earlier as reports or reenactments of a reader's individual engagement with a poem. Such interpretations may themselves be seen as specialized (that is, extended, and more or less formalized) versions of such common social activities as informal chatter about songs and stories, casual allusions to passages of poetry, exchanged recollections of characters and incidents in plays and novels, and the invocation of elements of particular literary works as illustrative analogies to currently interesting situations or as exemplifications of currently interesting propositions. In their most highly elaborated versions, the potential interest and value of such interpretations would consist not in the interpreter's putative identification of the historically determinate meanings of a work but, rather, in the intellectual subtlety and imaginative fertility that he displays in playing out various of its historically indeterminate meanings, and also in the general or immediate interest (for example, philosophic or political) of such propositions as the work may then be perceived to exemplify.

Conversely, to the extent that such an interpretation exhibits the intellectual crudeness and imaginative barrenness with which the interpreter has experienced the work, and also to the extent that the propositions or attitudes he uses the work to exemplify are themselves seen as shallow, vulgar, or otherwise noxious, the interpretation will be of little interest or value and disdained *accordingly*.

The two forms of interpretation described here are not, of course, clearly separable. Indeed, it is doubtful if either could be delivered in its pure form, that is, as an "explication" uncontaminated by the individual interests and pattern processing of the interpreter, or as a "reading" that reflects no assumptions about the historical determinants or intended meanings of a work. On the contrary, as I suggested in the last lecture, a significant source of the pleasure

152

and interest we take in our cognitive engagement with a poem is our presumption and projection (or hypothesizing) of the artist's "design," and a corresponding source of interest and pleasure for the spectator of such a reported engagement—or reenacted "game"—is precisely its consequent quality of *inter-play*. This is a quality, it might be added, that extends to the transaction between the interpreter and his own audience, since the latter will inevitably "match" his own experience of the work against that represented by the offered "reading," and, to the extent that the interpreter's game thus *itself* becomes an occasion for cognitive play, it serves an "aesthetic" function. Since a given interpretation may serve a number of functions simultaneously, there is no particular reason why, in any case, such separation or purity should be sought. Controversy inevitably arises, however, when the different claims that *can* be made by each are confused (either by the interpreter or his audience) or when the relatively distinctive sources of the interest and value of each are seen as opposed.

Which brings me to my concluding remarks. The two forms of publicly articulated "interpretation" that have been roughly delineated here (and other forms that could be seen as variants or variant combinations of them) are often set in polarized opposition to each other. As I have noted, each form serves more or less distinctive functions and each may be valued accordingly. While it may be observed that the functions served by each will *themselves* be valued more or less highly insofar as they are seen as instrumental to other valued ends (for example, political or intellectual, communal or individual), I do not myself believe that either has any absolute priority of interest or unique claim to value, nor do I believe that the functions served by each of them are necessarily competitive.

The effort to identify the historical determinants of literary works (for example, the cultural circumstances and personal motives that occasioned their composition and shaped their form; the linguistic and literary conventions in accord with which they were originally intended to be interpreted and experienced; the attitudes, values, or sentiments they may have been designed to exemplify and perhaps to promote) is a pursuit that clearly serves certain functions; and those functions are, to my mind, of considerable social value and intellectual interest. My argument with Professor Hirsch has not been an argument against the practice of "historicist criticism" but rather, as I stated at the beginning of this lecture, with the attempt to give certain forms of interpretation privileged status on what appear to me to be the extremely tenuous grounds of their unique claim to ethical propriety. As part of the counterargument developed here, I have sought to emphasize that whatever historical investigations *can* determine, they cannot determine the historically indeterminate meanings of a poem. Those meanings remain indeterminate by nature, the inference or "supplying" of them reserved for the individual reader as part of his engagement with and experience of the poem. I have also meant to suggest that it would be grossly impoverishing to restrict the activity of "interpreting" literary works to the establishment of their historically determinate meanings, no matter how much comfort we might take in the conviction that we had thereby banished, or branded in advance, all invalid or unvalidatible interpretations.

I should like to conclude by observing that the impoverishment alluded to here would be a quite radical one and, by thus making the universe a poorer place for ourselves and our fellow creatures, subject to a categorical imperative. For if, as I have suggested, it is at least in part as the occasion for individual cognitive activity that literary works acquire value for us, it would follow that any hermeneutic principle or pedagogic practice that aborted that activity would, to that extent, diminish the value of those works. Indeed, were it possible for the strenuous, concerted, and cumulative efforts of professional interpreters ever to persuade us that all the meanings that could be validly inferred from a poem were now "known," that poem would effectively cease to function as one. In short, if the ascetic view of interpretation against which I have argued here were somehow to prevail, not only would readers have little reason to read poems, but poets would have little reason to write them: they would be better advised (as, of course, they sometimes have been) to come right out and say what they mean.

III

LINGUISTICS AND
LITERARY THEORY

7

SURFACING FROM THE DEEP

It does not, I think, require an eye made especially sober by the light of too many setting suns to find in the word *new* a certain pathos. New clothes, new toys, bear beneath stiff folds and bright surfaces images of the tattering and chipping to come. The newborn and newlywed both figure forth in their very names the shadow of a temporality made more poignant by their own ignorance of it. Or, where a measure of self-consciousness must be presumed, as in the numerous recent announcements, from the expeditionary forces of literary study, of new approaches and new directions toward new horizons, there is pathos in such outbraving it in the face of the sorry destinies of so many of those who went before. Thus, confronted by this volume,[1] one might, even before opening its covers, find something unhappy in its subtitle—both for the reasons mentioned and also because, in implying obsequies for the old stylistics and thus acknowledgment of the brief life span of its most immediate forebear, it announces a birth manifestly tainted by genetic weakness. There is, of course, also belligerence and bravado in that subtitle: for the New Stylistics, cradled in the grave of the old, must, in laying claim to its inheritance, allay the natural suspicion that it will be, like its ancestor, subject to similar rapid obsolescence. Such a suspicion is, however, not altogether quelled by closer examination of the papers here assembled and thus christened.

157

The editor of the volume, Roger Fowler, has written an introduction to it and also contributed one of its seven papers. Since the burden of his introduction and the argument of his paper are closely related, I shall consider them together, below. It will be instructive, however, to look first at the two papers that precede Fowler's own; for one of the features that the new stylistics shares with the old is a frequent disparity between its general claims and its particular achievements, reflected in the present volume in the discrepancy between the actual character of a number of the articles in it and the editor's introductory comments on them.

I. Syntactic Strategies and Analytic Formulas

Donald C. Freeman's examination of "syntactic strategies" in three poems by Dylan Thomas ("The Strategy of Fusion: Dylan Thomas's Syntax") is offered both as evidence for a hypothesis concerning language in poetry and as a demonstration of a recommended method of critical analysis. The hypothesis, in its fullest formulation, is as follows: "One way in which poetic language differs from ordinary language . . . is that a poet's deployment of his language's transformational apparatus, its syntactic patterns, not only reflects cognitive preferences, a way of seeing the world; perhaps more importantly, it reflects the fundamental principles of artistic design by which the poet orders the world that is the poem" (19-20).[2] Aside from the noxious jargon, the most problematic terms here are "reflects" and "artistic design." *Reflects* could mean anything from "is determined by" to "manifests" or "instantiates" and seems, in the discussion that follows, to mean all of them variously and inconsistently. *Artistic design* is not only vague but radically ambiguous, its meaning hovering between something like the poet's aesthetic purpose (or intentions or ideas) and something else like the poem's aesthetic structure, and thus anything from the overall thematic principles by which the poem is organized to the specific meanings (or effects) the poet wishes to suggest (or create) or his vision of the universe. Thus although it is clear that Freeman wishes to hypothesize some relation between a poem's (or poet's) syntax and something else about it (or him), it is not clear to *what* the syntax is related and it is also not clear if the relation is one of causality (and if so, in which direction), correlation, covariance, or strictly anything at all.

Not only is the hypothesis itself so vague as to be vacuous but, since the evidence offered to support it consists of a series of analyses that assume it, the question is begged all through. Moreover, the analyses themselves, which Freeman offers as a model method by which we can "lay bare the deep form of particular poems" (39) and "gain a deeper insight into the poem's inner form and aesthetic center" (20), consist of the familiar tortuous parsings which, here, yield simplistic, dubious, or incomprehensible revelations which in turn, by yet another familiar circular route, are clearly restatements of the interpretations of the poems with which the analyst began. Freeman's summary gives the flavor of much of what precedes it: "I have tried to show how a number of syntactic strategies—first the yoking of immediate syntactic constituents which are contradictory; second, intensive relative clause formation and related transformations; and finally, various kinds of preposing transformations—have functioned with increasing force in three poems to help achieve the unity of man and natural process which is one of the central principles of Dylan Thomas's poetics" (39).

In the introduction, Fowler alludes to Freeman's paper as "typical of recent stylistics in adopting a powerful and complex central hypothesis as the point of departure." He continues:

> Freeman's chosen text—three poems by Dylan Thomas—is not offered as virgin territory to be explored by a perfectly neutral analytic machine [as presumably might have been the case in the old stylistics] ... Freeman approaches Thomas with a specific line of enquiry or field of interest: the poet's habitual synthesizing, identifying, generalizing preoccupations.... This preoccupation is assumedly encoded in the artistic design of Thomas's poems; and the artistic design both resides in the language and is discovered by the reader in his language-induced experience of the poems.... TG [that is, transformational-generative grammar] provides a delicate analytic apparatus for just the kinds of [syntactic] structures Freeman needs to describe.... Freeman shows how such structures, in Dylan

Thomas, arrest the reader and, as he unravels their contorted syntax, guide him to the heart of the author's artistic design. In the relation he sets up between grammatical model and critical problem, Freeman illustrates not a mechanical transposition of text into linguistic jargon, but a dialectical process in which the linguistics and the literature are mutually responsive (5–7).

It is true that in the new stylistics, unlike the old, "the reader" is conspicuously hooked into the machinery, so that whereas earlier we might have been offered simply a description of features and deviations, we are now to understand that the features and deviations are described by way of accounting for the reader's "language-induced experience of the poem." As in Freeman's paper, however, where the peculiarities of Thomas's syntax are alleged to be of interest because they "foreground" for the reader the most crucial features of the poet's "artistic design" (24), the hookup often simply attaches a new piece of apparatus onto the machine (here an ill-fitting cog imported from Russian and Czech Formalism) without appreciably changing either its product or efficiency. When, as before, the key concepts are vague, the assumptions dubious, and the aims confused or quixotic, the results of the analysis, despite the array of technical terms, tree diagrams, charts and formulas, will demonstrate nothing other than the operations of the machine itself. When logic is slack, it matters little how rigorous method is; and, in the new stylistics as well as in much of the old, the rigor continues to be misplaced, all of it being invested in the cranking of the machine and none in its casements and connections.

Before turning to the other essays in the volume, but with reference to them, I should like to make some further observations on Freeman's hypothesis and the analytic method that follows from it, the general form of which could be stated as follows: something in a literary work that is more or less manifest or "surface," S, bears some relation, R, to something else that is more or less obscure, inner, central or "deep," X; therefore, by analyzing S, one may discover X. Or, represented as a formula:

$$S \ (R) \ X \xrightarrow{\text{analysis of S}} X.$$

This, with some variations, constitutes the central argument of almost every paper in the volume. In Freeman's paper, S, the surface phenomenon, is "syntactic strategy"; in other papers, it is "syntactic patterning" or "phonological schemata" or "the language" of the poem or its "form" or "the observable patterns in a literary work" or simply "the text." X, that which is deep and which, in Freeman's paper, was the poem's "inner form," is elsewhere "the kernel theme" of a novel or story, or the work's "literary significance" or its "content" or "meaning." The relation, R, can be, as in Freeman, that S "reflects" X or, as in other papers, that it "mediates," "mimes," "encodes," is a "realization" or "concretization" or "actualization" of it, or is "generated" by it, or "expresses" it.

There is, of course, nothing surprising in the formula itself: it is a paradigm of many forms of analysis, from chemical to Freudian. Moreover, it is familiar from more traditional forms of literary analysis, particularly those performed over the past few decades by the legatees of the New Criticism, who commonly operated on the assumption that the "themes," "meanings," and "literary significances" of a work were "expressed" or "reflected" by its "form" or "language." In fact, the only thing that *is* surprising about the formula is how familiar it is, though the familiarity has been obscured by the new values given to its variables or, in some cases, by the new terms given to the old values. Thus, where S might, some years ago, have been image clusters or symbolism, it is now almost exclusively syntax. Or where it might, then, have been "sound patterns," it is now "phonological schemata," representing here, I think, not so much the greater precision of the analyst as his bewitchment by the sound pattern of those polysyllables. Of course, "encodes" is not quite the same thing as "expresses"; but perhaps it is not always altogether different either.

If, as I have been suggesting, there is discernible in the sounds of the new stylistics the melody of an old song, two conclusions might be drawn, depending on the degree of one's attachment to that song. One is that, since there is evidently nothing new under the sun, we might as well go back to bed. The other is that what is affectionately referred to as the form-content dichotomy continues, like the frequently reglued crack in an old teacup, to appear under pressure, and that its prominence among the essays in this volume is at least one indication of the weakness of the approaches they represent.

The issue itself is by no means avoided. Fowler remarks in his introductory comments on the second paper: "Epstein boldly confronts the age-old problem of the variability of literary form in relation to content. He assumes, as I believe one must, that it is possible to 'say the same thing' 'in different words' " (8). *Must* one assume it? I think not, though I also think the alternative should consist of more than the pious incantation of its denial or the repetition of credos concerning organic form or the indissolubility of form and content. What is needed, rather, is a richer conception of language than the one on which most criticism currently draws: a conception that does justice to the actual dynamics of verbal behavior generally, that permits a precise formulation of the *various* relations which, under various circumstances, obtain between the formal features of an utterance or text and whatever else (its causes or consequences, "meanings" or "effects") may be of interest to us, and that indicates where useful distinctions, in those regards, may be drawn among classes of texts or utterances, for example, "literary" and "nonliterary." Such a conception might, among other things, lead us to clarify what it means to "say the same thing" and explain under what circumstances we can or cannot say it "in different words." As long as we remain vague about the nature and identity of both that "thing" and its relation to the linguistic form of a text or utterance, no matter how precise or refined our methods of analyzing the syntactic, prosodic, or lexical features of a work, the analyses will remain pointless. Moreover, naming the thing "inner form" or "deep structure" and replacing "expresses" with "encodes" or "actualizes" simply obscures the vacuity of the exercise: the crack is still in the cup, the tea is still leaking into our laps.

II. SOUND AND NONSENSE

The sort of mischief it creates can be seen in the second paper in the volume, E. L. Epstein's "The Self-Reflexive Artefact: The Function of Mimesis in an Approach to a Theory of Value for Literature," which Fowler had praised for boldly confronting that "age-old problem." Toward the end of his paper, Epstein claims to have presented a method whereby judgments of poetic value, "now made on an intuitive basis," can henceforward be arrived at "by a comparatively objective procedure" (74). Encountered at its beginning, the heroism of such a claim would have induced immediate feelings of pity and terror: nothing but folly could be expected to support it and swift defeat is written in its face. Little but folly does support it, and if the defeat is not as swift or total as one might have expected, it is because the claim itself is so volatile that when, by the end of the article, it is actually made, it has already dispersed into thin air.

The method is derived from an assumed "model of language-production" that is, to my knowledge, unique:

> ... a speaker or writer first constructs a lexical constellation which mimes a state of affairs; this constellation is then realized in linear and segmental form syntactically, and then either phonologically or graphemically. This realization may be produced *automatically*, that is, with no principle of selection operating among its linear elements other than the style of the speaker or writer (and that style operating outside of awareness), in which case the final speech-act is casual prose. On the other hand, there may be *conscious* or quasi-conscious selection and arrangement of syntactic and phonological linear elements of form, in which case a "poetic function" is operating (40–41, italics in text).

Epstein's conception of the sequence of stages we follow in speaking or writing certainly gives one pause, as do the grounds of the distinction he draws between "casual prose" and "poetic function," and his peculiar use of the term *speech-act*. More significant, however, is his invocation of *mimesis*, a term which (with *mime*) is transformed here and throughout the article into an instrument of tendentious obfuscation. Epstein can make the curious statement that "lexical constellates" *mime* "states of affairs" not, as one might otherwise have suspected, because he holds to a primitive conception of words as images of things, but because *mime* is for him an all-purpose term that takes on whatever value is required to relate anything to anything else. Thus, when, in a particular analy-

163

sis, A is said to *mime* B, it is glossed or paraphrased variously as A "echoing," "corresponding to," being "analogous to," "reinforcing," "conveying," "expressing," and, to be sure, "imitating" B.

As we have seen, Epstein is not unique among stylisticians in playing fast and loose with key terms. Rather than linger over the point, however, we may proceed directly to a consideration of the method itself, which works as follows: On the assumption that the value of a poem is (or seems generally thought to be, or is felt to be "in this stage of history") directly proportional to the extent to which "the elements of its form" (specifically its "phonological and syntactic schemata") mime (or are "reflexive of" or "express" or "correspond to") its "content" (or "lexical constellate" or "the state of affairs" mimed by that constellate), and that "the highest grades" are assigned to works in which the most intensely "subjective" ("personal" and "emotional") content is most closely and thoroughly mimed by all its schemata, we may, by examining the degree of subjectivity in a poem's content and the degree of correspondence between that content and the poem's form, arrive at its poetic value.[3] In short, the sound (and syntax) must be an echo to the (preferably subjective) sense.

A full-dress demonstration of the method is offered for Blake's "The Tyger," "a work universally acknowledged as great" (60). Observing that all the "phonological structuring" in the poem is "non-mimetic" (for example, there is, in its "commonplace metrical and rhyme-schemes," "nothing that corresponds to claws, stripes, fire, roars, teeth, ferocity"), Epstein states: "What Blake achieves in *Tyger* [*sic*] is a subjective mimesis, based on syntax, for a very high degree of value. It seems obvious from the poem that what Blake is conveying is his own awe at a complete mystical perception of the energy that drives the universe and the poet, a force here symbolized in a tiger, a power beyond good and evil" (61–62). This much being "obvious from the poem," it remains for Epstein to provide a "close analysis of its syntax," which "reveals complex mimetic schemata which reinforce and convey this subjective state to the reader" (60).

Epstein's analysis of the poem, which Fowler characterizes in the introduction as "a sharply focused description" of the "significant features" of its "verbal particulars," selected "according to clearly articulated criteria of rhetorical significance" and "rendered in the reliable vocabulary of linguistic science" (8), occupies fifteen pages and is a tissue of absurdities. To be sure, it is rendered in "the reliable vocabulary of linguistic science," which, for Epstein, means a fatal attraction to the jargon of every literary and linguistic theorist from Aristotle to J. L. Austin. Nevertheless, the analysis is shot through with circularity and arbitrariness, and what would, under less scientific auspices, have been called the "reading" of the poem is marked by the belaboring of the obvious, heavy-handedness, literal-mindedness, and sheer silliness—as illustrated in the passages already quoted and in Epstein's summary:

> In the description of some structures in *Tyger* we have seen how two subtle, complex, and apparently contradictory emotional states, complete knowledge and questioning awe, are mimed, reinforced, and finally reconciled by the satisfaction and frustration of syntactic expectations in the reader. Not only does this entitle the poem to a very high grade of value; it actually makes the poem possible. It is difficult to see how just this highly subjective proportion of differing elements, awe and illumination, could otherwise have been conveyed (74).

Thus form and content, pried apart for analysis, are once more announced as ultimately inseparable, and Fowler's bold confronter finds it hard to see how, after all, the same thing could have been said in different words.

We recall, however, that the analysis is not itself the object of the article but only a demonstration of a method, though what it is a method *for* remains an open question. Specifically, it becomes increasingly unclear whether Epstein's comparatively objective procedure is designed to determine value or to explain value judgments. Thus, when he states, "in this paper, the second type of speech-act [that is, the one in which "a 'poetic function' is operating"] will be closely examined and analyzed, to [among other things] ... suggest a reason for formal mimesis of content as part of a criterion of value for literature" (41), the angularity of the last clause leaves one in doubt whether he plans to suggest a reason for *making* mimesis a criterion for value or the fact that (and/or a reason why?) mimesis *is* a criterion of value. Similarly, the conclusion characterizes the approach as "having the virtue of accounting for certain judgments of value" and, in the next sentence, as being "an [incomplete] indicator of value" and, finally, as being a "standard of value"— which, however, "applies mainly to varieties of Renaissance and post-Renaissance poetry from technologically advanced countries of Western Europe and America" (74–75). It appears, therefore, either that Epstein fails to appreciate the difference between a procedure (and/or set of criteria) for determining value and a theory that accounts for value judgments, or that he wants to have it both ways, or that he does not quite want to have it either way.

There is a difference, of course, and it is a significant one for literary theory. An objective procedure (even a "comparatively" objective one) for determining the *value* of individual poems is, I think, about as wild a goose as an objective procedure for determining the *meaning* of individual poems (of which, more below). A theory of value judgments, however, though hardly a tame goose, is both conceivable and perhaps worth chasing. Epstein does seem to recognize fitfully that we cannot account for value judgments solely by examining the objects that are valued. Hence the qualifications "in this stage of history" or "at least in a post-Romantic age," and so on. While these allusions are, in themselves, preposterously vague, they do reflect his acknowledgment of the existence of cultural variables among the determinants of value judgments (what Fowler refers to as his "generous cultural-historical premise" [9]). A theory that did attempt to account for judgments of literary value, however, would do more than make polite gestures toward cultural and historical variability. It would begin with the recognition that the sources of value in a literary work are numerous and variable and that individual value judgments are a function of multiple and subtle conditions. Neither "the culture" nor "the age" ever operates as a monolithic determinant of value *or* value judgments: there are many cultures within any "culture," and we do not all occupy the same "age" at any given historical moment. Moreover, individual judgments are always to some extent responsive to social and situational contexts and—in this respect like individual interpretations—

166

determined in part by the reader's personal history and experience. A theory of literary evaluation might be expected to attempt to identify all such relevant conditions and to determine the sources of variability and constancy among them—including, of course, what may be the independently describable properties of literary works. In doing so, it would presumably draw on the anthropology and sociology of art and on cognitive, perceptual, and developmental psychology—as well, no doubt, as on linguistics. Finally, it might be expected to be connectable to a general theory of aesthetic evaluation and, ultimately, to a general theory of evaluative behavior. It would be an enterprise of some magnitude, then, and one not likely to issue in the assignment of "grades" to individual works or in cavalier allusions to other folk elsewhere. It would, in short, be an enterprise that looked quite different from Epstein's.[4]

III. THE LIMITS OF LINGUISTIC DETERMINACY

Fowler's charitable characterizations of Freeman's and Epstein's papers are edged with a strong tone of defensiveness, perceptible elsewhere in the introduction and in Fowler's own paper. It seems clear that, after twenty years of large claims and minimal achievements, stylistics has sustained some telling blows—delivered by, now, two generations of critics and theorists, not all of whom could be dismissed as merely expressing reactionary sentiments or making "the standard objections to all professedly empiricist versions of induction in science" (81). The earlier tones of arrogance are now muffled, bold territorial claims are replaced by modest offers of assistance and collaboration, former errors are acknowledged and abjured, former standard-bearers are ruthlessly purged, and the truce is cemented by a marriage—or perhaps it is that overtures of alliance are made toward a bordering tribe that seems to be enjoying greater prosperity. In any case, the marriage or alliance is represented here in the volume's title (*Style and Structure...*) and in the yoking, within its pages, of three more or less conventionally "stylistic" papers (all on poetry) and four more or less "structuralist" papers (all on narrative). That the yoking is an uneasy and probably unstable one is suggested by Fowler's own characterization of the relation between the two groups of papers, a characterization

167

that distorts both and, I think, to some extent misunderstands the nature of the second, a point to which I shall return later.

In his own contribution to the volume ("Language and the Reader: Shakespeare's Sonnet 73"), Fowler joins party with those who have attacked the old stylistics for its "positivism," for its "presentation of poems as spatial (rather than temporal) and static (rather than engagingly kinetic) constructs" (89), and for its concentration on tallying up the "linguistic features" of a text without reference to any reader's potential or even possible experience of them (83). At the same time, he wishes to maintain some integrity of identity for stylistics and some rationale for its procedures, which he had described in the introduction as "assailing [the problems of literary criticism] with the equipment of an established battery of language sciences" (5). Thus, although he sees Stanley Fish's saturation bombing of stylistics[5] as "chiming" with some of his own "complaints" (89), he finds Fish's own literary analyses (in, for example, *Self-Consuming Artifacts* [Berkeley, 1972], deficient because, among other reasons, they do not, "where they involve syntactic considerations, make any specific use of the delicate metalanguage of syntactic description which has been developed by Chomsky and by his recent successors" (90). But, more generally, with respect to Fish and others who show proper regard for the reader's experience and for its "linearity" and "temporality," Fowler's central objection is that they "provide no guarantee that in following their technique we do not absolutely throw caution to the winds" (92–93). His own techniques, as demonstrated in his analysis of Sonnet 73, are designed "[to avoid] the limitations of all the above approaches," (93), that is, those of the old stylistics and of its recently developed alternatives.

Independent of the argument in which it is imbedded, Fowler's commentary on Sonnet 73 ("That time of year thou may'st in me behold . . .") is in many ways admirable: the reading he offers is rich and subtle, attentive to the poem's formal qualities and often illuminating in its description of them. These are substantial virtues, but they are also the virtues of literary criticism as practiced by sophisticated and sensitive readers. For the commentary to qualify as *stylistics*, it must offer something more or other than such virtues, and its problems lie precisely in what else it offers: namely, the sort of guarantee earlier found lacking in traditional literary criticism and even in "affective stylistics," a guarantee not only that caution has not been thrown to the winds, not only that the interpretation is more than "just any old response" (102), not even only that it is *"controlled by the verbal structure of the poem"* (102, italics in text), but that it is uniquely so controlled and controlled by nothing else. In spite of many disclaimers of the sort of spurious "objectivity" and "mechanical discovery procedures" associated with the old stylistics and some gestures of acknowledgment toward "the license of interpretive insight allowed to criticism" (120) and *"sets* of permissible readings" (102, my italics), Fowler makes it clear that he believes that the interpretation of Sonnet 73 that he offers *necessarily follows from* his analysis of its linguistic features. But of course it does no such thing, nor could it have; for no analytic method can produce an interpretation and none can validate one. Fowler's reading of the sonnet is extensive (almost thirty pages long) and thorough; it is not, however, "exhaustive." It is also plausible, but no more plausible than a number of others that he had earlier dismissed as not sufficiently controlled by the syntactic structure of the sonnet. Most significantly, it is no less vulnerable to charges of interpretive circularity than other readings he had derided for "assum[ing] that the poem's meaning is clear, known in advance" (102).

Briefly: after presenting a summary of how "commentators usually regard this sonnet" (that is, "as a dramatization of the horror of mortality; the poet reflects on his own imminent death, prettily figures it, and entreats his lover to love him the more for the inevitability; thereby the general reader is drawn into a depressing recognition of the fact of human transience" [102–3]), and remarking the tendency of those commentators to be distracted by the poem's formal symmetries and "spectacular" metaphoric structure and their "surprising" failure to consider the syntax more closely, Fowler develops his own reading of the poem, a reading which, as he had put it in the introduction, "shows how the linear organization of the syntax directs the reading process in the retrieval of meaning" (10). The upshot of the difference is that whereas other critics, preoccupied with what the poem ostensibly "states" and "figures," read it as *death-anticipating* and, in the couplet ("This thou perceiv'st, which makes thy love more strong"), *love-entreating*, Fowler, by paying close attention to "the lexical constituents which perform the figuring" (116), demonstrates that it is *lingering-vitality-affirming* and *love-ascribing*. The fact is, however, that there is considerably more variability (not to mention subtlety) among the interpretations offered by those other commentators than Fowler's oversimplified, distorted, and debased summary versions of their observations suggest and that his own interpretation constitutes neither a correction of their misemphases nor a supplying of their failures of attention, but simply another reading—and one that, for the points at issue, does not especially commend itself.

I shall not attempt here to pursue the details of Fowler's lengthy commentary on the sonnet. The nature of his difficulty in making good his claims, however, may be indicated by reference to what becomes a rather striking feature of his own style, namely the high frequency of self-qualifying locutions and, in conjunction with them, the recurrence of the formula S (R) X, where S is, as usual, a "surface" linguistic feature and X is the ascribed meaning, but here R, the relational term, is a word or phrase of exceptional vagueness. For example, S "might suggest" X (111); S "may well carry a secondary meaning of" X (111); "it is fair to suppose that" S "embraces" X (111); S "manages to connote" X (112); S "unexpectedly delivers connotations of" X (114); S "bears witness to" X (115); "there is a delicate suggestion of" X in S (116).

Now, there is, to my mind, nothing objectionable in Fowler's or any other critic's using phrases such as "might suggest" or "seems to connote" in referring to the relation between a linguistic feature and an ascribed meaning. On the contrary, such phrases are, I think, precisely descriptive. What is notable about their recurrence in Fowler's paper is that, if such expressions are not reflections of his timidity or evasiveness, they can only reflect his implicit appreciation of what he explicitly or otherwise refuses to appreciate: namely, that there is a significant aspect of meaning in the poem that is necessarily variable, irreducibly indeterminate, and, therefore, that although "the verbal structure" of the poem may *direct* one's experience and interpretation of it, that structure cannot "control," in the sense of unequivocally *determine*, either of them.

One may grant that, by virtue of the fact that a poem *is* a verbal structure, its meanings are presumably inferrable (and intended to be inferred) in accord with linguistic conventions, that we cannot "understand" the poem or read it "properly" unless we know and respect those conventions, that questions of meaning are properly settled by appeal to them and, where the relevant conventions are themselves in question, that philologists, cultural historians, and linguists may be called on to identify, recover, or specify them. Not all meanings are equally susceptible to coding, however, and some remain elusive and hazardous even in ordinary nonliterary verbal transactions: for example, those which arise from subtle features of the particular circumstantial and psychological context of an utterance, which might include the speaker's frame of mind or exact motives in speaking and his relationship to and attitudes toward his listener. ("He was awfully abrupt, but I'm not sure if he was angry or just distracted." "Don't you think that comment sounded sarcastic? ... disrespectful? ... flirtatious?") These aspects of meaning (which to some extent overlap with what speech-act theorists refer to as the "illocutionary force" of an utterance) are what, with respect to a poem, we sometimes speak of as its "tone"; and after the philologists, linguists, and cultural historians have provided their expert glosses on every word and grammatical construction in it, there is nothing that remains more resistant to agreement among readers. For, of course, it is that particular context that is, in a poem, least explicit and most open to surmise or, indeed (as I have argued elsewhere), understood to be historically indeterminate and thus, by convention, radically indeterminable, eternally open to constructive rather than reconstructive interpretation.

It is clear, I think, that the aspect of meaning I have been discussing here is precisely what Fowler refers to as "the superstructure of connotations" (117) in Sonnet 73 and from his "analysis" of which he derives his own particular angle on the tone of the sonnet. As I have suggested, however, the analysis is no analysis, but a set of construals, and the superstructure is indeed a superstructure, but one constructed by the reader (that is, each reader) upon the poem. The particular superstructure that any reader (including Fowler) constructs will reflect the particular choices he has made from among the numerous possible "connotations" of the poem's "linguistic features" and also the particular way he organizes and integrates them; and his choices will reflect who he is and *everything* he knows, not only about words but also about the worlds in which and out of which they are spoken. He may, of course, be absolutely convinced that his reading has been "controlled by the verbal structure" of the poem, for although he has made choices, he is usually not aware of having chosen them from among alternatives. There is perhaps no illusion so compelling as the sense one sometimes has of not only the propriety but the necessity of one's own construction:

> "But look! It's right there on the page—"
> "Whereon do you look?"
> "Do you see nothing there?"
> "Nothing at all; yet all that is I see."

Some note should be taken here of the set of notions associated with "the ideal reader," a creature who figures largely in Fowler's article and to some extent in a number of others in the volume. As we have seen, Fowler, though associating himself with Stanley Fish's demolition of the old stylistics, cannot accept Fish's own alternative, "affective stylistics." One reason is that, although Fish's "appeal to the analogy of generative linguistics" seems to be "a useful point of departure," Fish does not take the analogy seriously enough:

> ... we are invited to witness the reader responding se-
> quentially to language in literature, but the reader cannot
> be kept in decent communal order because he is not
> controlled by the constraints of precise communal syntax.
> The reader is not the "ideal reader" we might expect in a
> generative stylistics based on generative grammar, but a less
> organized, regrettably substantial, actual reader (90–91).

Similarly, in commenting on the work of Stephen Booth, who attempts to show how the reader constructs interpretive frameworks for responding to Shakespeare's sonnets,[6] Fowler finds "indecisive and evasive" Booth's imperturbability in the face of "incompatible," "variable," and "switching" interpretations, and he is forced to question the qualifications of Booth's blithely unqualified "[*the*] reader": "How can we be sure that the reader Booth employs to lead us through the sonnets is the right kind of reader" (92)? By contrast, the "interpretively significant formal structures" that Fowler analyzes in his own reading of Sonnet 73 are "validated in the 'ideal reader's' experience because they reflect culturally coded knowledge activated in the process of reading" (93).

Of all the courts of appeal ever proposed for the ultimate *validation* of an interpretation, none could be more sublimely imposing than that presided over by this ideal reader. Who can gainsay his decisions? Who could accuse him of fallibility, subjectivity, or partiality? Above all mortal battles and free of all mortal limits, all natural or historical contingencies, he simply *reads* and *knows*. Have mortal readers been at odds for years on the reading of a line? a passage? a poem? Bring them to court: the ideal reader will settle the case, cracking the message by consulting the cultural code. But, it may be asked, how will the ideal reader make his knowledge known to us? Since his sole mode of being consists of reading and knowing, how can he express himself? The answer is evident: through his mediator, the real but totally self-effacing critic. Only the ideal reader knows for sure, but only the critic knows for sure what the ideal reader knows.

Put briefly, my point here is that, as invoked by Fowler, the ideal reader cannot rescue us from the hermeneutic circle because he constitutes merely another loop in it. I shall return to the subject below, in connection with another article in the volume by Jonathan Culler. While we still have Fowler's article before us, however, I should like to comment on his enthusiastic association of himself with critical positions and analytic techniques that emphasize the "linearity" and "temporality" of "the reading experience." It is certainly important to recognize that reading is a process and that it occurs in time. Fowler, however (and some other critics and theorists whom he cites, and some whom he doesn't), goes far toward transforming that recognition into a new critical dogma, attended by a new set of critical pieties. We do, of course, usually read the words of a text sequentially, but (1) we normally scan as we read, taking in (and anticipating) more than one word at a time; (2) our expectations and recollections are organized not only linearly but also hierarchically, comprehending and subsuming simultaneously a number of structural patterns of various unit sizes, for example, from phoneme to canto, from morpheme to total semantic field; (3) we continuously modify our impressions—recollections as well as expectations—as we read; (4) we often reread a text, sometimes immediately, especially such brief texts as sonnets; and (5) we always perceive a text spatially *as well as* temporally and, in verse, the specific array of words on the page usually contains information that affects our expectations and recollections. In other words, we do not perceive or experience texts as "strings" of words or the way one pulls in wash off the laundry line; "temporality" and "linearity" do not control the reader's experience with the rigidity that Fowler et al. sometimes suggest, nor is the reader locked once and for all into a given linear sequence.

IV. STRUCTURALISM AND THE LINGUISTIC MODEL

In the introduction to the volume, Fowler takes explicit note of the two approaches to literary study reflected in its title and represented in its pages by, on the one hand, the three papers already discussed here and, on the other, the four that follow. His characterization and contrast of the stylistic and structuralist papers is even-handed and he evidently regards the two approaches as "complementary" (10): both "can be attached to a basically Saussurean model of language" and both "assail [problems in literary criticism] with the equipment of an established battery of language sciences": while one "entails close attention to the surface structure of literary texts," the other investigates "deeper, more abstract patterns"; while one "emphasizes particularity, individuality, concreteness," the other "is more given to generalization and abstraction"; and while one makes the individual work "more recognizable," the other makes it "less recognizable" (10–11). As that last apportionment suggests, the evenhandedness is sometimes a bit strained, but Fowler is certainly generous and sympathetic in his remarks on the structuralist papers—to the point, indeed, where he suppresses what some structuralists themselves are often at pains to make clear, namely that the two approaches are not complementary but, at least in their own view, something closer to antagonistic.

The nature of the antagonism and the degree of its sharpness can be indicated by quoting some observations made elsewhere by one of the volume's contributors, Jonathan Culler:

> The type of literary study which structuralism helps one to envisage would not be primarily interpretation.... Rather than a criticism which discovers or assigns meanings, it would be a poetics which strives to define the conditions of meaning.... The study of literature, as opposed to the perusal or discussion of individual works, would become an attempt to understand the conventions which make literature possible (viii).... Granting precedence to the task of formulating a theory of literary competence and relegating critical interpretation to a secondary role, [structuralism] leads one to reformulate as conventions of literature and operations of reading what others may think of as facts about literary texts.[7]

As I shall explain below, Culler's views of how literary study should be pursued are themselves not altogether unproblematic. For the moment, however, we may note (1) that he sees structuralism not merely as another "approach to literature" but as a new definition of the total enterprise of literary study; (2) that the enterprise is conceived of as comprehensive rather than atomistic: it is literature as a whole (or, as the structuralists often put it, "as a system") rather than individual works, even the total corpus of literary works, that is the subject of study; and (3) that he views the objective of literary study not as the elucidation, evaluation, or even description of individual texts, but as the explanation of literary phenomena generally. Structuralism, in other words, is not a new(er) criticism; it does not offer to do better (more "objectively," "rigorously," or "solidly") what literary critics attempt to do; it offers to do something else. Moreover, unlike literary criticism *and* the new stylistics, it is not essentially pedagogic in aim or justification: the "understanding" it seeks would be valued, not as ancillary, but as such.

So characterized, there is much in the structuralist program that commends itself. Moreover, much of the work done in its name is, I think, engaging and impressive. I believe, however, that the program generally and the individual studies pursued in furtherance of it are, at present, in a state of captivity—specifically, captivity to its own intellectual origins—and that it cannot truly prosper until it manages to shake itself loose from the egg that hatched it.

The egg, of course, is linguistics,[8] and the nature and consequences of the captivity happen to be illustrated fairly dramatically in Culler's own contribution to the volume, an article that manages, with great intelligence and elegance, to draw a set of interesting and valuable conclusions from a set of highly questionable premises and distinctly strained arguments.

The immediate aim of the article is indicated by its title, "Defining Narrative Units"; its broader aim is to contribute to the development of a general theory of narrative structure. In view of the number of such theories recently proposed, Culler observes that it is necessary "[to think] seriously about the criteria to be used in evaluating competing approaches and hence about the goals of an analysis of plot structure" (125). After considering and rejecting the grounds on which other theories have been promoted—for example, that they provide a "metalanguage" which "enables the analyst to describe a range of stories" or that "there is evidence about the general validity of the presuppositions on which [the] theory might be thought to be based" (126)—he proposes his own set of criteria:

> ... the only was to demonstrate the superiority of a theory of plot structure is to show that the descriptions of particular stories which it permits correspond with our intuitive sense of its plot and that it is sufficiently precise to prohibit descriptions which are manifestly wrong.... In short, competing theories of plot structure can only be evaluated by their success in serving as models of a particular aspect of literary competence: readers' abilities to recognize and summarize plots, to group together similar plots, etc. This intuitive knowledge constitutes the facts to be explained, and without this knowledge, which we display every time we

recount or discuss a plot, there is simply no such subject as the analysis of plot structure because there is nothing for the analyst to be right or wrong about (127).

To illustrate these points, Culler presents three plot summaries of Joyce's story "Eveline," ranging from a single sentence to a brief paragraph; there would, he maintains, "be substantial agreement among readers about what ought to be included at a particular level of generality" (128). There is, he concludes, an "implicit knowledge which enables the reader to process the text," that is, "rules and procedures he is unconsciously following when he picks out the crucial items in the plot"; and these "intuitions of the reader" are what "a theory of plot structure ought to explicate" (130).

Culler then discusses and evaluates a number of competing theories of narrative structure proposed by, among others, Lévi-Strauss, Greimas, Todorov, and Barthes. He concludes the article by formulating the outline of a theory of plot structure which, while drawing on and combining key concepts that (by one set of terms or another) had appeared in each of the theories discussed, nevertheless satisfies better than any of them those criteria he had initially established.

I shall return below to Culler's final formulation. First, however, I should like to examine more closely the process by which he arrived at it, particularly the origins of that set of criteria. As the quoted passages suggest, Culler uses a number of terms—"competence," "intuitive knowledge," and so on—that are familiar from transformational-generative linguistics. These reflect more than terminological contagion, however: they are the consequence of Culler's quite explicit conviction that if literary theory is to become a fruitful discipline, it must model itself after "the theory of language"; and the borrowing of terms is only a small indication of the thoroughness and consistency with which Culler does in fact hew his work in the image of Chomsky's. The sources and implications of this conviction are detailed in his *Structuralist Poetics*, the following passage from which is a central statement of the reasoning behind it:

... since literature itself is a system of signs and in this respect like a language, one postulates a poetics which

would study literature as linguistics studies language, taking
its cue from linguistics wherever that seemed possible.[9]

To one who is not a true believer, this statement is striking for the
number of questions that it begs and the flagrancy of the *non
sequitur* at its center. *Is* literature a system of signs? Is a *language* a
system of signs? If so, and they are in that respect alike, does the
inference still follow? Specifically, are the differences between
literature-as-a-whole and a language of no significance for the
nature of the discipline that studies each? Is linguistics a monolithic
discipline? Specifically, is it equivalent to transformational-generative grammar? If not, is Chomsky's theory of language and the
transformational-generative grammarians' pursuit of its study the
only and/or the most suitable model for the theory of literature and
the pursuit of *its* study? And, in any case, are the assumptions,
procedures, concepts, and conclusions of linguistics themselves so
well established, so free from internal problems or external criticism
that literary theorists are well advised to adopt and apply them
unreflectingly?[10]

Since a good case could be made for answering every one of these
questions no, the premises of the argument are at least dubious.
Moreover, even if one would answer some of them yes, the argument
itself remains illogical. For, in accord with such reasoning, one
could just as easily begin with a different characterization of
literature, but one of presumptively equal validity—say, as a form of
art or form of human behavior—and go on to observe that it is "in
this respect like" any number of other things—say, painting or
sex—and conclude that the study of literature should "take its cue"
from some method by which one of those other things was studied—
say, iconography or the investigation of animal sexuality. Or, if one
does begin by characterizing literature as a system of signs, one
could just as easily, and rather more logically, conclude (as, in fact,
some other theorists have concluded) that the study of literature is
properly the domain of the general study of sign systems—that is,
semiotics or communications theory—where it would take its place
beside the study of its sister sign systems, including natural
languages.

One might expect some fairly peculiar things to follow from such premises and conclusions, as indeed they do in the hands of other theorists similarly captivated. As it turns out, however, they serve Culler surprisingly well for, like the basically honest but happily inept character in a comic "caper" movie, he almost always manages to pull the job off anyway or at least to end up with something of value to show for his efforts. He does this, I think, partly by either strategically or unwittingly misunderstanding Chomsky, even when he literally parrots his words, and partly by failing to produce exact counterparts in the analogies he draws from linguistics to literary theory. The cumulative effect of the individual discrepancies is quite substantial and have permitted Culler to make some strikingly original and fruitful contributions to literary theory in spite of his unpromising convictions. As is evident in the present article, however, the cost of those convictions is the expenditure of a certain amount of wayward energy.

For example, alluding to the alleged facts that, when asked, we all produce comparable plot summaries and that we agree about what should be included in a summary at any level of generality, Culler writes:

> These examples illustrate the kinds of facts that a theory of plot structure ought to explicate. A theory is "descriptively adequate," to use Chomsky's phrase, "to the extent that it correctly describes the intrinsic competence of the idealized native speaker." *The structural descriptions which it assigns to a text must correspond to the intuitions of the reader*, or to put it the other way around, *the theory must account for the intuitions of the reader by providing a model of the competence which enables him to perceive structure* (130, italics mine).

The angularity of the italicized passages is explained by their source, a passage in Chomsky's *Aspects of the Theory of Syntax*, which it will be useful to have before us:

> A grammar can be regarded as a theory of language: it is descriptively adequate to the extent that it correctly describes the intrinsic competence of the idealized native speaker. The structural descriptions assigned to sentences by the grammar, the distinctions it makes between well-

179

formed and deviant, and so on, must, for descriptive adequacy, correspond to the linguistic intuitions of the native speaker....[11]

The nearly wholesale appropriation is obvious; what is less obvious but more significant are the discrepancies, which is to say the off-the-mark analogies.

1. The difficulty begins with the term *theory* itself: although taken in the broad sense of an explanatory model or set of explanatory statements about something, Chomsky's own *theory* of language is quite far-reaching, embracing everything from children's acquisition of language to linguistic universals and what they allegedly reveal about the human mind. Chomsky also uses the phrase "theory of language" in a much more restricted sense, as here, to refer specifically to a generative grammar. It is clear that Culler has taken Chomsky's perhaps reasonable criteria for an adequate *grammar of a language* as his model in formulating criteria for an adequate "theory of plot structure" (and, in *Structuralist Poetics*, for a general theory of *literature*). *A language*, however, is a very different sort and order of thing from *plot structures*, and there is no good reason to assume a priori that the specific criteria for a *grammar* of one would be at all relevant to a *theory* of the other. It is not surprising, then, that Culler, having adopted Chomsky's criteria for evaluating grammars, is obliged to take a very circuitous route toward his own very different destination. Thus, whereas it makes sense for Chomsky to invoke the intuitions of the native speaker regarding well-formed and deviant sentences as both the facts to be accounted for by a generative grammar and as validating the rules it specifies (for it is the specification of those rules that, by definition, constitutes the *grammar of a language*), it makes little sense to extend that aspect of the theory of syntax to a theory of narrative structure, and Culler's efforts to do so produce some of the most tortured argumentation in the article.

2. What is referred to in Chomsky's own work as the native speaker's "intuitions," "tacit knowledge," or "competence" is understood to reflect a substantial component of literally *innate* knowledge, more or less activated by a certain amount of pure

"exposure" to a particular language. Indeed, Chomsky is often at some pains to emphasize (*contra* learning theorists) that language is not, in his view, acquired by "learning" (that is, conditioned generalizations and discriminations, and so on) and certainly not by explicit *instruction*. For Culler, however, "intuitive" seems to bear no implication of innateness, and *literary* competence is seen as the product of a variety of cultural experiences, not excluding formal education. In *Structuralist Poetics*, for example, he observes:

> That achievement [that is, of literary competence] requires acquaintance with a range of literature and in many cases some form of guidance. The time and effort devoted to literary education by generations of students and teachers creates a strong presumption that there is something to be learned.... [In studying literature] one gains not only points of comparison but a sense of how to read.[12]

One need have no quarrel with Culler's observations here, as such. On the contrary, one may observe that whereas Chomsky's own appeal to innate mechanisms often has the consequence of closing the doors to inquiry prematurely, Culler's emphasis on the cultural transmission of literary conventions permits an empirical definition of literary competence and encourages an empirical investigation of its nature, origins and the processes by which it is acquired. Nevertheless, it is from Chomsky's view of the relation between linguistic competence and a speaker's intuitions that Culler derives his criteria for a theory of plot structure, particularly the very troublesome suggestion that what such a theory must do is specify the rules and procedures that readers intuitively follow in *describing* and *summarizing* plots. We should note that if this principle were extended, the theory of literature would end up accounting not for the characteristic nature or functions of literary works or the characteristic ways in which we experience them, but rather the characteristic ways in which we have learned to *talk about* them. That a theory of literature modeled after a theory of how we talk should end up telling us only how we talk about literature is perhaps not so surprising. Because Culler, however, really is interested in the nature of literary texts and literary behavior, he eventually transforms the essentially misbegotten concept of literary "competence" into an exceptionally useful instrument for investigating both.

3. Although Culler does not, as do Fowler and others, invoke "the ideal reader" to validate interpretations of literary works, he does conceive of him along distinctly Chomskian lines as analogous to "the idealized native speaker." One notes, however, that whereas the native speaker is also presumably a native listener, the ideal reader cannot be presumed to be also an ideal writer. Indeed, if the analogy from linguistics to literature were strictly pursued here, it is the *writer* (who would be not only also a reader but presumably a highly competent one) whose intuitions about plots would have to be accounted for. Moreover, since those intuitions would seem to be most obviously "displayed" in the plots of actual literary narratives actually constructed by actual writers (assuming that those constructed by less-than-ideal writers would not have survived as "literature"), the theorist of plot structures would seem to be justified in concerning himself directly with the structure of actual plots rather than having to approach his subject by way of putative readers' putative intuitions invisibly manifested in putative text processings or occasionally displayed in elicited plot summaries.

To be sure, there are good reasons why a theory of literary narrative or any theory of literature should be particularly concerned with the knowledge, expectations, and responses of *readers*, and good reasons to maintain that any theory of narrative structure that did not account for, or take into account, the ways that readers experience narratives would be to that extent incomplete. None of those reasons, however, are supplied by a conception of literary theory derived from linguistics. All of them, in fact, derive directly or indirectly from the *differences* between literature and language. I would suggest, then, that Culler's disanalogy here is perfectly justified and that, in developing his theory of narrative structure, he might have avoided some strained arguments and angular formulations had he recognized that it *was* a disanalogy.

As it is, Culler's insistence on locating both his "facts" and the source of his theory's validation in the reader's intuitions saddles that theory with an altogether gratuitous double burden that notably impedes its forward motion. For it not only creates the problem of how one is to identify those intuitions or locate their manifestations (and there certainly seems to be something more vagrant and variable about readers' constructions and assessments of plot summaries than there is about the speech of native speakers or their assessments of the well-formedness of sentences), but also raises or begs the questions of *whose* intuitions are being accounted for and/or who has the competence to validate *them*. Culler's example of "Eveline" does little to persuade one of the generalization it is designed to illustrate, namely the "substantial agreement" alleged to obtain among readers regarding the propriety of plot summaries (and, obviously, adding the qualification, "*ideal* readers," would do nothing but beg the question directly). The extent to which we produce comparable plot summaries may have a good deal to do with who "we" are and how we learned both what "plots" are and also what it means to "summarize" them. It is doubtful, for example, that a South American tribesman would produce the same plot summary of one of his myths as would Claude Lévi-Strauss. Or to put it another way, wouldn't our explaining to the tribesman (or, of course, to a child) what we wanted when we asked for a "plot summary" be the same as telling him how to "process" the story the way "we" have learned to? In any case, the derivation of narrative units and universals from the hypothesized plot summaries of hypothetical ideal readers is justified only by a series of analogies in which narratives are identified with sentences, plot summaries with the intuitions that comprise literary competence, literary competence with linguistic competence, and readers with native speakers, each of which is strained and the sum of which is highly dubious. That Culler ultimately arrives at his destination, that is, a plausible and fruitful theory of narrative, owes to the fact that his instincts are better than his maps.

We may now consider Culler's concluding observations. Following Barthes,[13] he writes: "It is when the reader begins to place actions in sequences, when he perceives teleologically organized structures, that he begins to grasp the plot" (137). He goes on to postulate that in "processing the text," that is, in reading the story *or* summarizing its plot, the reader's perception of narrative units "is governed by his desire to reach an ultimate summary in which the plot as a whole is grasped in a satisfying form"; and, following the suggestions of Lévi-Strauss, Greimas, Kristeva, and Todorov,[14] he suggests that, at its most fundamental level of generality, that form is always something like "the modification of a situation" or "a passage from one situation to another." Consequently, "the incidents of the plot must be organized into two groups and these groups must be *named* in such a way that they represent either an opposition . . . or a logical development. . . ." Finally, "each of the two groups can in turn be organized either as a series of actions with a common unifying factor which serve as a *name* for the series or as a dialectical movement in which incidents are related as contraries and *named* either by a temporary synthesis or by a transcendent term which covers both members of a contrast" (139, italics mine). Culler adds that a model of this sort might prove more fruitful than the usual taxonomical approaches to narrative structure because it "would lead us to think seriously about the expectations of readers and their role in the perception of plot structure" (140).

Aside from the curious emphasis here on *naming* (which evidently reflects Culler's conviction that the reader's "processing" of a narrative always issues in some more or less explicit verbal formulation and/or that a theory of plot structures can only account for how readers talk about plots), these hypotheses are plausible, their formulations are precise enough to permit testing and modification, and they are likely to be fruitful for literary theory for pretty much the reasons Culler states: that is, they suggest the dynamic interplay between the fundamental features or structure of literary narratives and the fundamental features or structure of human perception and cognition. (The interplay, I would add, operates in both directions: we respond to narrative structures in a certain way because of certain psychological predispositions, and so on, but also literary narratives are constructed to conform to and gratify those predispositions.) In short, the theory of narrative with which Culler emerges in this article has many things to recommend it. Validation from linguistic theory is, however, not among them. Indeed, one cannot avoid remarking that his concluding observations and proposals may be understood and defended quite independently of their origins in the Chomskian model and, inspirational effects aside, could have been formulated without that model.

I should like to make one further point about Culler's conclusions, namely that their generality may be both more limited and broader than he indicates here: more limited in view of the fact that there are obviously genres of fictional narrative (for example, "postmodern" works by Beckett, Robbe-Grillet, Sarraute, and so on) the structures of which cannot be so described and are not so perceived; and broader in that many, perhaps most, nonfictional or *nonliterary* narratives can also be so described and are also so perceived. In fact, it may be that the innermost kernel of narrative structure is simply "our" (Western? modern? ... universally human?) shared sense of what it means for *something* to have *happened*, and therefore equivalent or related to the basic motive and occasion for all [story]telling (= *narrare*). I shall return to and expand this suggestion below.

V. GENERATING THEORIES OF NARRATIVE

As we have seen, although Culler appropriates for a theory of narrative Chomsky's criteria for a theory of language, he does not, as Chomsky sometimes does, equate "theory" with "generative grammar" and thus does not call for or propose a *grammar* of narratives. A number of other theorists, however, do just that, among them the authors of the next two papers in the volume, L. M. O'Toole and John Rutherford. O'Toole, in his "Analytic and Synthetic Approaches to Narrative Structure: Sherlock Holmes and 'The Sussex Vampire,' " observes:

> Just as linguistics cannot limit itself long to the study of syntax alone, but must constantly refer back to semantics, so poetics ... must analyze not merely the formal patterns but what is being expressed by those patterns.... [O]ne definition of the literary work of art might be that it is the syntactic expression of a deep semantic opposition (145).

Accordingly, and also in accord with the work of two contemporary Soviet structuralists, A. Žolkovskij and Y. Ščeglov (cited, 148), one seeks to provide a "generative model" of narrative structure, "mapping the 'transformational history' of narrative texts and episodes much as the generative linguist maps the transformational history of a sentence" (148).

He continues: "The starting point for such a process must be some kind of 'kernel' in the deep structure of the work"; this kernel may be called its "theme," "a scientific abstraction, a formulation in a more or less abstract 'metalanguage' of the irreducible meaning of the text" (148) or, in the words of Žolkovskij and Ščeglov, "that invariant of which everything else in a work is a variation ..." (quoted, 148-49). By "illustrating how elements of plot, character and the object world are generated through various operations on the theme," we may "account adequately for many features of the style of a work" (148-49).

The argument of O'Toole's article can obviously be represented as a variation of our formula

$$S \ (R) \ X \xrightarrow{\text{analysis of } S} X,$$

where S = the surface features of the text (here plot, characterization, and "object world" as well as more specifically verbal features), X = the kernel theme, and R = "is generated by." As the title of the paper suggests, however, the analysis is here supplemented by a synthesis:

$$S \ (R) \ X \xrightarrow{\text{synthesis from } X} S,$$

with X, the theme, arrrived at provisionally by "a combination of analysis and intuition" and seen as "a hypothesis which can then be tested through the process of synthesizing the text" (149).

O'Toole demonstrates the operation of the method by analyzing and synthesizing Conan Doyle's story, "The Sussex Vampire." Initial analysis suggesting that the kernel theme is "the triumph of reason over the irrational," this provisional statement of it is tested systematically "against various structures in the work represented by the labels: *Fable, Plot, Narrative Structure, Point of View, Character, Setting*" and found to hold good (150-51, italics in text). That is, it is possible to see in each of these aspects of the story—even, O'Toole notes, in the "oxymoron" of its title—that

186

"basic semantic opposition." The synthesis of the story follows, in pursuit of which the theme is further analyzed into a set of antithetically related key factors (for example, adventure-security, apparent-real) which are shown to be "realized" through various "operations" (for example, combination, repetition, juxtaposition), in numerous elements of the story, ranging from the array of characters and their respective traits to the antithetical structure of specific sentences.

The synthesis is, however, little more than an extension of the analysis to other features of the story: the only difference is that the second part of the analysis is explicitly directed toward demonstrating the tyranny of the kernel theme whereas, in the first part, it was directed toward demonstrating the propriety of the identification of the theme. And, of course, for all the fantasies of genetic or biochemical engineering suggested by such terms, O'Toole does not "generate" the text of "The Sussex Vampire" either. Obviously the same kernel (that is, "the triumph of reason over the irrational") could have (and has) sprouted numerous other stories, and the "mapping of the transformational history" of the story is what would elsewhere be referred to as showing—methodically, to be sure, and in great detail—how that theme is "reflected" (here, "realized"; in Rutherford, "actualized" or "concretized") in various aspects of the story.

Nevertheless, the demonstration is in many ways impressive: the analysis (whether in forward or reverse gear) *is* systematic and thorough; and although the apparatus involves the familiar algebraic abstraction and notation, it is handled with some geniality and tact. O'Toole's own style is lucid and energetic, and he is certainly an attentive reader. The analysis is, in fact, persuasive in its details and quite intriguing to follow (in somewhat the same way as the text which is its subject and, perhaps, for some of the same reasons), and one finishes it with the sense that something quite neat has been accomplished.

What has been accomplished is the question. Without doubt O'Toole has discovered what is, in effect, the formula for "The Sussex Vampire." One may suspect, however, that what he has thereby demonstrated is the extent to which that story (which, as he had himself pointed out earlier, "is one of a vast series of stories of a very highly stylized and conventionally structured type" [151]), was written to formula. In other words, the neatness of the demonstration seems to be a function of the neatness of the material, and the generality of both the method that it illustrates and the model of narrative fiction that it assumes remain dubious.

John Rutherford's article ("Story, Character, Setting and Narrative Mode in Galdós's *El Amigo Manso*") seems to be in some measure designed to answer this objection—or, as Fowler remarks of the article in his introduction, "the technique of structural analysis is here demonstrated in relation to a full-length novel in the modern European realistic tradition: an implicit rebuttal of the Anglo-Saxon criticism that structuralist analysis 'works' only for exceptionally schematic narratives (detective stories, fairy-tales) or exceptionally short ones" (17).

Although the article is cluttered and its central argument somewhat fractured and diffuse, Rutherford's major concern is to describe a set of methods for analyzing narrative fictions, illustrating them through an examination of *El Amigo Manso*. In the course of the examination, he draws explicitly on O'Toole's study of "The Sussex Vampire," observing:

> O'Toole has necessarily taken a simple example to illustrate the theory he expounds; yet the same theory is applicable to complete texts, in which there are more basic (or "deep") themes and hence many more possible permutations (182–83).

And, a bit later, he remarks that "the same method of analysis that was used for the simple characterization of 'The Sussex Vampire' can, without strain, be applied to rich narrative texts" (184). For reasons I shall outline below, however, I believe that the application not only strains the method but cracks it at its weakest point.

Like almost every other contribution to this volume, including the editor's introduction, Rutherford's article is marked by an exceptional degree of methodological self-consciousness. Thus, although the major portion of the article is an analysis of a particular novel, and the immediate aim of that analysis is to illustrate a set of analytic methods, Rutherford's broader purpose is "to tackle the fundamental and elementary . . . problem of the global segmentation of narrative texts" (178). The problem arises, he writes, because "Even though the aim of structural or semiological poetics is the comprehension of literature as a system. . ., the poetician can hardly dispense with the analysis of [individual] texts as a basis for his investigations"; and although the problem of segmentation ("What are the component parts of literary works?") is not great "at the purely verbal or stylistic level," nevertheless "narrative literature has another dimension which is to some extent independent of language" (177). Aside, however, from the conviction that there is nothing that is not the better for being examined by way of analogies from linguistics, there is no reason to suppose that this other dimension of narrative texts (= "all that which can be paraphrased" [177]) *has* "segments" corresponding to those which linguists identify in their verbal level. The units of linguistic segmentation—phoneme, morpheme, word, sentence, and so on—are more or less discrete entities that can be more or less precisely identified and defined and which, moreover, are linearly and hierarchically ordered with respect to one another. (Other significant aspects of verbal structures, for example, prosodic and intonational features, are, for good reason, referred to as "supra-segmental.") What Rutherford proposes as the "segments" of the nonverbal dimension of literary narratives—namely, story, character, and setting, with narrative mode (= "all that which concerns the presentation of the world of the novel, rather than that world itself as the reader is invited to imagine it" [178–79]) as a "bridge" between the two dimensions (179)—are not segments in that or, in fact, in any other sense, and further analogies drawn from linguistics on the basis of an implied correspondence between the two are therefore unjustified.

Segmentation, however, is only one aspect of Rutherford's broader purpose. A second one is suggested by the following passage:

Poetics [as opposed to "traditional novel criticism"], concerned to formulate the norms governing literature as a system of communication, must direct its attention towards that which is specific to literature; and so the poetician's task is not to calculate the degree to which a novel apparently copies life, but rather to establish the principles according to which the novelist, consciously or unconsciously, makes a selection for the purpose, possibly, of giving the impression of a copy of life. The poetician will, then, look for non-psychological and non-sociological ways of discussing character, non-historical ways of discussing story, and non-geographical ways of discussing setting (178).

It is in accord with this curiously negative formulation of the poetician's objectives that Rutherford proposes a set of four analytic methods (one per segment) "that seem to offer interesting possibilities" (179) (presumably for doing things differently from literary critics), illustrating each method with reference to each segment of *El Amigo Manso*.

Rutherford prefaces the analysis of the novel with a two-page summary of it, noting: "The only important parts of the text I have omitted in this summary are its anti-realistic opening and closing chapters.... It is not, however, my purpose here to discuss this fascinating aspect of the narrative mode of *El Amigo Manso* ..." (181). (One might point out, in passing, that the acknowledgment of such an omission, when added to the extraordinary flatness and awkwardness of the summary itself, suggests the interesting possibility of unreliable poeticians and, of course, renews one's skepticism concerning the degree of "general agreement" Culler had ascribed to the construction and assessment of plot summaries.) He then analyzes in turn the characterization, setting, story (= plot), and narrative mode of the novel. It is in the analysis of characterization that Rutherford draws on O'Toole's method, observing that "what it points towards is ... a system which has certain affinities with the analysis of distinctive features in phonetics" (184). Accordingly, "the basic characterization" in the novel (of which "the actual characterization in the text is an expansion or elaboration") is represented in tabular form, each character being assigned a plus or minus with regard to his (or her) possession, in reality and in appearance, of four traits: rationality, superiority, nobility, and worldliness. Noting that two question marks appear in the table, reflecting the fact that, in the novel, "the question of the moral status [that is, "nobility"] of Irene's and Manso's behavior is left unanswered," Rutherford goes on to state: "This type of ambiguity is, of course, characteristic of literature, and any method of analysis should take it into account" (185). And nothing further is said of the matter. This is, however, surely facile and evasive; for since poetics was earlier defined as "directing its attention towards that which is *specific to literature*," such a characteristic, rather than something to be "taken into account" is presumably what is to be accounted for. Moreover, precisely because such ambiguity or indeterminacy of classification *is* so characteristic of the traits of literary characters, the more specifically "literary" the characters, the less useful the distinctive-feature model, for all the entries on the table would then tend to be question marks!

As I suggested above, the fact that such a method worked well for O'Toole's analysis of "The Sussex Vampire" may tell us more about the formulaic quality of that story than about the general validity of the method. And, to the extent that the method can be applied by Rutherford to *El Amigo Manso*, or by any other analyst to any other novel, it can tell us only something about the stereotyping of that novel's characters or about the analyst's insensitivity to their literary qualities. The "Anglo-Saxon criticism" is, then, by no means rebutted.

Rutherford's observations on the setting of the novel are perfunctory or, at best, not notably more revealing or interesting than comparable observations in more traditional forms of literary criticism. The analysis of "story" brings us to familiar analogic grounds: "Just as the linguistician who is concerned with syntax has the task of discovering the principles governing the strings of words that we recognize as sentences, so the poetician who is concerned with story analysis should try to discover those strings of actions and situations which we recognize as stories" (186). The analytic method that follows from this argument is adopted from Todorov's

Grammaire du Décaméron, in which stories or story sequences are taken as analogous to propositions, characters to nouns, their attributes to adjectives and actions to verbs. Analysis produces an algebraic formula that represents an abstract model of the novel's story, such that "the incidental details can be seen as expansions or elaborations of the underlying structure it reveals" (192). The justification of the production of such abstract models of individual novels and stories is that "they give the poetician, in principle, the chance of constructing a finite number of models which, together with the application of a set of transformational rules, will generate all the stories possible in narrative literature" (192). Well . . . just a *chance*.

The analysis of the novel's story is followed by an analysis of the fourth of its segments, narrative mode, defined by Rutherford as "the ways in which the novel's objective world of character, story and setting may be actualized in the text itself" (195). He observes: "The interest of many narrative texts, *especially modern ones*, is centered on narrative mode rather than story, character or setting" (196, my italics). As I shall suggest below, in connection with other more general questions raised by the article, it might have seemed more to the poetician's point to observe that the "especially" in this respect is probably not so much *modern* texts as, in fact, *literary* ones.

The article concludes with the hope that "the reader will now . . . be in a position to judge whether the division of texts into these four segments, and the methods of analysis I have suggested for each of them, show possibilities of contributing to a general theory of narrative" (211), and with the observation that, although the methods do not meet the criteria set forth by Culler—insofar as "they do not provide any direct explanations about how a reader assigns meanings to a text as he reads it" but only "after he has read it"—nevertheless, "the two approaches complement each other" (211–12).

The three structuralist papers in the volume discussed above (the fourth, by Seymour Chatman, is anomalous among them and will be considered separately, below), both individually and taken together, have, I think, a better claim to the attention of literary theorists than do the papers offered by the stylisticians: they reflect a more spacious and sophisticated sense of the possibilities of literary theory; the general objectives for which they argue are explicitly and interestingly related to each other; and, although I believe each of them is radically flawed or limited, their authors do not seem, as do the stylisticians, to be running in place at a dead end. As I have been suggesting, however, it may be that in their attachment to linguistic models and attraction to linguistic analogies, the structuralists represented in this volume have created unnecessary obstacles for themselves and taken strangely circuitous routes toward their destinations.

In that connection, I should like to consider briefly two of Rutherford's central assumptions, beginning with the one that is apparently fundamental to the structuralist use of the linguistic model, namely that literature, like language, is in some sense a system—a "system of signs" in Culler's characterization, a "system of communication" in Rutherford's. One may agree that our expectations of and responses to various verbal structures are shaped by distinctive sets of conventions and, moreover, that it is possible to regard and study "literature" as the system constituted by one set of such conventions. It does not follow, however, that that system is directly analogous to the one that constitutes a natural language or, more importantly, that literature is, like language, a system of communication. On the contrary, one may observe that there is a fundamental way, in this respect, in which they differ, and that its implications for the pursuit of literary theory are substantial: for the distinctive characteristics of the system that defines and constitutes "literature"—the conventions in accord with which a verbal structure does become or is regarded as literature—originate in and continue to be shaped not by a communicative function but by an aesthetic one. Thus, whereas the conventions that constitute a language (or any essentially communicative system) exhibit characteristics—such as relative stability, economy and perspicuity—that reflect its fundamentally instrumental functions in communication, the conventions that constitute literature exhibit rather different characteristics—such as relatively continuous innovation, "uneconomical" elaboration, and semantic ambiguity or indeterminancy—that reflect its aesthetic functions.[15]

The significance of the distinction becomes apparent when we consider another of Rutherford's assumptions, also familiar in structuralist writings, namely, that poetics "must direct its attention to that which is *specific* to literature." We recall that, for Rutherford, this implied that the poetician must attempt to establish "the principles according to which the novelist ... makes a selection from life and orders that selection for the purpose, possibly, of giving the impression of a copy of life" (178). It is difficult to see, however, how that implication follows. Is it the selection and ordering from life that is "specific to *literature*"? Are not all narratives, literary or otherwise, selections and orderings from life in accord with some principle? And is it the purpose ("possibly") of that selection and ordering to give the impression of a *copy* of life?—that is, is verisimilitude *ever* the basic principle or purpose of the novelist's art? By way of ansewring the questions raised here, and also to draw together some points made earlier in connection with the articles by Culler and O'Toole, I should like to offer some general observations on narratives and some suggestions for an alternative conception of narrative theory.

It is, I think, quite possible that every "story," fictional or non-fictional, has what could be called a kernel theme or indeed a "generating" principle, in accord with which its elements have been selected from all the possible things the narrator could at that moment have said or written: something quite close to what, with regard to a conversational anecdote or news-story, we speak of as its "point," and which could also be seen as its motive or, most simply, the reason why it was told. If, as I suggested earlier, the basic or minimal *plot* of every story (change, reversal of fortune, or *peripeteia*, as structuralists from Aristotle to Barthes have maintained) can be reduced to the assertion "something happened," then its basic *theme* or generating principle would seem to constitute the reply-in-advance to the listener's always potential question, "So what?"; and both basic plot structure and basic theme could be seen as indeed universals of narrative, grounded in the recurrent occasions, contexts, dynamics, functions, and motives of one of the most universal of all forms of verbal behavior (or "speech-acts"), namely *telling*.

In ordinary verbal transactions, we do not tell stories (for example, relate personal anecdotes, repeat news events) merely to inform our listeners that something happened: things are *always* happening, but there is not always any reason to tell them to someone. One reason we do sometimes tell them is that the fortunes of those involved in the story (for example, the speaker himself) are presumably of some independent interest to the listener. If that is not the case (and of course it is usually not the case in *fictional* narratives), the story is usually told because it exemplifies or indicates (or apparently contradicts) some general proposition— again, one that is presumably of some interest to the listener—which may or may not be explicitly stated.

Like nonfictional narratives, fictional ones also relate something that happened; and what happens in them also commonly illustrates or indicates (or subverts) general propositions, for example, that loveless marriages encourage adultery, that sublunary events are providentially designed, that friends in need are friends indeed. Not all fictional narratives are (or are designed to be) "literary," of course: whatever aesthetic interest they may have, parables, myths, and fables obviously also serve didactic or socializing functions and, as I think we now recognize, the "literariness" of a verbal structure is always both a relative and variable matter. Nevertheless, if we are seeking for that in narratives "which is specific to literature," we might reasonably begin by looking for those characteristic modifications of narrative universals that seem most clearly to be shaped by—or to serve—an aesthetic function. Among the more prominent of such modifications are the following:

1. In the elaboration of "what happened," the structure and formal linguistic features of the narrative themselves secure the listener's interest and become sources of gratification. For example, the "suspense" that is potential in any narrative is, in literary narratives,[16] characteristically enhanced by that structure of "enigma" described by Barthes in *S/Z*; and what would otherwise be the listener's natural impulse to prod the speaker to "get to the point"

is, with respect to a literary narrative, characteristically countered by the pleasures of getting there.

2. The general propositions that are exemplified or indicated by the events of the narrative are characteristically left unstated and therefore indeterminate, the construal or inference of them by the individual reader being among the characteristic sources of interest in literary narratives.

3. In accord with one of the central conventions of "the system of literature," the act of narration is itself understood to be fictive and the entire verbal structure of the work is understood to be not a tale told but the representation of a telling—a modification that simultaneously establishes and protects the aesthetic function of the literary narrative as well as serving it.

This list could obviously be extended and each item in it elaborated and refined. I offer these observations not as a theory of narrative but to suggest that a theory along such lines could be pursued and, furthermore, pursued without direction or analogies from the criteria, objectives, or analytic or synthetic methods of transformational-generative grammar or, for that matter, from concepts or methods in any other discipline, from physics to philosophy, occasioned by and designed to solve quite different problems. I would suggest, then, that a *general* theory of narrative might offer to discover the social and psychological functions of all tellings, to relate the characteristic features of narratives to those functions, and to locate universals and account for variations among those functions and features; and that, in association with it, a theory of *literary* narrative might offer to investigate and describe characteristic modifications of those features that appear to serve and be shaped by specifically aesthetic functions. While those who pursue such theories of narrative might be expected to draw on linguistics for whatever understanding of language it may provide that is actually relevant to their enterprise, and would also be expected to draw on the data of, and integrate their own findings and formulations with, studies in anthropology, folkloristics, sociology, psychology, and communications, they nevertheless would not define their

196

domain or objectives or devise their methods of analysis in the image of those of any other field of study.

VI. CONCLUSION

Seymour Chatman's article, "The Structure of Narrative Transmission," is the last in the volume and, to my mind, the most substantial: its subject is sharply focused, its aims plausible and clearly defined, and, although Chatman, like his co-contributors, is concerned with methodological questions, he is not consumed by them. Thus the major part of the article is neither a methodological warm-up exercise nor a dress rehearsal, but a full-fledged performance or (the article being one section of a larger study) at least the complete scene of one.

The questions that Chatman's study is, at least in part, designed to answer are as follows: for any narrative work, if a narrator is present, how is his presence recognized and how strongly is it felt by the audience; and, more generally, since "in all but the scenic arts—like drama and the ballet—pure mimesis ... is an illusion," how is this illusion achieved, "by what convention does a reader, for example, accept the idea that it is 'as if' he were personally on the scene, though the fact is that he comes to it by turning pages and reading words" (215). Two assumptions, not completely self-evident, are implied by this last question: that the idea *is* accepted (or the illusion of pure mimesis experienced) by the reader, and that the illusion is achieved by some "convention." With regard to the first, one might quibble over the terms *illusion* and *mimesis* and suspect that the purity of either is rare, but I would be inclined to grant that we do, when we read literary narratives, experience something like an imaginative substantiality (or "real presence") and that our doing so is of significance in the value those narratives acquire for us and thus for literary theory. With regard to the second, the assumption is justified in the subsequent discussion, in which the term *convention* is used in a nonmetaphoric sense with reference to the basis on which quite specific linguistic features of a text direct and control the reader's quite specific inferences and experiences.

Chatman observes: "Preliminary to any discussion of the structure of discourse in literary narratives is an understanding of the linguistic and linguistic-philosophic basis for reports of speech, thought, physical action, and so on" (in effect, those conventions, strictly linguistic and other, that govern the inferences we draw from narrative statements generally), "since it is at least partly on these grounds that the reader makes his decision about who is speaking, thinking or whatever, and in particular whether there is an express narrator or not" (218). This is somewhat awkwardly stated, but the point is, I think, clear enough and important. In elaborating it, Chatman draws on the theory of speech-acts developed by J. L. Austin and John Searle and on Richard Ohmann's distinction, based on that theory, between fictive and nonfictive narrations.[17] The borrowings here, though digressive and perhaps not strictly necessary, are nevertheless tactful and discriminating, and permit Chatman to describe, with impressive precision, the conventions that direct our identification and interpretation of narrative statements in literary discourse.

The methodological concerns of the article are reflected in Chatman's trenchant critiques of studies by Ohmann, David Lodge, and F. Stanzel,[18] and in the contrast he notes between his own descriptive analysis, based on the assumption that there is a variety of "discourse features" which combine in various ways in individual works, and taxonomies that propose to establish a finite number of "homogeneous and fixed genres" (233). He observes:

> Variety among narratives is thus [that is, in his own analysis] accounted for in terms of various mixtures of independent features, not by an endless proliferation of categories or a Procrustean reduction of instances into normative types. Literary theory in general and narrative theories in particular have suffered from too powerful a reduction into a small number of genres, with the consequence that the full discursive complexities of individual cases are missed because they don't "fit" or get interpreted somehow as exceptional, or even worse, aberrant (233–34).

Since Chatman is not himself given to self-promotion, it should be added that among the salient virtues of his own taxonomy are the following: that it is sparing in its assumptions and that those assumptions it makes are drawn from what is relatively well established in our present understanding of language and the dynamics of communication; and that, because they are based on clear and consistent principles systematically pursued, its categories are genuinely parallel, comprehensive, conceivably exhaustive, and lend themselves readily to refinement and elaboration by other theorists.

In the article, Chatman develops only one section of what is ultimately to be "a description of the variety of narrative transmission," specifically that section which deals with "structures with the least presumption of a narrator's presence" (233), that is, narrative works and passages close to "unmediated story or pure transcript or record" (237). Accordingly, he describes how sources of narrative transmission are implied and inferred (1) in those forms of literary narrative, such as epistolary novels, that imitate written records and "reduce the implied author to a mere collector of documents" (240); (2) in those, such as Faulkner's *As I Lay Dying*, which imitate a transcription of speech and in which "the implied author is presumed to be nothing more than a stenographer" (242); and finally (3) in those, such as passages in Joyce's *Ulysses* and Woolf's *Mrs. Dalloway*, in which a character's thoughts and feelings, or "consciousness," are represented without the overt mediation of a narrative voice.

The distinctions here are sharp, but admit of subtlety, and the generalizations are uncluttered and persuasive. Without making much ado of the fact, Chatman consistently relates distinctive linguistic features to their characteristic implications or expressive effects, supporting his observations in these regards neither by invocations of the competence of ideal readers nor by allusions to cultural or linguistic codes but by demonstrating, with concrete examples from a number of novels and stories, how variations among those features produce corresponding differences of implication or effect. Also, it might be noted that although the general framework of the analysis as well as its details reflect Chatman's command of the contemporary study of language, its domain, objectives, and methods are neither derived from nor validated through analogies to linguistics.

In fact, Chatman makes only one direct allusion to transformational-generative grammar, but it is, for our present purposes, an instructive one. In the course of examining the narrative functions and effects of certain linguistic features in the opening sentences of *The Brothers Karamazov*, among which are a number of passive constructions, Chatman observes that "in the early versions of transformational grammar, passive constructions were derived from their active counterparts." He continues:

> But fundamental narrative units—the story statements— are not to be equated simply with the underlying deep structures of sentences. On the contrary, the transformations whose effects appear on the surface manifestation of literary narratives may be clearer indications of narrative structure (223).

Although the specific point is given substance in the discussion that follows, it is made essentially in passing; that is, it is not further explored as a methodological issue. A more general point is suggested, however, and it is one of considerable significance, not only for Chatman's study and the broader investigation of narrative but also for the general pursuit of literary theory: namely, that the methods used by linguists to analyze, explain, and represent the grammatical features of verbal structures may be quite irrelevant to the analysis and explanation of their literary functions and effects, that the employment of those methods may in fact obscure rather than illuminate the literary theorist's subject and, finally, that it may be in the investigation of the "*surface* linguistic manifestations" of literary texts, rather than in the effort to locate any putative "*deep* structures" in them, that the labors of the literary theorist will be most rewarded.

It is pertinent to observe that Chatman's article resists reduction to a variation of our formula

$$S \ (R) \ X \xrightarrow{\text{analysis of } S} X.$$

Or, put another way, in his study of the conventions of narrative transmission, X drops out of the formula and R is the relation not of

surface phenomena to deep matters but of various linguistic features to their convention-governed implications and, thereby, to
their literary-narrative functions and effects. The relation here, we
might note, is not a vague or volatile one, such as "reflects" or
"actualizes," but the relatively unambiguous, stable, and reversible
one of *implication*, here of the type specified-implication-in-accord-
with-specified-convention. Moreover, since both the features and
their effects are *manifest*, open to direct observation and even to
manipulation (as when, by altering a feature slightly or comparing it
to a slightly different one, Chatman demonstrates the alteration or
difference of its effects), he can concentrate his efforts on the
precise and systematic *description* of those features and can provide
an *explanation* of their functions and effects in various (and
potentially *all*) narrative texts. Deep-sea diving is not required at any
point.

I do not wish to overburden Chatman's article with praise. Its
aims and achievements are relatively limited, its claims modest.
Nothing in its revelations is startling or altogether novel, which may
be part of the reason why it reads so easily, invites so few objections,
and occasions so little exasperation. Nor do I wish to suggest that all
that is admirable and exemplary in the article owes to the fact that
Chatman, uniquely among the contributors to the volume, has not
felt compelled to dog Chomsky's tracks. Nevertheless, reaching this
article at the end of a volume in which so much that is new is old,
and so much of what is both new and old is dismaying, one might
very well come to the conclusion that only by surfacing from the
deep can we discover the salutary pleasures of air and light, acquire
a less subterranean and more sunlit view of the continents there are
to explore, and have the hope of dry land at the end of our journeys.

NOTES

CHAPTER ONE

1. Nelson Goodman, *Languages of Art: An Approach to a Theory of Symbols* (Indianapolis and New York, 1968).

2. Since the classifications offered here are not based on simple considerations of aesthetic "merit" or cultural significance, this first class would include the works of Herodotus as well as the note for the milkman. What distinguishes the literary or linguistic *artwork* is what I describe below as "fictiveness" and have elaborated elsewhere as the distinction between *ahistorical* (or mimetic) and *historical* discourse (*Poetic Closure* [Chicago, 1968], esp. pp. 14–23). There are certainly borderline and otherwise difficult cases, for the distinctions we are dealing with here are not strictly logical ones, but involve those "antecedent classifications" that Goodman sometimes acknowledges, that is, cultural traditions and conventions that govern how any utterance, on any particular occasion, is conceived of by its speaker (or author) and "taken" by its audience.

3. That is, if such texts exist. This third class would also include all instances of uninscribed oral "literature" and, of course, all nonce works of verbal art such as the rhymes a child might compose while playing. By making no provision for these events or neglecting to acknowledge their logical and historical relation to inscribed works of verbal art, Goodman secures a spurious simplicity for his own class of "literary works" in *Languages of Art*.

4. Goodman conceives of the relation between natural discourse

203

and "the world of objects and events" as identical with the relation between scores and their compliant performances or inscribed characters and their phonetic compliants. Since this conception seems to partake of all the defects of any referential theory of language, I find it patently unserviceable. [The nature of the causal relation between utterances and "the world of objects and events" is elaborated below (pp. 16, 21–22) and developed more fully in part 2 (pp. 86–100) in connection with a nonreferential conception of "meaning."]

5. Goodman does not, to my mind, give sufficient attention to the extent to which our response to a work of art, as opposed to any configuration or occurrence of natural events, is determined by our recognition of it as an artifact. When we "interpret" a work of art— that is, hypothesize its generating or structural principles, or ascribe causal relations to it—we are engaged in a cognitive activity with possibilities and limits significantly different from those which obtain for the scientist interpreting a set of natural events. For example, we inevitably experience and interpret works of art in a characteristic cultural context and at least partly in terms of previous experiences with the genre and style of the work, considerations that could be extended to the interpretation of natural events only by gross metaphor.

6. Goodman suggests that "scientific systems" are as "artificial" as works of art (cf. his reply, "Some Notes on *Languages of Art*," *The Journal of Philosophy* 47 (1970): 563–73). The sort of scientific system he has in mind, however, is presumably not a disembodied concept but a theory or hypothesis made available to us in the form of a discursive statement or set of statements. Such statements are artificial only in the restricted sense that they are the products of human activity. They are surely not artificial, however, in the sense of constituting a fictive nature; for the scientist does intend, and his audience will understand him to have intended, that his alludings be taken as real alludings. That is, the conventions determining or indicating fictiveness do not operate for the statement of scientific systems any more than they operate in my note for the milkman. Would Goodman really wish to maintain that there was no relevant difference between the account of the motion of the planets in Copernicus's *De Revolutionibus* ("hypothetical" though it was) and the account of the motions of The Flying Island of Laputa in *Gulliver's Travels*?

The phrase "nature proper" is perhaps ambiguous. There is an obvious sense of *nature* which any aspiring monist, myself included, would have to grant embraced cultural artifacts, including artworks themselves, along with all other objects and events. I am not using *nature* in that sense here, but in the other familiar sense that *contrasts* "nature" with artifacts, the natural object or event with the artificial one that may be taken to represent it.

CHAPTER TWO

1. *Poetic Closure: A Study of How Poems End* (Chicago, 1968), esp. pp. 14–25, and "Literature as Performance, Fiction, and Art" [above, pp. 3–16].

2. [Since the population denoted by that "we" is not delimited in any way here, the consequent implication could be that "we" are everyone and/or that "actually *do*" means "actually *should*." It was not my intention, however, here or below, either to invoke what would certainly be a very questionable universal or to present a normative statement in the guise of a descriptive one. As I point out later in the study, especially in parts 2 and 3, what "we" actually *do* depends a good deal on who we actually are and on the circumstances in which we do it; and what I allude to below as the conventions and assumptions that direct "our" experience of verbal structures must be understood as themselves historically, culturally, contextually, and otherwise *variable.*]

3. Since the term *context* has been acquiring increased currency in comtemporary aesthetics and linguistics, I should point out that it is not my intention here to quarrel with or qualify the sense it bears for other theorists. It might have been better to discover or devise another term altogether for what I am here defining and later elaborating, but the alternatives that presented themselves seemed just as likely to create comparable confusions, and I confess to a temperamental loathing of neologisms. It should also be noted that, in proposing that we view the context of an utterance not merely as its physical setting but as the totality of its determinants, I am not so much broadening the ordinary reference of the term as affirming the existence and significance of a particular *relation*, namely causality, between a verbal event and the universe in which it occurs. Defined in terms of that relationship, the "context" of an utterance inevitably refers to something more extensive than what the common use of the term suggests, but also something more particular.

4. I have considered the matter elsewhere: see "The New Imagism," *Midway* 9 (1969): 29–44.

5. "Private or personal utterance" may be extended to include not only overt but interior speech. The representation of the latter, particularly in romantic and modern lyrics, is discussed in *Poetic Closure*, pp. 139–50.

6. I should emphasize that I am not specifically referring here to those formally and publicly articulated "interpretations" of poetry that we associate with academic or professional criticism, but rather to the informal and often enough private activities of the reader as such, or what we might otherwise speak of as his response to or experience of the poem. Of course much formal criticism is an extension of these informal activities, but the very fact that professional critics are offering public statements entails other concerns and responsibilities, and I am not presuming here either to limit or to account for them. See, however, pp. 38–39, below.

7. *The Sonnets, Songs, and Poems of Shakespeare*, ed. Oscar James Campbell (New York and Toronto, 1964), p. 136.

8. [That is, with respect to those conventions. As I emphasize later, the reader is not constrained in any absolute sense by the poet's assumptions, and interpretations of a work that are "inappropriate" in that respect may yet be "appropriate" in relation to other emergent functions, conventions, and conditions of encounter.]

9. [It is dealt with at length in part 2.]

CHAPTER THREE

1. Comparable observations may, of course, be made with respect to the term *literature*. For a discussion along somewhat the same lines as presented here, see Christopher Butler, "What Is a Literary Work?" *New Literary History* 5 (1973): 15–29. [See also John Ellis's recent and illuminating discussion of the definition of literature in *The Theory of Literary Criticism: A Logical Analysis* (Berkeley, 1974), pp. 24–53.]

2. [An analysis of the child's functional discrimination of fictive discourse is presented in greater detail in part 2, pp. 124–32.]

3. The distinction initially outlined in "Poetry as Fiction" is redrawn here with some modifications.

4. I have in mind here statements such as the following:
No literary theorist from Coleridge to the present has succeeded in formulating a viable distinction between the nature of ordinary written speech and the nature of literary

written speech. For reasons I shall not pause to detail in this place, I believe the distinction can never be successfully formulated, and the futility of attempting the distinction will come to be generally recognized (E. D. Hirsch, Jr., "Three Dimensions of Hermeneutics," *New Literary History* 3 [1972]: 260).

Since nobody has ever managed to devise any workable criterion for distinguishing "poetic language" from "ordinary language", it seems foolish to retain a spurious terminological distinction which effectively denies common sense (Roger Fowler, "The Structure of Criticism and the Language of Poetry," *Contemporary Criticism*, Stratford-upon-Avon Studies [London, 1970], 12:183–84).

[I return in part 2 to "skeptical monism," and consider more closely Hirsch's statement and the argument that attends it (pp. 133–54.]

5. *The Concept of Mind* (London, 1949), pp. 16 ff.

6. Signals and cues for the classification of utterances, and the possibility and consequences of misclassification, have received extensive treatment in the works of Gregory Bateson and Erving Goffman. See Bateson's notion of "frames" and "metacommunication" in "A Theory of Play and Fantasy," *Steps to an Ecology of Mind* (New York, 1972), pp. 177–93, and Goffman's most recent study, *Frame Analysis: An Essay on the Organization of Experience* (New York, 1974), esp. pp. 40–47.

7. Terms are troublesome. In what follows, I shall use the terms *poem* and *poetry* to refer to (1) those compositions commonly and readily so designated, and (2) a particular subset of fictive utterances characterized later in the discussion, the members of which usually, but not necessarily, correspond to (1).

8. [The terms *ahistorical* and *noncontextual* are subject to some misunderstanding. As I observed earlier (pp. 33–34), I am not suggesting that a fictive verbal structure comes into being independent of any human agent or historical context. I do distinguish, however, (*a*) the historical and contextual act that constitutes a *natural* utterance, (*b*) the historical and contextual act that constitutes the *composition* of a fictive utterance, and (*c*) the ahistorical, noncontextual *structure* that constitutes a fictive utterance.]

9. The contrasts drawn here between paintings and pictorial illustrations will not, of course, hold good for all paintings and all

illustrations, even if we confine ourselves just to the "representational" ones. A number of painters have cultivated a deliberately flat, anti-illusionist quality (Matisse, for example, or Milton Avery), and others (for example, Roy Lichtenstein) have been interested in suggesting the pictorial quality of—or, in fact, in *representing*—precisely the sort of illustration described above. The analogy does not require a hard-and-fast distinction between paintings and illustrations, however, because the distinction between poems and verbal illustrations is not itself a hard-and-fast one. All fictive structures are, by definition, to some extent mimetic, but not all to the same extent. What may be called "mimetic *repleteness*"—that is, the degree to which a fictive structure not merely represents an identifiable member of a certain general class of things but also evokes the illusion or impression of its historical particularity—is a relative matter, and will vary from poem to poem, from painting to painting, and from illustration (visual or verbal) to illustration.

10. [Not *all* audiences, of course, especially not those, such as children, who have not yet learned the conventions. (See pp. 212–13, footnote 7.)]

11. Compare the greeting-card message printed above with these lines from Theodore Roethke's "My Papa's Waltz":

> The hand that held my wrist
> Was battered on one knuckle;
> At every step you missed
> My right ear scraped a buckle.

(*The Collected Poems of Theodore Roethke* [New York, 1961], p. 45)

12. *The Singer of Tales* (Cambridge, Mass., 1960), esp. pp. 30–67.

13. The examples given here have been adapted and simplified from Lord's, pp. 50–53, and some consist of wholly invented analogues.

14. Reprinted in *Concrete Poetry: A World View*, ed. Mary Ellen Solt (Bloomington, Ind., 1968), p. 114.

15. Of all the relations a speaker may have to someone else's words, perhaps the most interesting is his *performing* of them, as when an actor recites the lines of a play or when we read a poem, either aloud or to ourselves. "Performing" is quite distinct from either quoting, depicting, or referring to an utterance—or, of course, saying it. The relation is, however, a complex matter in its own right. A brief discussion of literary performance within the

theoretical framework of the present study may be found in *Poetic Closure* (Chicago, 1968), pp. 9–10 and above, pp. 5–8.

16. London, 1924, p. 5.

17. *Answer Back* (New York, 1968), p. 33.

18. ["Parabolic" meaning is explored further in part 2, pp. 141–44.]

19. *The Proverb* (Cambridge, Mass., 1931).

20. It may be worth pointing out, in connection with our earlier discussion of advertisements, that advertising slogans often achieve the semblance and acquire the force of household "sayings" at least partly because, like those sayings, no one knows who first said them. Thus, electronically transmitted *gnomes* infiltrate and swell the store of culturally transmitted proverbs and maxims until we can virtually regulate our entire lives in accord with what some totally and eternally unidentifiable "they" say.

21. *The Proverb*, p. 169.

22. *Oral Literature in Africa* (Oxford, 1970), p. 424.

23. [The topic is treated at length in part 2.]

24. Harold G. Henderson, *An Introduction to Haiku* (New York, 1958), p. 112. The translation given above is adapted from the two translations of the poem provided by Henderson.

25. [The characteristic activity of interpreting a poem is not *confined to* the construing of contexts. Other distinctive aspects of literary meaning and interpretation are considered in part 2, esp. pp. 121–24 and 137–54.

CHAPTER FOUR

1. I allude here to the following studies: Roman Ingarden, *The Literary Work of Art* (orig. pub. 1931), tr. George G. Grabowicz (Evanston, Ill., 1973); Käte Hamburger, *The Logic of Literature* (orig. pub. 1957), tr. Marilynn J. Rose (Bloomington, Ind., 1973); Robert Champigny, *Ontology of the Narrative* (The Hague, 1972); Richard Ohmann, "Speech, Literature, and the Space Between," *New Literary History* 4 (1972): 47–64; John R. Searle, "The Logical Status of Fictional Discourse," *New Literary History* 6 (1975): 319–32.

2. Studies by Roger Brown and Camille Hanson support the suggestion that parental approval and disapproval do not, in themselves, operate as "selection pressure" for the increased "correctness" of a child's speech. See "Derivational Complexity and the

Order of Acquisition in Child Speech," *Cognition and the Development of Language*, ed. John R. Hayes (New York, 1970), pp. 155–207, and the discussion by Brown in *A First Language* (Cambridge, Mass., 1973), pp. 410–12.

3. The quantity of information conveyed by an event is always relative to a particular "receiver" at a particular time. Thus, while the assertion that the George Washington Bridge is intact may contain no measurable "news" for most listeners, it may be highly informative to someone who had recently planned or chronically fears its collapse.

4. So distinguished, the meaning of symbolic events is close to what H. P. Grice terms "non-natural meaning" ("Meaning," *The Philosophical Review* 64 [1957]: 377–88, and "Utterer's Meaning and Intentions," *The Philosophical Review* 78 [1969]: 147–77). The formulation of the distinction presented here, however, differs in several respects from Grice's. For a view of convention-governed behavior more in accord with the one developed in the present study, see David K. Lewis, *Convention: A Philosophical Analysis* (Cambridge, Mass., 1969).

5. The "two persons" may, of course, be the same person, that is, we may respond to our own symbolic acts as symbolic events, as when we leave notes for ourselves.

6. During the past decade, considerable effort has been directed to remedying this deficiency. The effort is reflected in the work of speech-act theorists (J. L. Austin, *How to Do Things with Words* [New York, 1965], and John R. Searle, *Speech Acts* [Cambridge, England, 1969]) and in studies such as Erving Goffman, *Relations in Public* (New York, 1971); Gregory Bateson, *Steps to an Ecology of Mind* (New York, 1972); Robin Lakoff, "Language in Context," *Language* 48 (1972): 907–27; Dell Hymes, *Foundations in Sociolinguistics* (Philadelphia, 1974); Roy Turner, ed., *Ethnomethodology* (London, 1974), esp. Turner's article, "Words, Utterances and Activities," pp. 197–215.

7. Gregory Bateson's discussions of "metalanguage," "metacommunication," and, generally, of "the messages that identify what sort of message a message is" (see especially "A Theory of Play and Fantasy" and "Epidemiology of a Schizophrenia," *Steps to an Ecology of Mind*, pp. 177–200) correspond very closely to the observations outlined in this paragraph. Schizophrenia is, of course, a more serious misfortune than social embarrassment, but readers familiar

with Bateson's theory of "the double bind" will appreciate the relation between mistaking the spirit and force of an utterance and being given contradictory messages about them.

CHAPTER FIVE

1. What is described here as the potential multiplicity of function of any verbal structure is evidently similar and perhaps equivalent to what Jacques Derrida refers to as the "iterability" of all "written signs" or all "marks." See "Signature Event Context," *Glyph* 1 (1977): 179-80.

2. As the heavy qualifications indicate, I am not offering here to provide a definition of "artwork" or "aesthetic," nor, as will be seen, am I suggesting or assuming that there is some kind of activity or experience uniquely evoked by artworks or some single function that such works serve. Moreover, I should emphasize that the "cognitive activities" described below are not to be thought of as specifically "intellectual" or "mental." Although there is still much to discover about the mechanisms by which we acquire (or "process") information, it is clear that they involve the entire organism and that, with respect to our engagement with artworks, no distinctions can be drawn between purely intellectual responses and either sensory, emotional or physiological responses.

3. Cf. Eleanor J. Gibson, *Principles of Perceptual Learning and Development* (New York, 1969): ". . . getting information from the environment is intrinsically rewarding, not secondarily so" (p. 127). Gibson does not, however, break down that "getting" into a process and end (that is, *learning* as distinguished from *knowing*), which appears to be why she finds puzzling or "paradoxical" the fact that subjects in studies of perception seem both to enjoy uncertainty but also to be rewarded by a *reduction* of uncertainty (p. 128). She solves the problem, improperly I think, but suggestively, by concluding that those experiments in which subjects appear to enjoy uncertainty are "artificial."

4. I borrow the term *relational richness* from Leonard B. Meyer, to whose studies of musical structure I am indebted here at many points. See especially his discussion of "conformant elements" and "hierarchic structures" in *Explaining Music: Essays and Explorations* (Berkeley, 1973) and "Grammatical Simplicity and Relational Richness: The Trio of Mozart's G Minor Symphony," *Critical Inquiry* 2 (1976): 693-779. Recent studies that illustrate the pos-

sibilities of multiple pattern-processing in literary works include Stephen Booth, *An Essay on Shakespeare's Sonnets* (New Haven, Conn., 1969); Roland Barthes, *S/Z: An Essay* (orig. pub. 1970), tr. Richard Miller (New York, 1974); and Benjamin Hrushovski, "Segmentation and Motivation in the Text Continuum of Literary Prose: The First Episode of *War and Peace*," *Papers on Poetics and Semiotics*, no. 5 (The Israeli Institute for Poetics and Semiotics, Tel-Aviv University, 1976).

5. In the very process of composing a poem, the individual author continuously tests its effectiveness as an artwork on *himself* (by assuming the role of a stand-in for some presumptive or potential audience), and he shapes or revises his text accordingly. He may also, of course, explicitly "try it out" on various associates, and further revise it in the light of their criticisms and reactions. Similarly, the folkloric work is continuously being tested by and tried out on the various successive audiences to whom it is presented in the context of performance, and the responses of those audiences enter into the successive shappings and revisings of the work.

6. See Susanna Millar, *The Psychology of Play,* (London, 1968) for a useful historical introduction and a review of recent research. A number of later studies of specifically verbal play and a comprehensive bibliography of the subject may be found in *Speech Play: Research and Resources for Studying Linguistic Creativity*, ed. Barbara Kirshenblatt-Gimblett (Philadelphia, 1976).

7. It should be emphasized that I am concerned here specifically with how children learn to discriminate natural and fictive *discourse*, that is, verbal and, for the most part, vocal acts and events. Although there is reason to believe that children learn to discriminate all fictive acts and events in comparable ways, a thorough study of the question would require special attention to technologically, especially electronically, mediated events. For example, it seems clear that the identifying *signals* of fictiveness in popular magazines, motion pictures, and radio and television broadcasts are not as reliable as those in discourse, not only because they are sometimes deliberately more ambiguous (cf. the discussion above, pp. 55–57) but also because they are relatively less well-established and less culturally redundant. Moreover, while the child learns language through social transactions and under a wide variety of conditions, his encounters with magazines and television screens are more likely

to be solitary and to occur under relatively invariant conditions. The opportunities for corrective cognitive feedback are therefore minimal, and the differential *consequences* of fictiveness in "the media" are certainly far less "im-mediate."

CHAPTER SIX

1. *The Aims of Interpretation* (Chicago, 1976), pp. 90–91.

2. Hirsch tends to speak not of readers but of interpreters, for example, "those who practise interpretation," and "we who interpret as a vocation," and seems to imply that there should be not merely readers who engage professionally in the public articulation of their interpretations (as teachers, "critics," essayists, and so on), but a corps of highly disciplined exegetes who serve as self-abnegating mediators between authors and the laity. As I suggest below, however, it is not clear why such a ministry should be necessary or what useful functions its devotees would perform that are not already performed by literary philologists and cultural historians. On the question, see also pp. 38–39, above.

3. See esp. pp. 47–50, above.

4. The propositions exemplified by a work may, of course, be propositions about anything, and at any level of generality. Thus a novel may exemplify propositions about the nature of *narrative* as well as the nature of society; and, as we know, much "postmodernist" poetry can be seen as exemplifying propositions about *language*. (Propositional exemplification is also considered in part 3, pp. 195–96, in connection with theories of literary narrative.)

CHAPTER SEVEN

1. Roger Fowler, ed., *Style and Structure in Literature: Essays in the New Stylistics* (Ithaca, N.Y., 1975). Numbers in parentheses below refer to its pages.

2. The first clause of Freeman's sentence is indebted to an observation made by Richard Ohmann in *Shaw: The Style and the Man* (Middletown, Conn., 1962), p. 22. Freeman dubs it "the Ohmann hypothesis" and states that it is among the aims of his article "to expand this principle with reference to aspects of the grammar of poetry, a topic so far little studied from a transformational generative point of view" (19).

3. Epstein himself does not explicitly describe the method or

indicate its relation to its assumptions. The statement provided here is a compendium of points scattered between pages 41 and 60.

4. Among recently published studies that exhibit something of the scope one would expect from the kind of theory described here are Jan Mukařovský, *Aesthetic Function, Norm and Value as Social Facts* (orig. pub. Prague, 1936), tr. Mark E. Suino (Ann Arbor, Mich., 1970); Morse Peckham, *Man's Rage for Chaos* (Philadelphia and New York, 1967); and Hans Kreitler and Shulamith Kreitler, *Psychology of the Arts* (Durham, N.C., 1972).

5. "What Is Stylistics and Why Are They Saying Such Terrible Things about It?" *Approaches to Poetics*, ed. Seymour Chatman (New York and London, 1973).

6. *An Essay on Shakespeare's Sonnets* (New Haven, Conn., 1969).

7. *Structuralist Poetics* (Ithaca, N.Y., 1975), p. 128.

8. It would be Fowler's contention, one presumes, that stylistics was hatched from the same egg or that the two approaches are at least fraternal twins. Historically, that is more or less true. Nevertheless, insofar as stylistics *defines* itself as the application of linguistic methods of analysis to problems of literary criticism, it is more essentially tied to linguistics than is the structuralist program for the study of literature, at least as projected by Culler in the passage quoted above. Of course, characterizations of stylistics and literary structuralism and accounts of their historical and intellectual forebears and siblings vary considerably among those who have undertaken to describe either or both of them and to trace their joint or respective lineages (cf. Karl D. Uitti, *Linguistics and Literary Theory* [Englewood Cliffs, N.J., 1969]; Fredric Jameson, *The Prison-House of Language* [Princeton, N.J., and London, 1972]; Robert Scholes, *Structuralism in Literature* [New Haven, Conn., and London, 1974]; Morton W. Bloomfield, "Stylistics and the Theory of Literature," *New Literary History* 7 [1976]: 271–311).

9. *Structuralist Poetics*, p. 96.

10. Comparable questions were raised by Gerald Prince in his excellent review of *Structuralist Poetics* in *PTL: A Journal for Descriptive Poetics and Theory of Language* 1 (1976): 197–202.

11. Noam Chomsky (Cambridge, Mass., 1965), p. 24.

12. *Structuralist Poetics*, p. 121.

13. Roland Barthes, "*Introduction à l'analyse structurale des récits,*" *Communications* 8 (1966): 1–27.

14. Claude Lévi-Strauss, *Anthropologie structurale* (Paris, 1958)

and *"L'analyse morphologique des contes russes,"* *International Journal of Slavic Linguistics and Poetics* 3 (1960): 122–49; A. J. Greimas, *Sémantique structurale* (Paris, 1966); Julia Kristeva, *Le Texte du roman* (The Hague, 1970); Tzvetan Todorov, *Grammaire du Décaméron* (The Hague, 1969).

15. The precise nature of those "aesthetic functions" are not, I realize, self-evident. For the present discussion, one need only grant that a set of distinctive functions exists. An interesting and valuable analysis of the aesthetic use of language (drawing a good deal from East European literary theory) appears in Umberto Eco, *A Theory of Semiotics* (Bloomington, Ind., and London, 1976), pp. 261–76. [See also the discussion above, pp. 116–24.]

16. Rather than "in literary narratives," here and below, it would be more accurate, if more cumbersome, to say: "to the extent that a narrative is, or can be, regarded as 'literary.' "

17. Austin, *How to Do Things with Words* (New York, 1962); Searle, *Speech Acts* (London, 1969); Ohmann, "Speech Acts and the Definition of Literature," *Philosophy and Rhetoric* 4 (1971): 1–19.

18. Ohmann, "Speech, Action, and Style," *Literary Style: A Symposium*, ed. Seymour Chatman (London and New York, 1971); Lodge, *Language of Fiction* (London, 1966); Stanzel, *Narrative Situations in the Novel* (Bloomington, Ind., 1969).

INDEX

Acts. *See* Symbolic acts; Utterances, as acts; Verbal acts

Advertisements, 55–57, 209

Aesthetic experience, 11–13, 57, 116–24, 211. *See also* Language, aesthetic functions of

Ahistorical structures, 15–16, 18, 21, 51, 56, 70, 95, 138, 207

Aristotle, 8, 13, 14, 20, 39, 41, 42, 117, 165, 194

Art: and cognitive activity, 11–13, 116–24; and competent audiences, 150; and illustration, 52–55, 56, 207–8; impersonality of, 115; literature as a form of, 3–9, 13, 24–28, 32, 119–24; medium, concept of, 25–27; vs. nature or natural events, xii–xiv, 11–13, 204–5; and perception, 26–27, 32–33, 48–49, 52–55, 116–24 *passim*, 211; and play, 116–24, 131–32; visual, and poetry, 25–28, 32–33, 52–55, 208. See also *Mimesis*; Representation

Artistic design, 12, 39, 122–23, 145,

148–50, 153. *See also* Intentions, authorial

Audience. *See* Listener; Reader

Austin, J. L., 93, 165, 198, 210

Autobiography and memoirs, 8, 31, 48, 49, 136

Avery, Milton, 208

Bacon, Francis, essays of, 84–85

Bakhtin, Mikhail, xvii

Barthes, Roland, xviii, 177, 183, 194, 195, 212

Bartlett (anthology of quotations), 67–68

Bateson, Gregory, xviii, 207, 210–11

Beckett, Samuel, 185

Biography, 4, 8, 10, 29–30, 44

Blake, William, "The Tyger," 164–65

Bloomfield, Morton W., 214

Body motion. *See* Gestures

Booth, Stephen, 172–73, 212

Boswell, James, *Life of Johnson*, 48

Brown, Roger, 209–10

Browning, Robert, "The Bishop

217

ON THE MARGINS OF DISCOURSE
The Relation of Literature to Language
Barbara Herrnstein Smith

"Barbara Herrnstein Smith is one of a very few outstanding theorists of literature writing today, and her new book, *On the Margins of Discourse: The Relation of Literature to Language*, is a major contribution to the contemporary critical debate. She writes with a rare combination of elegance, verve, and logical precision. The issues she deals with are among the most central in the theory of literature, and many currently fashionable notions do not survive her incisive analysis. This book is a joy to read."
—John M. Ellis, University of California, Santa Cruz

In this centrally focused collection of articles and lectures, Barbara Herrnstein Smith examines a fundamental problem of literary theory: the location of its own subject, "literature." Through an analysis of the dynamics of verbal behavior, she argues that while terms such as "literature," "fiction," and "poetry" resist clear-cut and stable definition we nevertheless learn to make functional distinctions among various verbal acts and events. Smith asserts that an appreciation of the nature and significance of those distinctions is crucial to our understanding of literature and to the methods and goals of literary study.

In Part One, Smith introduces the distinction between natural discourse and *fictive discourse*—verbal structures that function as representations of natural utterances. She also deals with the relation of utterances to inscriptions and of literary *mimesis* to representation in other art forms. In the title essay, Smith explores a number of borderline cases, including "found poetry" and proverbs, and considers the distinctive ways in which we experience and interpret fictive verbal structures.